Mastering Niche Marketing

A Definitive Guide to Profiting From Ideas in a Competitive Market

Learn the Same Strategies & Techniques That Prominent Marketing Experts Utilize To Create Massive Streams of Passive Income.

A Globalnet Publishing Product

By Eric V. Van Der Hope

Published by Globalnet Publishing
» Los Angeles «

Globalnet Publishing • 10514 National Boulevard • Los Angeles • California • 90034

Mastering Niche Marketing

A Definitive Guide to Profiting From Ideas in a Competitive Market

Copyright © 2008 by Globalnet Publishing & Eric V. Van Der Hope.
Website: www.GlobalnetPublishing.com | Email: support@globalnetpublishing.com

Cover Design: Nu-Image Design
Book Production: Lulu | www.Lulu.com

All Rights Reserved under International and Pan-American Copyright conventions.

No part of this report may be reproduced or transmitted in any form whatsoever, electronic, or mechanical, including photocopying, recording, or by any informational storage or retrieval system except as permitted under Section 107 or 108 of the 1976 United States Copyright Act, without the prior written permission of the Publisher (dated and signed by Publisher), except for the inclusion of brief quotations in a review. Requests to the Publisher for permission should be sent to: Globalnet Publishing, 10514 National Boulevard, Los Angeles, California 90034.

First Edition (Digital Version 1.0) January 2008
Second Edition (Paperback Version) July 2008

Library of Congress Cataloging-in-Publication Data

Van Der Hope, Eric., 1970-
    Mastering Niche Marketing: A Definitive Guide to Profiting From Ideas in a Competitive Market / author, Eric V. Van Der Hope.
        p.cm.
    Includes numerous resources and bonus material.

    ISBN-13: 978-0-9779684-2-8 (alk. paper)
    ISBN-10: 0-9779684-2-1

1. Small Business. 2. Entrepreneurship. 3. eCommerce. 4. Internet Marketing. I. Title

LIMIT OF LIABILITY/DISCLAIMER OF WARRANTY: The publisher and the author make no Representation or warranties with respect to the accuracy or completeness of the contents of this work and specifically disclaim all warranties, including without limitation warranties of fitness for a particular purpose. No warranty may be created or extended by sales or promotional materials. The advice and strategies contained herein many not be suitable for every situation. This work is sold with the understanding that the publisher is not engaged in rendering legal, accounting, or other professional services. If professional assistance is required, the services of a competent professional person should be sought. Neither the publisher nor the author shall be liable for damages arising herefrom. The fact that an organization or website is referred to in this work as a citation and/or a potential source of further information does not mean that the author or the publisher endorses the information the organization or website may provide or recommendations it may make. Further, readers should be aware that internet websites listed in this work may have changed or disappeared between when this work was written and when it is read.

Printed in the United States of America

10 9 7 6 5 4 3 2 1

Acknowledgements

My success in business did not happen overnight nor did it come from hard to come by resources. What I've learned, I've used and Put Into Action! If there is only 1 lesson you learn from this book - it should at least be this - start taking action now! You can use the same methods I used and learn from the same success-minded individuals I modeled my business from.

As I look back over the past eight years or so, I feel the need to express my thanks to those fine individuals who have been instrumental in my success. If it weren't for them - I wouldn't be in the position I'm in now! It may seem a bit odd to some individuals who notice their name and my thanks, even though they might not have thought they'd helped me - they did, in one form or another!

First, I'd like to thank my mentors:

Ted Nicholas - 'the Legend' and the greatest marketer I've ever had the honor of meeting and talking with! His record speaks for itself - he has produced over 5.9 billion dollars in sales with his own companies as well as through his clients.
http://www.tednicholas.com

Anthony Robbins - for my motivation and inspiration.
http://www.anthonyrobbins.com/Home/Home.aspx

Joe Sugarman - on how to motivate & influence potential buyers using psychological techniques.
http://www.joesugarman.com

Mark Joyner - for my business philosophy.
http://www.markjoyner.name

Corey Rudl - exemplified what it meant to follow my passion.
http://www.marketingtips.com/corey_bio.html
http://www.remembercorey.com
http://www.marketingtips.com

I'd like to thank my teachers:

Shawn Casey - on the importance of creating my own products and growing my business through Joint Ventures.
http://www.shawncasey.com

Frank Kern - introduced me to internet marketing and the importance of growing my business with little known, small, 'virtual real estate' niche markets.

Mike Litman - "Best-Kept Secret of the Rich" - success hinges on the partnership of like-minded individuals doing even more than you.
http://www.mikelitman.com

Joel Christopher - the "Master List Builder," - enough said! ☺
http://www.joelchristopher.com

Tom Antion – for improving my speaking abilities.
http://www.antion.com

David Garfinkel - taught me how to write my own sales copy.
http://www.davidgarfinkel.com

Derek Gehl - taught me the importance of testing products before they're launched.
http://www.marketingtips.com

Raleigh Pinskey - for helping me build credibility through branding.
http://www.raleighpinskey.com

Glenn Hopkins - on the importance of building a 'list' of eager students & customers.
http://www.glenhopkins.name

Alexandria Brown - on the importance of connecting with my readers with ezines.
http://www.alexandriabrown.com

Rick Beneteau - for helping me realize that I can make a difference in other people's lives.
http://www.interniche.net

Yanik Silver - how to profit from selling information that people are searching for and want!
http://www.yaniksilver.com

Ewen Chia - the 'Master Affiliate' marketer.
http://www.ewenchia.com

I'd also like to thank my business partners/colleagues:

Jason Oman - http://www.jasonoman.com
Patric Chan - http://www.patricchan.com
Ryan Deiss - http://www.drivingtraffic.com
Ken McArthur - http://www.kenmcarthur.com
Jason Cox - http://www.jasonjcox.com
Rosalind Gardner - http://www.rosalindgardner.com
Duncan Carver - http://www.onlinemarketingtoday.com
Leo J Quinn Jr. - http://www.leoquinn.com
Mike Mograbi - http://www.imnewswatch.com
Jeff Smith - http://www.highertrustmarketing.com
George Katsoudas - http://www.frankensteinmarketing.com
Ian Herculson - http://www.ianherculson.com
Charlie Lafave - http://www.websiteer.com
Terry Telford - http://www.terrytelford.com
Gary Durkin - http://www.doubleedgemarketing.com
Paul Myers - http://www.talkbiznews.com
Michael Senoff - http://www.hardtofindseminars.com
Michael Nicholas - http://www.orderbuttontriggers.com
Dr. Mani Sivasubramanian - http://www.moneypowerwisdom.com

Richard Osterude - http://www.marketingdad.com
David Zohar - http://www.netcustomercenter.com
Barry Richardson - http://www.totalmarketer.com
Dave Jenyns - http://www.meta-formula.com
Don R. Monteith - http://www.howtogetyourdreamjob.com
Karon Thackston - http://www.marketingwords.com
Chris Malta & Colette Marshall - http://www.worldwidebrands.com
Jens Clever - http://www.daytradingcoach.com
Jeremy J. Burns - http://www.jeremyburns.com
Jim Edwards - http://www.ebookfire.com
Leslie Householder - http://www.thoughtsalive.com
Louis Burleson - http://www.louisburleson.com
Martin Franzen - http://www.siteselling.com
Max Rylski - http://www.maxcovers.com
Michael J. McGroarty - http://www.learnfrommike.com
Michael Rasmussen - http://www.michaelrasmussen.com
Roy Oron - http://www.makelinks.com
Sen Ze - http://www.senze.com/business-blog
Tahir Shah - http://www.no-hype-no-fluff.com
Theodore Hansson - http://www.thansson.com
Ross Stokes & Kathy Crockett - http://www.227UnusualBusinessIdeas.com
Wayne M. Davies - http://www.yousaveontaxes.com/ultimate-guide.html
Anthony Fesalbon - http://www.hypercover.com
Charlie Page - http://www.charliepage.com
Merle - http://www.merlesworld.com
Anne Ahira - http://www.anneahira.com
Eva Browne-Paterson - http://www.evieb.com
James Andrews & Valerie Hasara - http://www.oyesucan.com
Don Richter - http://www.profittips.com

You know what? - There's more . . . ! But I'm sure you get the point . . . you don't experience large amounts of success by going about it by yourself, it comes from the help of your friends, partners and colleagues who are also trying to excel at what they do! ☺

We can improve on how we live our lives by surrounding ourselves with like-minded individuals. So make it your goal to surround yourself with 'better' people than you and you'll be able to learn tremendous lessons from them and discover that there are no limits to your own definition of success, whether it be in business, or in how you live your life! ☺

Praises For Mastering Niche Marketing

"Reading this book was like reading an autobiography of the very steps I took to become a highly successful internet marketer myself. A successful business relies on a solid foundation, but what most failed business owners neglect, is the importance of setting realistic milestones, developing the desire to achieve those goals, having a vision and focusing in on it and most important, the necessity of taking action to achieve the desired results. Eric has been able to emphasize these points while systematically describing how to build a marketable online business from an idea in seven crucial phases! This is an extremely thorough book - WOW!"

- Jason Oman
#1 Best-Selling Author of 'Conversations with Millionaires'
www.JasonOman.com

"Many entrepreneurs, marketers, and want-to-be infopreneurs struggle with finding a niche that they can profit from. In this book Eric removes that obstacle and teaches you HOW to profit from them!"

- Glen Hopkins
#1 Best-Selling Author of 'Lucrative List Building'
www.GlenHopkins.name

"I just wanted to let you know how impressed I was with your book. It is well thought out and jam-packed with fantastic information on all the areas of online marketing. Very impressive!

Picking the niche that's right for you is a very important part of building your business. The information you provide is a must for online entrepreneurs."

- Colette Marshall
Marketing Director
www.WorldwideBrands.com

"Congratulations! Your book really is an incredible source of information! ☺ In fact, there's so much killer material in there it's more like a home study course than a book!

As we all know there are an unlimited number of niche markets in the world, but that doesn't mean that they will all be profitable!

You have taken out all the guesswork at finding potentially profitable niches by using your "5 Niche Sourcing Qualifiers" to systematically weed out all the 'rubbish' and reveal the hidden treasure. Best of all, that's just one of the strategies you cover in the book.

It's bound to be an instant classic. Keep up the great work and I look forward to reading more of your material in the future! ☺"

- David Jenyns
Trader, Author And Coach
www.freetradingsystems.org

"I find your book *'Mastering Niche Marketing'* one of the most thorough books on the niche topic out there.

You really go into great detail showing how to find profitable niches then drill it down to everything needed to begin creating cash flow from them.

Another very interesting thing is you go beyond what other internet marketing books teach where you show how to set up a business. You give all the details online marketers want to know and I think that's a great bonus-worth of information to make available (it answers the important questions new marketers ponder on setting up their business).

I'm sure anyone interested in the niche marking will find your *'Mastering Niche Marketing'* book a valuable resource and solution to making their niches profitable."

- Michael Nicholas
Read The Newsletter The Gurus Read!
http://www.ImpactInfoMarketing.com

"Hi Eric,

It's Terry Telford from TerryTelford.com. I just wanted to write you a quick note to compliment you on your new book, *'Mastering Niche Marketing.'* Although I was very impressed with the detail you've given, I think you got the title of the book wrong. I would suggest, "If you read this book and apply the principles, you will make money . . . Period." Although my title is a little longer than yours! ☺

In all seriousness, Eric, this book is a must read for anyone who is considering using the internet to earn an extra income, or even making a career of it. The step-by-step detail you've covered leaves "no stone unturned."

I feel this book will be beneficial for 2 types of people. The first group of people who need to read this book are people who are just beginning online and are floundering because they don't have an easy to follow, step-by-step strategy to follow. The second segment of the market who can benefit from your book are the people like myself, who already make a good living online, but want to tack on an extra income stream. Quite often a back to the basics approach does wonders from revitalizing a company's cash flow.

Thanks for putting together a solid tutorial that will benefit people and make an impact in their lives.

Talk again soon.

Enjoy your day!"

Terry ☺
www.TerryTelford.com

"What can I say WOW you've covered EVERYTHING there is to cover to start from scratch and build a successful business. This is like the absolute Online Business Bible. Wow, . . . you've done a ton of research here. Well done & Congratulations!"

- Richard Osterude
The Marketing Dad
www.marketingdad.com

"There is no way in the world any newbie can succeed online without choosing the right niche market and focusing on it. This is an excellent book to help any newbies research and zero in on the perfect niche. Side note: I love the screenshots throughout the book."

- Mike Mograbi
Internet Marketing News Watch
www.imnewswatch.com

"Just wanted to drop you a line to congratulate you on the creation of such a wonderful resource!

With 100% conviction I can completely recommend *'Mastering Niche Marketing'* to anyone who is considering purchasing it. This guide is not one of the normal get rich quick books or read how I made millions books - it is truly unique.

Now absolutely anyone will be able to follow your step-by-step formula to finding a niche based upon their hobbies or passions. One of the greatest things I found is that you really go into such detail in every single step. I have to admit that I was skeptical when I started to read it but I was absolutely blown away - I really did not expect the level of detail which you have gone into.

I love the way that you guide people by the hand - there are going to be loads of people who have you to thank for helping them to become successful at making money on the internet.

I went through your guide with a fine tooth comb looking to find something which was missing. No matter how hard I looked I was not able to find one. Everything is there - market research, product creation, website setup, copywriting, traffic - everything.

Let's face the facts, making money on the internet is not as easy as it used to be – however, you have identified every single area which the 'newbie' needs to know about. With this information in their arsenal they can avoid all the pitfalls and start making money fast based upon a product which they are actually interested in.

To be absolutely honest I do think you have actually made a mistake, this is not a guide - this is a complete home study course!

Well done Eric - you have done it again - you have managed to create a resource which is designed to help people.

If only this had been around when I started all those years ago!"

- Peter Cunningham
Scarborough, U.K.
Editor - Salt Water Aquarium/Aquarists Online
www.AquaristsOnline.com

"This is a very good book and was laid out so logically even a beginner could follow along. You offered an easy process with great information about what to do and not to do when evaluating and choosing a niche. The step-by-step process of actually developing a niche was enlightening and you offered excellent resources for researching viable niches. Great job!"

- **Karon Thackston**
Author of 'How To Write Successful PPC Ads'
http://www.writeppcads.com

The *EXCLUSIVE* Supplemental can be YOUR own virtual ATM Cash Machine!

One of my main goals for providing this valuable resource is to make sure you receive the information that most marketers tend to NOT include in their teachings! So I've decided to give you what you've been missing in your education - the most essential element in setting up your business!

Businesses have failed because this information you are about to read has not been put into practice! Don't make the same mistake!

Another reason for this supplemental report is to provide you, the reader, a simple alternative to making cash . . . ! And here is how:

I've published a digital version of The *EXCLUSIVE* Supplemental and I'm making it available to you for free. All you'll need to do is get that document branded with your own personal referral link. Then, once you start recommending or referring that report to others and they purchase my book, it'll become your 24 hour, 7 days a week, 365 days a year - ATM Cash Machine!

All you need to do is get your own personal link - and this will cost you nothing as well! So, to get your link, you must sign up as an affiliate (otherwise, you will not receive any of the commissions as a result of those you refer). ☹

> **STOP!** - before you continue, make sure to join my affiliate program. You will get paid a **70%* commission** for each sale you refer! So sign up at the following website: http://www.nichesourcing.com/affiliate.htm
>
> It's highly recommended that you do this **NOW** before you soon forget! Action takers will be rewarded with an extremely generous commission! ☺ Put this book down NOW and surf to the website above!!

All you have to do is visit the website indicated above, sign up to the affiliate program and receive your own digital version of The *EXCLUSIVE* Supplemental. You can then give it away to others for free as an incentive to acquire subscribers. You'll grow your opt-in list and every individual that receives that document will increase your chance of making generous commissions!

Absolutely No SPAM can be used to promote this report!

* Regular affiliates will be rewarded a commission of 50% until they have successfully referred 9 sales. As an incentive and reward, affiliates will earn 70% on all additional sales made. I believe in rewarding individuals who are action takers!

Table of Contents

------ Eric V. Van Der Hope's *EXCLUSIVE* Supplemental ------

THE GROUNDWORK: Success Starts With the Proper Conditioning

Part 1: Thorough Planning and Proper Mindset

Part 2: Design Your Business With A Proper Foundation

- Sole Proprietorship.
- Corporation.
- Partnerships.

- Properly File Your Business Name.
- Obtain a Business License.
- Obtain a Sales Tax Permit (optional depending on your type of business).
- Obtain a Resale permit (optional depending on your type of business).

Part 3: An Ingredient To Success - Doing Something YOU enjoy!

------ End *EXCLUSIVE* Supplemental ------

PHASE 1: Finding A Niche Market

Chapter 1: Niche Sourcing 101

Chapter 2: 'Shooting blanks'? Choose From 9 Effective Business Models

Chapter 3: Decision Time – Choose the Niche You Want to Focus On

Chapter 4: Purchase Your Virtual Storefront

PHASE 2: Creating the Product

Chapter 5: Choose Product Format/Package

Chapter 6: Create & Design Your Niche Product

PHASE 3: Developing the Offer

Chapter 7: Designing Your Niche Website / Salesletter

PHASE 4: Creating the Back End Product

Chapter 8: Increase Your Profits Exponentially – Develop Your Backend

Chapter 9: Testing Phase – then Go LIVE!

PHASE 5: Generate Targeted Traffic

Chapter 10: Traffic Control

Chapter 11: Keeping Your Customers Happy – Exceed Their Expectations

PHASE 6: Duplication of Process

The Wrap Up: Afterthoughts

ADDITIONAL RESOURCES

Foreword

In your electronic "hands", you hold the key to a virtual kingdom. When you finish reading this very complete guide to creating and marketing a product online, you'll know what to do, how to do it and when to do it.

But . . . will you do it? Will you follow through and take the steps that will lead to your success, the kind of success that will allow you and your family to enjoy life on your terms? Or will you simply continue to follow the same path you've been on, doing the same old things and getting the same old results.

Presuming that you're looking for a change . . . an improvement . . . something different in your life, we should discuss the difference between those who succeed and those who fail.

Amazingly enough, it generally comes down to one simple word: Action.

You either take Action or you don't.

If you take Action, you move forward towards the change, the improvement in your life. If you don't take Action, you remain stuck where you are. If you're exactly where you'd like to be in life, being stuck is just fine. But I'll bet you'd really like to be somewhere else.

That somewhere else might be the joy of being your own boss and working from home, or the fun of buying a new car, or the pleasure of new home, or just being able to relax when the bills come in the mail because you know you've got them covered (and then some!).

I believe it's in the human nature to want to accomplish more in our lives . . . to move forward . . . to face new challenges.

I also believe that when we're not doing that, we are unsettled, uneasy and not at peace with ourselves. Sure, we can pretend that we're happy with our "lot in life." But that's just make believe. We can make excuses for where we are in our lives, but the uncluttered bottom line to this is simple.

You can make money or you can make excuses.

You can't do both.

So I urge you to take Action . . . to move forward in your life toward some goal you want to achieve. The hardest part of taking action is taking the first step. The next hardest part is building sustainable momentum.

Here's the simple way I like to approach this:

Make a commitment to yourself that you'll take at least one small step every day towards achieving your goal. No matter how bad your day was, or how long you had to slave at your other job, don't make excuses. Take at least one step each day. On good days, do more. On bad days, do less, but take at least one step forward.

If you'll do this for yourself, then you'll be amazed at what's happened by the time you reach the end of the first month. You'll have taken at least 30 steps forward in your business. For many people, this is 25 (or 30!) more steps than they've ever taken before. You'll have positive momentum. You'll start to see results. With this momentum on your side, you'll be pretty much unstoppable now. You'll let nothing stand between you and success.

It all starts when you do two things: (1) take the first step. (2) Make the commitment to do something - no matter how small - every single day.

I feel, however, that it's only fair to warn you that when you get started, you'll have a lot of days when you feel like you're not getting anywhere. You might feel like you're in the deep end of the pool and you're just treading water. You're not moving forward.

It's natural to feel this way. Don't let it stop you from continuing to take those positive steps each day. Because you are moving forward, it just takes a little time to build enough momentum that you can feel the progress.

It's natural that all of us want leap from having no business to having a thriving business that brings in the big bucks. But it doesn't work that way. You can't earn $10,000 a month, until you first learn how to make the first hundred dollars. And then make $1,000. You have to start at the beginning. Everyone does.

For example, when I started publishing my newsletter and building my opt-in list years ago, I only had 1 subscriber . . . me. To get the second subscriber, I registered with Hotmail for a second email address. Now, since I've steadily built the list over the years, my list has over 1,000,000 subscribers. But I had to start with just 1 before I could grow to a million.

As I mentioned, during the early days of your business, you'll often feel like you're making no progress. When that happens to me during the early phases of a project, I think back to the childhood story of the person who has a choice between receiving $1,000,000 or the value of a penny doubled every day for 1 month. Of course, we all know now what the penny can grow to - way more than $1,000,000 at $10,737,418.23 when you add up the 30 days.

But did you ever think about how that penny being doubled looks in the early days?

Day 1 - $0.01
Day 2 - $0.02
Day 3 - $0.04
Day 4 - $0.08
Day 5 - $0.16
Day 6 - $0.32
Day 7 - $0.64

Look at that! After 1 week, that penny has only grown to $0.64. It hardly seems worthwhile. In fact, it's hard to believe that in just 3 more weeks, you'll be looking at over a million dollars. But you will.

When you feel like you're working away at your business, but you don't see huge progress, remember this story. You're just in the early days of those pennies doubling and gaining momentum to grow into something really valuable. If you quit in the early days, you'll be left with virtually nothing.

But when you keep moving forward - taking Action - you'll achieve whatever you want.

It all comes down to Action. As you read this book, take notes and refine them into your Action Plan. Then, start doing the steps in your Action Plan right away. Do them every day. Do this and . . .

I know you're going to be a great big success!

Shawn M. Casey, J.D.
www.ShawnCasey.com

How To Get The Most Out Of This Book

Before I get into the 'meat and potatoes' of this book, I'm going to be quite frank with you on a couple of facts about running a profitable business. So I'm going to get straight to the point here! ☺

If you feel that you can run a business without a budget (MONEY), you are in for a seriously rude awakening!

I cannot tell you how many people have asked me if they could start something with absolutely nothing, or someone does not have enough money for food but they are willing to spend their last few dollars to start what they feel is a great opportunity!

If someone is in this most unfortunate circumstance, action must first be taken to fix that situation before anything else!

Now, don't get me wrong . . . I'm not saying it's not impossible for some people to actually start and run a profitable business from nothing, but the chances are very, very slim. Most people don't have the willpower nor a burning desire to make it happen.

Actually, you may or may not have already heard this - but for the most part if you haven't heard, you're going to have to come out from under the rock you've been hiding under!

Success results from your ACTIONS!

You must put to use the methods I've discussed within this book or you will not reap the benefits!

Let's compare this to completing a race . . .

Obviously the goal is to win the race. However, if you can't accomplish this, you should at least complete it! If you don't actually start - you will never finish! This is obvious - right?

The point I'm trying to get across is that if you fail to take action to complete the necessary steps, you will never finish your race!

You must absolutely take Action, there is no other way.

Your success is up to you. How much does it mean to you? Do you want it bad enough? Only you can answer that . . .

If you can't get past this barrier, than going into business for yourself may not be for you!

Seems kind of harsh, but I'm being realistic.

Whether your goal is to be like a Bill Gates, an Oparah Winfrey, a Donald Trump, a millionaire, or a successful businessperson, you need to have guts, have to practice patience, need a tremendous amount of will power, be an action taker, be a good listener, a good learner, an adventurer, an opportunist - the list goes on and on!

I'm a firm believer in not "reinventing the wheel twice". If your wish is to be successful at something - then imitate someone who is doing it successfully!

I'll admit, I'm not some 'big named' guru making millions of dollars, but I am the guy that's finding success at making small niches profitable and as a result creating a steady stream of passive income that continues to grow to this day!

Throughout this book, I'm going to recommend that you use specific tools or resources that will be beneficial for your business. Some tools will be free & others will have a cost associated with them. Either way, I will always recommend something that I've successfully used in the past, am currently using or it's from a source that I know and trust. The tools that I've recommended have contributed to the growth of my business.

But there is a catch . . . ! You've got to use them! It will be up to you to decide if investing in these resources will make an impact on your business. Only you will be able to decide if these tools will fit into your budget and ultimately help you with your business.

Let me reiterate for you, you've been gravely misled if you feel that your business doesn't need money or that this whole business idea is going to be a "cake walk" without any effort!

Business people can expect to spend hundreds of thousands of dollars on a storefront business. Therefore, going into this kind of business is out of reach for the normal person that has the aspirations of succeeding as an entrepreneur.

The advantage of developing a business online makes it extremely possible for everyone - no matter who they are, to operate and manage something meaningful. The costs involved are extremely low compared to the "traditional" business.

Understanding that there will be costs associated with the services needed to operate your business increases the probability that you'll be successful as your business grows.

The more tools you have available to help in the growth of your business, the better chance your business will continue to grow.

However, this doesn't mean that the more money you have will guarantee the growth of your business! It's basically up to you, your wants, needs, your desires - it all comes down to if you are willing to WORK AT IT by taking ACTION!

Other benefits to managing an online business other than the obvious low cost is that your 'virtual storefront' is open 24 hours a day, 7 days a week, 365 days a year! Also, your market is now open to the world. A "traditional" business is limited to marketing within its local area. These two benefits alone increase your profit potential exponentially!

This book does not promise you that by reading it you will make thousands of dollars, or that you'll make hundreds of dollars, or for that matter any money at all! There is no quick money or quick fix here . . . this is solely up to you! I'm sure you've heard the biblical quote: "you reap what you sow". This is so very true. Whether its building a website, making money or creating wealth - it all comes down to what YOU do, not someone else! The more effort you put into your business, whether it's hard work, resources, or investments - the more chances that you and your business will thrive.

The possibilities are unlimited!

My hope in writing this book has been to create a down-to-earth resource that will be easy to understand and provide a foundation to start your very own business.

In order to get the most from this book, could I humbly make a suggestion? ☺

If you have the digital version of this book, please print it for ease of reading, hole-punch the pages and organize it into a binder. Now, you are not limited to reading your book from the computer. You'll also have the opportunity of taking notes as you follow along with your reading. Make it your workbook - mark it up, highlight it - whatever it takes to get the most use out of it!

If you have the paperback version of this book - excellent! You can read this book from anywhere, so go ahead and use it as a workbook if you'd like . . . by marking it up, highlighting it - however you think it'll help you learn everything within this book!

I'll show you in 6 steps how to identify, create and promote a high demand product, so you will notice that the book is divided into 6 phases. From beginning to end I'll discuss and explain the topics within their chapters during which I'll describe what you should do. At the end of each section, additional resources, tidbits of useful information and suggestions will be provided.

You'll begin to understand, if you do not already know, that your success will depend on a combination of (but not limited to) the following attributes:

- The proper planning.
- A deep-seated desire.
- Mentally visualizing your goal.
- Willingness to ACTUALLY TAKE ACTION!

What this book will do for you is limited to how far you are willing to go, how determined you are and what your priorities are!

So what are you waiting for . . . !?

Let's get started! ☺

Introduction & Overview

The purpose of this book is to outline the most effective ways to turn your interests, hobbies, or talents into key components of an online business. Particularly when you have the right tools to hand, you are in an incredibly strong position to achieve success in a niche or specialist market, when you run a business that's related to something you're passionate about.

Exactly what it says on the tin, this book will take you step-by-step through the process of setting up your own successful business. It'll provide you with the essential pieces of information you need to turn your passions into a profitable business from the start. The rest is up to you.

Before we go much further, it's important to consider exactly why niche marketing is such a great approach to doing business. A number of old adages apply here. Stick to what you know is the most significant and the most direct. When you do something you know, whether it's playing a particular sport, studying a particular subject, practicing a particular profession, or, yes, running a particular business, you are much better off when whatever you're doing is a reflection of something you are genuinely interested in.

Ask almost any successful person about their career choice and they'll probably tell you that they are doing exactly what they dreamed of doing for much of their life, or, at the very least, if they didn't have that much foresight growing up, they are at least doing the only think they can imagine wanting to do for the rest of their life.

Job satisfaction, or, perhaps more accurately, career satisfaction, is a key component to personal success. That doesn't just mean financial success, of course, because perhaps you want desperately to be a teacher. Most teachers aren't well paid but that doesn't mean to say all teachers are destined to be frustrated with their professional lives. Quite the contrary.

Combining your talents, hobbies, interests, and passions, incorporating them into your profession; this is a very powerful step towards becoming a happy and whole human being. It may sound a little weird, but at the end of the day, personal happiness makes a difference to a life in so many ways.

This book will present you with just about all the information you need to set up a successful business targeting a market niche related, one way or another, to you; what you know or do best. However, before we begin to look at what you need to do to set up a successful business, it's as well to consider a few points about what not to do.

At the end of the day, rule number one, if you want to have a business, you have to have some way to facilitate the exchange of money. Specifically, you need something - a product or a service - that's compelling enough that people want to give you money in exchange for it. The way to ensure that this exchange is facilitated one way or another is to find a way to serve customers. Particularly when you're looking at niche marketing, serving your customers is about identifying and ultimately helping to fulfill a need of theirs. Part of your business and marketing strategy, as we will see shortly, will focus on identifying and exploiting niche markets.

What is a niche market?

The formal definition is generally along these lines: it's a small but potentially profitable market segments for which it is possible to design and provide a form of custom-made products or specialized services.

At this point, it's helpful, before we look at how you can go about tapping a niche market, to get a better understanding of what we're talking about. First, the word "niche" was originally used by ecologists to describe the position of a species and its use of resources within a given environment. What the term implies in a business context is a situation or activity that is ideally suited to a particular person, group of people, or personality type.

So what does it generally take to become a successful niche marketer? Believe it or not, the notion of niche marketing is fairly old but it is gaining new significance in the world thanks largely to the development of the internet. Think for a moment about what the internet is allowing the modern world to do and you can immediately begin to see the connection to niche marketing. Now, you don't have to run a business online to be a successful niche marketer, however, these days, running a business online is not only easy, it tends to be pretty cost-effective as well. The internet, however, opens up the whole world. People in Europe can connect instantly with people in the United States, Australia, Africa, Asia. Virtually anywhere, with anyone, so long as there is an internet connection and some kind of console, such as a computer or even a mobile cell phone or PDA system that allows an internet hook-up. Bringing people together like this, the internet effectively tears down or negates the geographical borders between individuals around the world. Someone interested in Star Wars and who lives in Asia, can connect in seconds to someone else with the same interests virtually anywhere in the world.

Everyone is unique, with their own unique set of needs and interests, but the internet, in particular, makes specialist knowledge more accessible to individuals in general. It also draws together existing niche markets, people with special interests, and provides businesses with a means of reaching significant numbers without having to spread their business out over a large area.

At the end of the day, niche marketing is about targeting. The internet makes the target market larger, more accessible, but the principles are the same whether you are developing a niche market business online or offline.

This book will help you set out in the right direction, not just to set up a successful business but to establish a business that will bring you great personal and professional satisfaction in addition to great personal and material wealth. Above all, keep in mind that, as an entrepreneur, your chief obligation is to be true to and to balance both the creative and the practical aspects of who you are.

Wherever the road takes you, enjoy the journey from here on in; good luck!

------ Eric V. Van Der Hope's *EXCLUSIVE* Supplemental ------

The Groundwork:
Your Success Starts with the Proper Conditioning

"Time & time again, I've noticed that most marketers completely 'miss the boat' on this critical element while they try to explain how to set up a business - it's almost scary! Furthermore, they are doing YOU an injustice by not including this within their teaching! So - learn this information and then use it!" --- **Eric V. Van Der Hope**

Part 1
Thorough Planning and Proper Mindset

i.i   Preparing Your Business The Right Way.

What is the right way to prepare a business?

Before you make any decisions about your business, it is essential that you understand and attend to some of the most fundamental aspects of good business practice. Business, your professional life, like your personal life, requires a lot of work, a lot of constant vigilance, affirmation, and reaffirmation for you to stay on track. One way to look at the process of planning and setting yourself up for a new business is to consider that the right way to start a business depends on whether or not you have the right attitude.

The right attitude for business includes willingness and a reasonable comfort-level for spending money. Most entrepreneurs also benefit from a desire to educate themselves in a given area relating to their business. Along the same vein, it is also helpful to be ready and willing, not to mention able, to learn and take action based on what you have learned in a given situation. Above all, entrepreneurs must be patient. Businesses take time to develop. It takes time to tap a market, even a small and specialized market. You need to be patient with your business and with yourself; you've also got to be patient with your customers and any other individuals with whom you have contact as a business person.

The best businesses are the ones that receive the devotion, care, and attention of their owners without the owner becoming too invested in the outcome. A lot of very successful business people experienced a trial-and-error phase in their career; they tried out some business ideas, invested money perhaps, which ultimately did not bring any or much of a return on investment (ROI).

Good business planning boils down to preparedness. It's about mental preparedness and practical preparedness as well as individual preparedness and general preparedness for a given venture. It's also about cultivating and maintaining a positive mental attitude towards your business and about not letting yourself become too invested in the outcome. Because you can't predict the direction of your life, you can't assess whether or not a business venture or how you approach challenges in life, is a success or failure. Every step you take in life leads down a road, on a journey to a destination you cannot precisely identify or predict. Planning a business the right way is about focusing your thoughts in a positive way to make the most of whatever experiences you have.

Essentially, in order to manage your business, you must have the right attitude, have the desire to continually learn and you must be patient and willing to prepare.

i.ii   Focusing Your Mental Attitude: Focus the Power of Your Thoughts.

In 1910, a writer by the name of Wallace D. Wattles published a book entitled "The Science of Getting Rich". The content of that book has recently been revived and represented, repackaged, if you will, into a book relatively new on the market, known as "The Secret".

Despite something of a cloak and dagger routine about the main idea it presents, the book actually discusses nothing more complex or unknown than the fairly well recognized and circulated principles of the law of attraction. One of the most fundamental and powerful reasoning of philosophers at any given time, the law of attraction contends that "like attracts like". The principle applies in many areas of life and has ultimately been considered one of the most powerful principles in the universe for some time. Many people believe this particular wisdom stretches all the way back to as early as 3500BC.

We can apply the law of attraction to generate the best possible business experience for ourselves by focusing on what we think and feel at a given time, by channeling these thoughts and feelings to bring into our lives the things we want.

By accepting that we create our own circumstances by the choices we make in life and that those choices are fueled by our thoughts, we begin to accept responsibility for our actions, gain greater control over our lives, and thus establish our mental attitude as positive and receptive to new experience, thoughts, feelings, and desires.

i.iii   Start by Setting Goals: In Order to Reach Your Full Potential.

First of all, let's define a goal. A goal is something that makes a positive change in your life. It's something that forms a new habit or changes an existing habit; it improves or develops a skill, talent, or ability. It might help you to focus on realizing a dream or improving your performance on a task or activity.

One of the most effective ways to focus your thoughts to achieve what you want is goal setting. The best way to 'set' your goals is to simply write them down. Unfortunately, this is easier said than done for most people. Those that do try goal setting are often discouraged by the process when things don't turn out as they expected.

What the vast majority don't realize about goal setting: a few golden rules must be followed otherwise your goals are going to be unattainable. If you're goal is to be a millionaire, for example, you're unlikely to achieve this goal unless you actually think - emotionally, physically and visually expressing the ideas in your goal setting - the several steps you must take to become a millionaire. You have to consider, for example, that you should **a)** become extremely good at money management; **b)** find a great business idea; and **c)** more likely than not, you need an efficient investment strategy to make money on money so that you can develop residual income. In other words, you have to be realistic.

You should consider the following as general rules for setting your goals:

1) You should set goals for every area of your life to reflect the general direction in which you want to go. Those general areas can be categorized along the following lines: Financial and Career, Family and Home, Spiritual and Ethical, Physical Health, Social and Cultural, and Mental and Education. Goal setting in each area of your life will help to ensure that you are balanced. It will also help you to look closely at the fundamentals of your every day life, which should allow you to see what you need to change.

2) You must make sure your goal is something you actually want to achieve. Everyone is different. When setting goals, it is essential that your goals are consistent with your values.

3) A goal should not contradict any of your other goals. One good example: wanting to purchase a $750,000 house with an income goal of $50,000 per year. This is a classic example of non-integrated thinking and ultimately, it will sabotage any and all work you put in to earning your goals. You should really work hard, instead, to eliminate clashing ideas from your thinking to achieve your goals.

4) You should write your goals in a positive voice instead of a negative voice. For example, say "I will be rich" instead of "I will not be poor"; "I will be successful" in stead of "I won't be a failure". Your subconscious mind is a very powerful tool. The more often you use positive instructions, the more often you will see the achievements of your goals.

5) You must write your goal out in complete detail. One of the keys to effective goal setting is detailed thinking. Think about your objectives in detail and make sure that you write all those details down, as if you are using your mind like a magic wand. You have to be specific about what you want to achieve. Instead of writing "I want a successful business" write something like, "I want a successful online niche marketing business". Instead of writing "I want a new home", write "I want a three bedroom apartment on the Upper West Side" or "I want a five bedroom, two-storey family home with two bathrooms, and 4,000 square feet of space". This well thought out, detailed thinking will help your subconscious mind achieve what you want.

6) It's important to make sure your goal is high enough. There IS such a thing as setting a goal too low. Your goals should be realistic but it should also be something that you can aspire to; something you can work towards.

7) You should definitely write down your goals. Write down your goals to create a roadmap. Instead of just writing down your goals, you must review your goals frequently; if you haven't written them down, it's unnecessarily difficult to do this. Plus, the more focused you are on your goals; the more likely you are to achieve them.

The benefits of goal setting are numerous. First of all, they give you a target to aim for, which many authorities insist is very important for achieving goals. One author, Dr. Maxwell Maltz, author of Psycho-Cybernetics, said that human beings have built-in goal seeking mechanisms in their subconscious minds. This part of our minds, the success mechanism, helps you search for ways to reach your targets and find answers to your problems. Also according to Maltz, people work and feel better when their success mechanism is engaged. Goals provide your successful mechanism with clear targets of your own choosing.

Goals can also help you concentrate your time and efforts. Typically, goal setters achieve outstanding results when they have learned how to focus and concentrate time, energy, and resources on a single objective. The concentrated power produces results that are much greater than those achieved through the diffused and unfocused energy.

Another advantage of goal setting is that each goal you set provides motivation, persistence, and desire. The famous illustration of this is of Thomas Edison failing over one thousand times before he discovered a way to make the light bulb work! Almost without exception, high achievers keep picking themselves up after each of their falls and continue to work steadily towards their targets until they are reached.

Goals help you to establish priorities and they can provide a roadmap to take you from where you are to where you want to be. Strategies that are focused help you stay focused as well.

An expert estimates that only 10% of people actually think about goals for their life on a regular basis. Less than 3% actually bother to write them down. Position yourself within this small percentage and you'll more than likely achieve what you set out to do.

Now that we've discussed the importance of goal setting, I'd like to share with you a goal setting model that I've modified from several sources over the years and that has proven to work quite successfully in my life. I call it the **"6-Step Action Plan to Success"**:

Step #1: Set your "3-5 Year Goals"
Step #2: Set your "Yearly Goals"
Step #3: Set your "Quarterly Goals"
Step #4: Set your "Monthly Goals"
Step #5: Set your "Weekly Goals"
Step #6: Set your "Daily Goals"

Step #1: Set your "3-5 Year Goals"

If you are having difficulty coming up with goals, you must 'set the tone,' and get into the right frame-of-mind! The following are a few suggestions to get your mind thinking. In the next 3-5 years, visualize where you want to be in your personal development. Economically and financially, where do you want to be? Where do you want to be in your business?

You can't hold back here . . . think big but be reasonable! ☺

Also, you must be specific in developing your goals. For example, if you say "I want to be making lots of money," this is not specific enough - you must state an actual amount.

Step #2: Set your "Yearly Goals"

Now that you've decided on your primary goals, it is essential to break these goals down into smaller, 'bite size' objectives that will be more manageable to achieve.

Again, ask yourself questions to activate your thought process. Start with asking yourself: "What should I do within the year to meet the expectations I set for myself to achieve my 3-5 year goals?"

This is YOUR time to brainstorm - so don't hold anything back!

Write down as many goals as you can think of.

Done . . . !?

Now, you probably have too many goals on your list - right!?

No problem! This is your chance to trim down what is most important to you. At this point you should single out, in order of importance to you, 5 main goals you'd like to get completed.

Don't overwhelm yourself with a big list of goals - the reason why I'll suggest only 5, so keep it simple and manageable! ☺

The goals you've decided to work on for the year will ultimately help you attain your primary goals. I cannot emphasize enough the importance of achieving these milestones/goals. By achieving them you are well on your way to reaching and enjoying your primary goals.

Step #3: Set your "Quarterly Goals"

After setting your yearly goals, you've probably grumbled to yourself after realizing that these goals may seem too big to accomplish! ☹ So, your quarterly goals will give you the opportunity to set smaller, more attainable benchmarks that will set the foundation to reaching your yearly goals.

Before each quarter starts, you should review what you were able to accomplish in the last quarter and then decide what needs to be done for the next quarter in order to keep up in a forward moving direction towards the completion of your yearly goals.

Keep in mind, that as you continue to set your goals, milestones or benchmarks, they should all be reasonable and attainable and most important - specific! If you can maintain this thought process, there is no reason that you cannot accomplish what you want! ☺

Step #4: Set your "Monthly Goals"

The same process that was explained in the previous steps should also be applied here.

Decide on the top goals you need to get completed in order to reach your quarterly goals.

Step #5: Set your "Weekly Goals"

Again, by repeating the same process as in the last step, you'll be able to reach your weekly goals.

Ask yourself what top goals or benchmarks need to be accomplished in order to reach your monthly goals?

Now that you've narrowed down the benchmarking to a weekly basis, it may be a bit more difficult to maintain a consistent 'Top 5.' It certainly wouldn't be out of question to have several minor goals or benchmarks that need to be completed by the end of the week. Therefore, you should review what needs to get accomplished at the beginning of the week to decide which are most important to get done first.

Step #6: Set your "Daily Goals"

By now, I'm sure you've seen a pattern emerge from these goal setting steps! ☺

That being said, your daily tasks are what you need to do in order to reach your weekly goals. Each of your steps will draw you closer and closer to your ultimate goals.

Can you see the method to this madness . . . !? ☺ Well, it actually works!

In order to get off on the right foot, but more important the right frame-of-mind for the entire day, you need to set time aside each day to create your 'to do' list.

In simple terms, create a list of things you need to accomplish that day that will get you nearer to your goal and or goals. Even if it's a list of 1 or 2 'actions,' you are moving in the right direction.

As a suggestion and to create a sense of urgency, you should accomplish this task before you do anything else in the morning, even before your daily routine of reading your local paper, watching your local news on T.V., even checking your 'snail' mail or for that matter - your email!

Set the tone for the day by actually telling yourself what's most important - you'll find that this will create momentum and propel you towards completing your goals.

Start making small steps forward. No matter how insignificant these steps may seem to you, as long as you keep moving forward, you'll achieve what you've set out to do. If you only have 45 minutes a day or 2 hours a week to commit to reaching your goals or the growth of your business - it's better than nothing at all! ☺

The fact is, if you fail to plan your goals and work towards reaching them, you never will. Put procrastination in the shredder and make the time - no matter how little you feel you have!

Soon, you will find that you've accomplished a significant number of tasks if you maintain a relatively active goal setting itinerary, in a short amount of time.

Once you have your goals planned out and on paper, you must remind yourself of them constantly or you will forget what you are trying to do! Make your goals available in a number of different places to remind yourself what you are actively pursuing.

Post stickies in as many places as you know you will be to remind yourself of what you want to get accomplished - your bathroom mirror, your refrigerator, your computer, your game room, near your T.V. - everywhere you think you'll be!

Ideally, your goals should not be collecting dust on your desk! Take action and quit the procrastination!

You are the only person in control of your destiny. So, you are the only person at fault if you don't get done what you planned. You have only yourself to blame, so - get rid of all the distractions and plan your day, weeks, and months accordingly! ☺

So, follow what's been outlined here, you'll be pleasantly surprised at what you can get accomplished in very little time. If you can get into this invaluable routine, you'll be well on your way towards success at whatever you do! ☺

i.iv   Develop Your 'Battle Plan': What Is It Going To Take For Success?

What does it take to be successful? Most people have no idea how to answer this question. That's exactly why they (and you) need a battle plan before you do anything else to turn your hobby into a business.

Of course, when we say 'battle plan' we're actually talking about several different documents that together map out your larger strategy. The most common documents are business plans, marketing plans, strategic plans, and financial plans. Less often than not, these documents are combined into one complete plan. For ease of reference, however, we're going to look at how to develop four separate documents.

Let's start off with the business plan.

A business plan basically explains your business idea to outsiders. Most of the time business plans are used to secure financial backing. They tend to be written to argue the case for the business. They're designed to explain and show why such and such a business idea constitutes a worthy investment.

The following sections make up the **business plan**:

The Executive Summary. As odd as this might sound, the opening section of your business plan should be written last. There is, however, one very good reason for this. The executive summary should summarize the main points of your business plan. You need to know your main points - and really nail them - to be able to summarize them. Even if you're creating a business plan for your own reference, you should make sure that the executive summary grabs your attention and convinces you that your business idea is a really good one.

The Company. You need to provide a company overview in your business plan. This section should basically describe how you plan to build the foundation for your company. It should include a brief history of your company, explaining what type of legal entity the company will form, and who will own the company. This section should also summarize the start-up costs of the company and give some indication of where the initial funding is going to come from. Even if you don't plan to do anything too fancy with your business, even if you want to fund it yourself and keep the profits to yourself, it's still a great idea to have a formal business plan that includes this type of information. It really will help you stay grounded! ☺

Your Products and Services. The cornerstone of your business is the product or service that you provide to your customers. In the third section of your business plan, in no uncertain terms, you should describe the products and services you intend to sell, explaining precisely (even if it's for your reference only) how you intend to sell these products and why customers are going to buy them. Make sure that you can explain the benefits that the service or product offers and how much it will cost to deliver what you're selling.

Your Market. The next task is to describe your target market. You should research your market's demographics, growth trends and predicted growth potential, plus any additional information about future markets. You should also furnish your plan with a chart detailing your market forecasting. It's also in this section that you should briefly describe the nature of the industry you plan to operate in, who your competitors are, and why your presence is needed.

Strategy and Implementation. Focus your strategy onto your particular market segment, in this case your niche market. Explain why the products or services you offer are going to address the particular wants and needs of the market you've identified. Explain how you're going to put your product or service out there on the market. You should also try to forecast your sales and calculate the basic costs you are going to incur for each sale. Try to combine all of this information and set yourself a series of milestones with dates. The dates are important. Set up your budget and, even if it's just you running the business, define the specific responsibilities you will have and how you will meet them.

Management Team. If it's just you, and if you're not planning on showing your business plan to anyone, feel free to skip this section. However, if you want a confidence booster, perhaps you'd like to feature the management section. What's required here is an overview of your business team. Generally, key members of a business team include the manager, CEO, and other key personnel, such as marketing specialists and financial advisors. Basically, you would name and describe each key member, explaining one way or another why they are perfect for the job they've been assigned within your company. You should also include a table to show personnel costs; about how much you expect to pay everyone. Then, if there are any vacant positions on your team, you should list those too.

Financial Projections. As the title of this section suggests, you need to describe the financial strategy of your company. The more detail you can provide in this section, the more organized you are going to be as you start to implement your 'battle plan'. The fewer unknowns you have in business, the better. You should include here a detailed overview of your financial strategy and evidence to support your projected growth patterns you're relying upon. You should also include your break-even analysis here; basically, this is the chart that shows when you're going to start making a profit, how long it's going to take. Then, you should also detail the fixed and variable costs of your business and make some representation of your projected profit and loss, cash flow, and overall cash levels. You should also feature a balance sheet somewhere to show the status of your business finances month-to-month for somewhere between one and three years.

The golden rule: this may sound like a lot of work but the more work you put into developing a sound, comprehensive 'battle plan', of which the business plan is a major part, the better prepared you are going to be to run your business.

Okay, next we have the **marketing plan**:

Since your intention is to offer a niche business, you really need to nail your marketing. A comprehensive marketing plan will really go a long way to helping you do this. As with the business plan, try not to flinch at the notion that this might require a bit of time. It will, but your return on investment will be very high and well worth the trouble! ☺

Here are the basic components of a marketing plan. Again, you should bear in mind that most businesses present their marketing plan formally, whether it's to investors or to loan officers at the bank. You can, and probably should, prepare your plan as if you were going to show it to investors, even if you're likely to be the only one to see it. The sounder your plan, the more likely it is to bring you business success.

So, here ya' go:

Step one in market plan creation: you must focus on your customer. Start out by defining your product or service. Explain the benefits in detail from the perspective of your customer. Next, show how your product or service differs from those of your competitors. For example, explain why your offering is more useful to the market. The more succinctly you describe your product, the better you'll communicate with your target market/customer. Look at your marketing plan as an exercise in effective marketing. Sounds really straightforward - doesn't it?

Step two involves describing your target market/customer. Every business has their ideal customer, their target. The most successful businesses have an exact profile of their target market/customer printed in their mind, generally due to an effective marketing plan. To be equally effective in your targeting, you should describe your customers in terms of demographics, age, sex, family composition, earnings, geographic location, and lifestyle.

Decide whether your customers are conservative or innovative? Leaders or followers? Timid or aggressive? Traditional or modern? Are they introverted or extroverted in their behavior and personal choices? Why do they like to buy? When do they like to avoid the shops? Believe it or not, everyone has their times of year for spending the big bucks and times of year that they just avoid shopping all together!

For step three, you should create a precise communication strategy. Focus upon how you're going to communicate with your target market/customers. At the end of the day, you can know everything about your target market/customer right down to the type of clothes they wear. It won't do you much good, though, unless they know you as well. Communication covers everything from the design of your company logo to your extended advertising, public relations, and promotional campaigns. You need to know what your target market/customers read and what they listen to. Nowadays, you really need to know which websites they go to and where they shop.

Then, added to all of this, you need to apply a model for your advertising. You need to decide your specific objectives as an advertiser. Do you want your customers to know your company by name? Do they need to know where you're located? You also need to plan how much money you have to spend on your marketing. Find out what media is available to you and how much it's going to cost you. Referring back to everything you know about your target market/customers, try to distinguish the type of marketing that will work best for your company. The last item on your marketing plan checklist is to make sure that you have a proven method for evaluating your marketing plans on a regular basis. The more regularly you check up on how your advertising budget is being used, the more likely you are to avoid costly mistakes and otherwise achieve a high return on investment for every cent you spend putting your message out there.

Now that you have your marketing plan down, we'll take a look at your strategic plan. Very similar to a business plan at first appearance, the strategic plan is actually a unique document with a very unique purpose. The focus of the strategic plan is the mission statement. The purpose of the strategic plan is to explain and establish the goals and business values of the company. The plan's objective is to provide you with a means to implement your values and goals into your daily business practice. Unlike the two other types of documents we've considered, the strategic plan is generally kept within the company. Most business owners and management teams use the strategic plan to communicate their values and goals to staff members. The ultimate objective of the strategic plan is to keep everyone involved in a business venture on the same page.

The mission statement is the first section of the strategic plan. It should mention the market upon which the business intends to focus, describe the type of customers identified for the business, define new types of products or services for development, identify the type of employees the company would look out for, decide what type of organization the company will form, and set challenges for short-term and long-term financial goals. An effective mission statement helps keep everyone within the company on the same page.

The last of the documents you will really need to make up your 'battle plan' is the financial plan. Its content is pretty obvious. Between your business plan and your marketing plan, you should have a lot of information about the financial make-up of your business, how long it's going to take to make a profit, and how much you expect to make. Of course, your financial plan can look at all of this in a little more detail and on top of that should clearly indicate where the money is going to go.

You can also create a financial plan for yourself. While this has little to do with your business specifically, it can help you plan to achieve financial independence and reach retirement when you want to, not when it's convenient for someone else! Part of the piece of the whole 'law of attraction' notion, a personal financial plan might do a lot to help you as you start up your niche market business.

If you decide to take a crack at this, you should divide your financial life into several categories. Each category should represent a staple element of your life, such as your home, your family, your other property. Under each category, set goals. "I want to live in a bigger house", "I want to put my kids through college"; that kind of thing. Then, with as much information as you have available, try to figure out roughly how much money you need to achieve that goal by a particular date. You can go by month and year, of course.

Fit your personal goals into your business battle plan and you only enhance your plan of attack.

Follow These Action Steps:

- Start your business off on the right foot!

  - Plan and prepare.

  - Educate yourself, be willing to learn everything you can in your niche - become an expert!

- Get into the right frame-of-mind.

  - Your success depends on what ACTION you TAKE!

  - Put aside the fear of 'screwing up' - and just DO it!

  - DO NOT PROCRATINATE!

- You will not reach your destination (your goals) if you don't know where to go!

  - You must begin by deciding on what your goals are & then implement them!

- Develop and plan your 'battle!'

  - Successful businesses start with a business plan!

Now that you've got into the right frame-of-mind, set your goals, and developed your business plan, it's time to decide on a business name, properly filing it and setting up a proper business account with your bank. By reading the next chapter, you'll learn what you should be accomplishing next in this process.

Part 2
Design Your Business With a Proper Foundation

ii.i   Give Yourself a Proper Business Name.

Shakespeare asked, "What's in a name?" For businesses, a name amounts to a first impression, often a lasting impression! A good, solid, relevant business name is as essential to the success of a business as virtually any other element.

Unfortunately, many people name their business before they have a complete concept of what they're setting out to do. This is a bad, if not entirely the wrong practice! If you really want to name your business efficiently and provide the proper foundation and mindset, you are best to determine your marketability and business niche and your overall business planning approach, before you settle on a name. These are all things you need to keep firmly in your mind when you brainstorm your business's new name.

One of the reasons so many people jump the gun when it comes to picking a name: the process is a lot of fun. You can exercise a high degree of creativity. More to the point, however, the naming of your business - like the naming of a child - is something of a rite of passage. Most of us feel, once our business has a name, that it exists as a separate and actual concept.

Picking a name, however, is far more complicated than simply coming up with something that you like, or something that seems cool and catchy to you. The name you give to your business determines the identity of your business. Your business name becomes the most prominent aspect of your public face. It is undoubtedly the way that people will remember your business and it also has a bearing on how people - potential customers - find you in the first place.

Your business name - even just one or two simple words - is as important as your business plan or your marketing strategy, if not more so! It transcends all of the elements and sets up a dynamic of potential success, mediocrity, or failure.

First, the name of your business needs to be a vehicle of communication. It needs to communicate to your customers, your potential market, precisely what your business does. Of course, every business is different.

An accounting firm, for example, is a serious financial business. A party promoter service, on the other hand, is a creative agency looking to attract customers in a more laidback setting. In terms of their names as well as their business models, these two businesses have entirely different needs.

On the one hand, the accounting firm needs a name to communicate professionalism, reliability, and even tradition, to a group of people who will be receptive to those inferences. On the other hand, a party promoter service needs to communicate a certain street-smart edginess and needs to appeal to the average party-goer or host.

For the accounting firm, a traditional naming structure would suit it very well. In fact, most of the accounting firms you see feature the names of the partners. This is a very effective way to communicate what the accounting firm does and what it values.

Young people won't be interested and engaged by a name like "Waldorf & Grey". However, they aren't the target market for your average accounting firm.

Myspace.com communicates the nature of what it represents. The company's target demographic is teenagers and twenty-somethings. The name implies individuality, personality, and uniqueness, which are all important attributes of that generational span.

A company name such as Simon and Schuster is going to attract serious-minded individuals. An accounting firm called Waldorf & Grey is going to attract clients with a similar disposition. Conversely, an event-planning group called something like Hip Hop Party Promoters might successfully target their twenty-something to teenager clientele. A part promotion company called Harvey and Fisher really wouldn't generate the same response.

The name of your company should define not only the attitude you intend to promote, but it should represent the intrinsic qualities you want to instill in your company and in your work.

Here are a few general points about naming strategies: business names should contain real words rather than invented ones because consumers can identify with real words more easily than they can imprint meanings on invented words. Abstractions are weak and names that are too specific are too restrictive of a business purpose. Particularly when a business outgrows its original model, a name that is too specific really does not serve well.

Put together a list of sample names. Verbalize each one out loud and see if it sounds good. The next test is your friends and family. Give each of your sample names a run past your friends and see if they **a)** have any problems pronouncing the word, **b)** can come up with any derogatory jokes, or **c)** have an idea what the name denotes about your business.

The next step in the name game process involves typing out your sample name and applying different fonts to see how it looks. Apply the different fonts and try a few fancy features to see how the name looks in print.

You should also try to get a name that's short and sharp for the most part, unless your business has other requirements that you can specifically justify. Make sure that you also run the name you've chosen through the proper legal channels. There's nothing like facing a lawsuit because you used a name that already belonged to another company.

Hiring a consultant to help you with the naming process can also be a step in the right direction. Such a company brings a range of benefits to your project. Not only do such firms expertly analyze word associations, connotations and inferences, they will be able to convey a much more complete understanding of the legalities of company naming practices.

To help you assess the need to hire a professional company, the next section will outline the requirements for properly filing a business name.

Disclaimer Reminder

Please understand that this is a brief introduction to setting up a business. Therefore, you should only refer to this information as a basic guide to get started. I'd encourage you to seek and consult with an attorney, lawyer or accountant experienced in this type of venture before you get involved in any business. Also, you'll need to inquire with your local establishments as the procedures could differ depending in what city, county, state, province and country that you live.

ii.ii   What Legal Structure of Your Business You Should Consider.

All new business owners should be concerned with how their business structure is set up in a legal sense. Since there is so much information on this topic I will not get into too much detail here. However, I'll give you a brief explanation of the options that you can consider.

Sole Proprietorship.

- ✓ 72.3% of American businesses are sole proprietorship.
- ✓ Easiest of legal structures to set up.
- ✓ Least expensive of legal structures to set up.
- ✓ Legal structure good only for an individual - You, or married couples.
- ✓ If you're thinking of having partners, this legal structure will not work for you.
- ✓ IRS recognizes you and your business as one entity. Therefore, you'll be able to report business income, loss, expenses, etc., on your individual tax form.

Corporation.

- ✓ A independent legal entity separating you from the legal structure.
- ✓ More difficult of the legal structures to set up.
- ✓ Expensive (Costs can range from $475 to $4000 or higher).
- ✓ Provides you limited liability.
- ✓ Pays taxes separate to you.
- ✓ Can be made up of shareholders.

Partnerships.

- ✓ Similar to a sole proprietorship but different in that you and your partners are co-owners of the business.

- ✓ Provides personal liability (this can be a disadvantage because if any of your partners decide to purchase something on credit in your business name, you will be held personally liable if any of them decide to stop working).

- ✓ If you and your partners have equal share of the ownership in the business, no one is quite in control. This can seriously hold back the growth of the business due to lack of forward decision making.

- ✓ It's not a home-based business.

- ✓ The chance that one partner will put more effort and work into the growth of the business than another partner is likely which could then result in disagreements, arguments and resentments. This ultimately results in conflict which could be detrimental to your business.

- ✓ If you don't like your partner, it may be impossible to get rid of him/her without breaking up the company in the process.

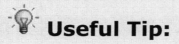 **Useful Tip:**

If you don't have any immediate plans to take on employees and you are just starting out, deciding on the route of a sole proprietorship would be most appropriate. Setting up will be easy and less expensive and you can pretty much start your business at any time.

ii.iii   What Legal Requirements You Should Be Aware Of.

I'm going to assume that you will start your business as a sole proprietorship. That being said, I'll only mention a few issues that you should be aware of (there are many, but would only apply if you decided to set up your legal structure differently).

Properly File Your Business Name.

Depending on the type of business you create, you must either file your business name as a DBA (Doing Business As) or when you incorporate your company.

If you're a sole proprietor or part of a partnership, if you're the only owner of the business or if you have just one or two people who are partners with you, all you may need will be a DBA. In fact, most business entities need to register and publish a DBA statement, also known as a fictitious business name, trade name, or assumed name. That is, unless the business operates under a name other than its owner's personal name or the name of a filed corporation or Limited Liability Corporation.

To file a DBA, you'll first need to identify the appropriate legal documents that you will need to file. For a DBA, that would be the Doing Business As Name Statement. Your statement generally needs to be published in a local newspaper. For example, this gives others the opportunity to object if the name somehow infringes on a business name of theirs.

You don't need to file a DBA if you operate as a corporation or if you have formed a Limited Liability Corporation (LLC). When you form one of these formal business structures, even if you're a sole proprietor, you've already gone through stages to ensure that your business name is unique. Part of the filing process for a corporation or an LLC (and the best way to form one of these entities is to secure the help of a seasoned lawyer or one of the reputable online businesses) involves searching for companies with the same or similar names, and thus verifying that your name is unique.

If all is well and good, a DBA or corporation/LLC formed, your business name is protected and available for you to use.

Obtain a Business License.

Many states and localities will require that you file for a Business License. This can usually be accomplished with your local city or county offices. In most cases you'll have to actually go in person to get this license. This is the easiest of licenses to get and usually requires a small fee of $15 to $45 depending on where you live.

Obtain a Sales Tax permit (optional depending on your type of business).

Depending on the type of business you've established, you may or may not need to file for a Sales Tax permit. You will need to inquire with your local city or county to see if your business requires that you pay taxes on your products or services that you will be providing.

Obtain a Resale permit (optional depending on your type of business).

If your business in involved in the reselling or making of products, any of your purchases may not require that you pay taxes. The reasoning behind this is that whatever entity is the final consumer of whatever it is that you've sold, will have to pay any taxes. Therefore, your suppliers may not require that you pay taxes on the services that you end up reselling to your customers.

Obtain an EIN (Employer Identification Number).

Once you have registered your business you will need to obtain you EIN. This is similar to like having a social security number for your business. This number is used as a means to help the government to separate you from your business.

ii.iv   Set up a Business Checking Account.

Even if you are operating as a sole proprietor, having a dedicated bank account - a checking account - for your business, is extremely advantageous. Why, you ask? Well, for many small businesses, one of the biggest and most destructive problems is not knowing where to start with business records. Poor record keeping often equates to no record keeping at all. Unfortunately, though, the need for income tax information is not the only reason to keep business records.

You need to keep records for yourself. Good records of your financial dealings provide the only accurate record of your business' financial performance. They allow you to monitor performance in specific areas, compile accurate income tax data, and plan well for the future of your business, both short-term and long-term.

The key to successful record keeping is a good accounting system. A good accounting system really depends on having the information you need separate, easily identifiable, and thus accessible.

Do not use your personal checking account to operate the funds for your business. This is good business accounting principle number one. A business checking account lets you monitor all your business transactions in one place. They will be well documented and you'll be able to easily oversee where your money is going and where it came from.

A business checking account also lets you monitor all your bill paying as well. That is, you can pay all of your bills by check and mark on the check what was purchased. This record-keeping method will give you the opportunity to better analyze your expenditures in more detail.

If you will be making small expenses, use petty cash, noting all such dealings for their significance to the business. You should have a separate account for your petty cash and, when the funds get low, you should simply write and deposit a check from your business account to cover the transactions.

Follow These Action Steps:

- Give yourself a proper business name.

- Properly file your business name.

- Obtain a Business License.

- Obtain a Sales Tax permit.

- Obtain a Resale permit.

- Obtain an EIN.

- Set up a Business Checking Account.

Tips & Suggestions:

I'm sure you've seen your share of the get-rich-quick schemes throughout the internet! So you have to be extremely aware of what's out there! There are scam artists around every corner, but don't let this discourage you . . . there are a bunch of good folks out there as well! So, be patient and start your business the right way, without falling into the traps as many have done so in the past!

So how you ask?

Well, I learned a great deal from Chris Malta of Worldwide Brands. When I first got started in business, a friend of mine recommended him and I haven't regretted it ever since! Chris helps individuals to get a solid grasp on the complexities of starting and running a business from home on the internet. But that's not all he does! Later on in this book, I'll tell you about, hands-down, the best resource for finding products to dropship! You will not find anything like this anywhere! Chris is the creator behind this valuable resource!

Anyways, Chris is willing to give you not just one, not 2 but 3 books, completely free, no strings attached, so that you can learn a few tricks on your way to success in business!

One of my favorite chapters in his book, "Starting Your Internet Business Right", is chapter 11. Want to be sure you're business is legal or if you are being cheated? Of course you do, so read his book! ☺

Like Music to Your Wallet! Download Chris Malta's FREE E-Book...
"Starting Your Internet Business Right!"

Just visit the following website: http://www.wwb.nichesourcing.com or if you are reading the digital version of this book, simply click on the picture above. You will be directed to Chris Malta's website where you can download his free books - in just one simple easy step!

Part 3
An Ingredient to Success – Doing Something YOU Enjoy

iii.i   What Is Your Hobby?

There's nothing more effective or powerful than doing something you love. That's why we're asking you a number of key questions in this chapter relating to the things you enjoy. "Do something you enjoy" . . . it is indeed an ingredient for success in business as much as in life.

So how do you go about profiting from a hobby? Wait a minute. How do you go about deciding exactly what your hobbies are? If you're like most of us, you probably don't have time to sift through every one of the activities you've participated in since you were a kid. Baseball, perhaps, tennis...maybe you used to play poker all night long at college. Who knows? The key question: which of your hobbies can you actually turn into an income stream?

Check out Serena and Venus Williams. Their dad developed a hobby for them and turned it into a multi-million dollar, one-way ticket to fame, fortune, and the WTA Pro Circuit. Think for a moment about Bill Gates. He was obviously really into computers in college . . . so much into them, in fact, that he dropped out of college to pursue his IT hobby full time. About 56 billion dollars later, having completely cornered the market with Microsoft for so many years, Gates is actually off to pursue his number two hobby. Would you believe he's planning to retire and play bridge? Clearly, Gates is a discerning man. Could he have made a fortune playing bridge? It's highly unlikely.

A few golden rules then, for distinguishing your bankable hobby.

1) You must be very good at your hobby.

2) You must be very enthusiastic about your hobby.

3) There's got to be something you know about the hobby that most others don't.

4) There's got to be some demand for knowledge, skills, or services relating to the hobby you're thinking about.

Let's think for a minute now about your hobby and how you might turn information into a profitable product in a creative way.

If you love tennis, for example, you don't have to turn yourself into the next Mr. Williams or even the next Ms. Hingis (mother of child tennis prodigy Martina Hingis). In fact, you could profit from this hobby by developing an e-book or a comprehensive website about tennis, approaching the subject from a profitable angle. Say you do some market research and find out that there's a pretty high demand among parents for books about how to pick a tennis coach or how to develop your kid's forehand. If you have the interest and the inclination, you can produce a product that targets one or other of these niche markets.

Say you happen to be a very good card player. Did you know that there's a whole subculture of card players out there? Not just poker players who burn the midnight oil but bridge players who tour the country and even the world playing major tournaments for titles and for money. You could easily target professional players and professional teams with a comprehensive e-book on team building: how to win tournaments with team spirit! A catch title like that will set you on the right track.

Of course, your hobby doesn't have to be anything like this. It's not necessary that it be something undertaken professionally in any capacity. Take the example of Mary McCarthy. Mary loved fine-food. It was very much her hobby to cook and dine out in high-class restaurants. She turned this into a very successful business targeting the niche market of fine food lovers (people just like her). Today she's recognized as the founder and CEO of Tutta California, which produces olive oil and cabernet wine vinegar.

Say you love cats or dogs? Why not develop a business focusing on teaching people how to take care of these animals. It may not appear as immediately profitable as an olive oil business or an IT-business concept, but you might be surprised in the long run.

Perhaps you love fish. Well, I like saltwater fish! In fact to be more specific, one of my hobbies is maintaining a reef eco-system that involves keeping saltwater fish, corals, invertebrate, etc. And YES, I have developed a niche business from it . . . Check it out here: http://www.reefkeepingbasics.com. I've also got a content-based saltwater fish related site here: http://www.saltwaterfishpets.com. There is a tremendous amount of interest in these hobbies, and the individuals involved in them are very passionate for it. This results in an excellent niche area to concentrate my efforts in and as a result it makes a good sum of money in the process! ☺

iii.ii   What Is Your Passion?

Hopefully we've got you thinking about how your interests can actually turn into good business. Now let's consider what you're passionate about. Apparently it's easier said than done for most people. On a recent Oprah Winfrey poll, from thousands of respondents, an amazing seventy-percent indicated that they had no idea what their life's passion is.

So how do you go about identifying your passion if you don't yet know what it is? Well, what do you really enjoy in life? What topics of conversation get you all riled up about? How would you spend your time if you had the choice to do anything?

If you can answer these questions honestly, you should have a pretty good idea about what your passions are. You might be passionate about your work. Perhaps you're passion is your family life; maybe you live spending time with your spouse and your kids. Maybe you love reading or writing. Perhaps you're a serious sports fan. You might well be passionate about your hobby, whatever it is.

The next question you need to think about: how do you apply your passion and turn it into a sound business idea. It is so important to be passionate about your job, about your work, yet so many people overlook this simple fact. Look at any famous actor or actress, any singer or sports person; a regular celebrity. The chances are, even before they were famous and rich, they just loved what they were doing.

You can identify people who are passionate about their job by their attitude. People who are doing something they love tend to be so much happier in general than those who don't have the luxury or the presence of mind to do something they can get excited about.

Throughout this book, we're going to be emphasizing the importance of using what you know and what you love to make money. The whole premise of niche marketing is essentially that everyone has something they love, something that really interests them.

iii.iii   What Is Your Expertise?

Why have we been talking about your hobbies and your passions? The chances are that your hobbies and your passions also represent your areas of expertise. People who are passionate about sports, after all, tend to know a lot about it. Anyone who loves their job is more than likely to know the ins-and-outs of their company and their industry.

Combine your knowledge of your hobbies and passions and decide where your real expertise's lie. What do you know that others don't know?

Say you love to travel. Not only are you passionate about packing up a knapsack and hitting the road, you've done it a number of times. You're a seasoned traveler. It would probably be fair to assume you have pretty good knowledge of how to go about hitting the road on a budget. That's your expertise and you can easily tap into that.

iii.iv   Will People Benefit From What You Can Offer?

"It's a big red flag when someone outlines the size of the market - multibillion dollars - but doesn't clearly articulate a plan for how the idea will meet an unmet need in the marketplace," said Aaron Keller, an adjunct professor of marketing at the University of St. Thomas.

People benefit from all sorts of products and services but if you want to be successful in business, you need to be able to point out exactly how they're going to benefit from what you're offering. Before you do anything to try to turn your hobby, passion, or expertise into a business, you have to ascertain who can benefit from what you have to offer and how.

There are plenty of ways to answer this question. One of the best ways is to conduct market research. Although many people jump to the conclusion that market research has to be a very expensive and time consuming proposition, a small number actually realize that the only market you really need to think about is made up of serious-minded, honest, friends. Take a group of these friends and test out your business idea.

If they seem to think it's a good idea, spend a little more time honing your idea and look to test it again on a slightly larger group of friends and family.

iii.v   The 'Burning Question': Can Your Hobby, Passion or Expertise Fulfill a Demand?

This burning question is all about market research. Once you've identified that your product or service can benefit people, you need to find out whether or not there are other products and services that are providing the same benefit. Don't worry if there are a few businesses out there doing what you're planning. At the end of the day, there might be a hundred businesses similar to the model you have in mind. But if you have a strong model that provides benefits in a new and better way, you have very little to worry about. A strong plan and offering great benefits to customers will help you take control of even the toughest market.

Having a bit of competition is also a good thing, even if you think otherwise.

Ask yourself a few of these questions to be sure:

- ✓ Do you have hobbies that you're very well acquainted with?

- ✓ Have you traveled to some interesting place about which you had a strong desire to know more?

- ✓ Where would you like to be right now? How familiar are you with the place you're thinking of?

- ✓ Do you have work experience that has allowed you to develop some unique skills?

- ✓ Do you have a particular area of interest that is served by a variety of products? Are you familiar and passionate about one or more of these products?

- ✓ Do you enjoy a particular activity, either alone or with friends?

- ✓ Are there times that you simply don't want to work? What would you prefer to be doing? Do you know enough about the activity you have in mind to share your ideas?

- ✓ What are you particularly good at? Can you give advice to others to help them become competent in the area you're strong in?

- ✓ Is there something you have always wanted to learn? Are you determined enough to learn about it? Could you become acquainted well enough with the subject to educate others?

Make a list of the ideas that come to mind as you answer these questions for yourself and as you brainstorm the moneymaking ideas. By following through with this, you will eventually come up with something you'll know is worthwhile to pursue.

Follow These Action Steps:

- ◔ The success of your business will have a direct relation to your hobby, to your expertise or to your passion!

  - ▶ If you love what you do, if you are an expert at what you do or if you have a passion for it - then there is no reason that you cannot be extremely successful with it!

  - ▶ We can safely assume that we don't just have one thing we like or that we have only 1 hobby . . . so start thinking, writing and deciding what hobbies, or things you enjoy doing or a specific passion you may have that you feel could actually benefit others.

- ◔ If there is a demand for it - then there is a market for it!

- ◔ If you don't think you can personally offer something that will benefit others or if you feel that there is no demand for it - it's not the end for you! ☺

- You can also search for niche markets that people, other than you, have a sincere passion for. Those would be invaluable markets to tap to say the least!

- Find what people want - and give it to them!

PHASE 1:

Finding A Niche Market

Chapter 1
Niche Sourcing 101

1.1   What's a niche?

Niche is a word that is commonly used in marketing. You've probably heard the term, niche marketing, even before you picked up this book. Very few people really understand what these terms mean, though. Basically, a niche is used in marketing to refer to a group with identifiable and specific tastes and lifestyle preferences. We might add to this the condition that the group, with their specific preferences, presents a viable business opportunity for individuals or businesses with a mind to focus their attention.

Niche marketing involves targeting a group using information about their specific preferences.

Let's talk examples.

Some people really love to take exotic vacations. They love to travel spontaneously and without much fuss. They like to be left to their own devices to explore far away destinations. Okay, so think about this for a moment. Most vacations take one of two forms. Either you are traveling to a place you've never been and you rely heavily on a travel agent or a company like Expedia.com to plan the details, or you travel somewhere you've been before; you have substantial knowledge about the place, a favorite hotel, perhaps you're even staying with relatives. You don't really need suggestions about what to do when you get there, stuff like that.

People who want to take exotic vacations as we described at the beginning of our example, they're taking an approach that's entirely different. They have specific needs. They might need chartered planes. They might need special guidance. Perhaps only a handful of companies actually deal in vacations to the chosen destination.

To organize and sell exotic vacations in remote locations, a company has to have specialist knowledge. A company that goes to the necessary lengths to acquire that knowledge is essentially targeting a niche.

Another example: some real estate companies in New York City deal specifically and exclusively with clients interested in acquiring large buildings worth an excess of several million dollars. Only a handful of people want to invest in real estate this way. Companies that deal with this type of business, they are also targeting a niche.

If you decide your hobby is tennis and you'd like to see more kids involved in the sport at a competitive level, you could write and publish a guide for parents or tennis coaches to show them the best ways to get kids enthusiastic about the game. You would be targeting a niche if you did something like this.

1.2   Research thoroughly.

Literally thousands of ideas are out there just waiting to be turned into something more. So many things are yet to be created, so many needs yet to be met. However, there is a catch. We've talked already about what a niche market is. To summarize the definition we came up with we can apply a few keywords. Words that aptly describe a niche market include "specific" and "contextual". A niche market is something that rests upon the preferences and needs of a very specific group of people that operate in a certain context. People who like to take exotic vacations likely have their own behaviors and habits that impact their choice of destinations, how they choose their destinations for a given trip, when they prefer to travel, how they get their information about their chosen destination, and what they like to do to enhance their vacation experience.

If you want to tap this niche market in any way, you really need to understand as much about your group as you possibly can. You not only have to research your own business idea very thoroughly, you need to expand your research focus to look very closely at the characteristics of your target customers, your niche market creators. If you don't match your business idea and model up with the preferences of your target customers, you're facing a disaster.

Hands-down the foundation of your success in niche marketing is good, comprehensive research of your market and your business model. Do the two elements match up?

1.3   How To Identify Your Niche.

Find a market with little competition or narrow down your choice of market into a highly particularly focus group that your competitors often neglect.

According to many niche marketing experts, when it comes to choosing a niche market, people really don't put much thought into the process. What's the result? Well, we've more than hinted at it. If you don't properly research your niche marketing opportunity, if you don't really think about what your business is going to do to target your niche market customers, the chances are that you and your business won't be doing very much at all.

When trying to choose their niche market, most people do one of two things. Either they choose to try and operate in a market that is enjoying booming sales or they choose a market solely based on their own expertise, without any reference to the wants/needs of the customers they expect to have.

Of course, there are a number of problems with both of these methods. To properly identify your niche, you need to know what not to do as much as what to do. First of all, if you target a market that's doing well or that's saturated with opportunities to make money fast, you're going to really struggle to break in. A "new comer" in an already booming market is several steps behind their competitors and, as hard as you might be prepared to try, it's extremely difficult to catch up those extra steps.

You're also going to struggle to get any control in the market. A hot market, in which a lot of money is exchanging hands; it looks really good from a distance, but as soon as you get up close, you realize the struggle is fast and furious. Most of the business operating will have larger budgets than you, more staff, and the ability to just do so much more than you within a given period.

Even if you could break through with sweat and blood, why would you want to go to so much trouble? There are so many niche markets out there that haven't been tapped yet, there's very little sense in trying to push yourself into one that is completely or close to completely saturated already.

Okay, so perhaps you now leap ahead and make common niche marketing mistake number two. You choose a market that relates very well to your expertise. Actually, this approach isn't as bad as we've just made it out to be. You have a chance of making it very big by going into business blind and relying on your skills and knowledge base. You're looking at a possibility of achieving your dreams, making a lot of money with a business that requires very little work in the end. The flip side, however, is that you're also looking at your worst nightmare if - and the odds predict this happening - you miss the mark and don't, at the end of the day, have a good target focus on customers.

It's right that you should create a product or offer a service that relates to something that you know a lot about or that you can do very well. To be successful, however, at least, to guarantee success, you need to follow a couple of basic rules.

Number one: don't repeat the mistake of oh-so-many other would be niche market business people. Don't develop a product that looks great to just you. Don't go out and spend a fortune on advertising to target all the people you think are dying to buy your product. This is a bottomless pit. Nowadays it's way too easy to chase several thousand dollars - sometimes more - throwing all the money out into the universe and sitting back, expecting it to go forth and multiply only to return to you before too much time has passed. Don't think that money will ever do this. You cannot just spend money, generate advertising, and expect a product that only you have okayed to sell like hot cakes! ☺

Don't jump into any niche market. Don't make a move until you have considered all of the elements in the market.

So, how do you identify your niche and ensure it can be sustained, but more important be profitable?

That's a great question and I'll explain this next . . .

Eric's 5 "Niche Sourcing Qualifiers"

It's extremely important to note that success of a particular niche that you've decided to concentrate on depends on specific demands, what I'd like to refer to as - qualifiers. Once you've targeted a potential niche, it should at least satisfy 4 of the 5 qualifiers to increase your chance of developing the niche into something sustainable yet profitable.

1) The niche should be actively searched for on the internet - so it must be a craving market.

2) People must be spending money in this area of the market.

3) There must be at least some competition existing in the marketplace for this product.

4) The product you've chosen must have a long-term sustainability in the market.

5) Decide whether you will enjoy your choice if you decide to develop it as a business!

Of course, while you try to find or hone in on your niche, you should also look at the situation for evidence of a problem that people want to solve or a specific need that could be better addressed. Remember that you can always improve an existing product and let that be the basis for your business.

 Extremely Important:

Before we go any further, I'd like to emphasize how important my **5 "Niche Sourcing Qualifiers"** are. To put it simply - this will 'make' or 'break' your business depending on how you've implemented these factors in your research.

So, this is by far one of the most important lessons you should seriously consider and put into practice to ensure success of your business!

Now, to make sure you've fully grasped these guidelines, I'd like to explain step-by-step to further help you visualize how important these principals are.

The following will be a real-life case study of how I regularly use my **5 Niche Sourcing Qualifiers** to reveal a sustainable and profitable niche! ☺

Remember, if you find a niche that can match up with at least 4 of the 5 qualifiers - you've struck the 'mother-lode' of gold! ☺

Note: Obviously, I'm not going to reveal to you how I do this with all my niches! However, I'm comfortable taking you step-by-step with this niche. I'm confident you will not find a better product in this part of the market - so I'm not worried about competition! ☺

Case Study of a Niche Chosen by Eric - Saltwater Fish

Step 1: I started with something I knew about, liked and had a passion for - 1 of many hobbies I have (If you come up with a blank here, assuming you have no hobbies to start with, which I find highly unlikely, then the research, brainstorming, and Niche Sourcing Methods come into play here.)!

Step 2: I 'measured up' my chosen niche with my 1st Qualifier:

1) The niche should be actively searched for on the internet - so it must be a craving market.

One of the best indicators on gauging a potential market is through search engines. The more activity and 'hits' your niche receives, the bigger chance that your niche has plenty of potential! ☺

There are a couple of good resources that I use to measure the popularity of my niche. They are also essential for keyword research.

The first tool I use is software called - Good Keywords. You definitely NEED it, it's necessary . . . You can download it from my site here:

http://www.resources.nichesourcing.com

(Yes - it's FREE! No sign-ups required - just download it to your computer and install)

After you've installed the software on your computer, run it and I'll 'walk' you through the important aspects of how to use it.

See image below (this is what Good Keywords should look like when running).

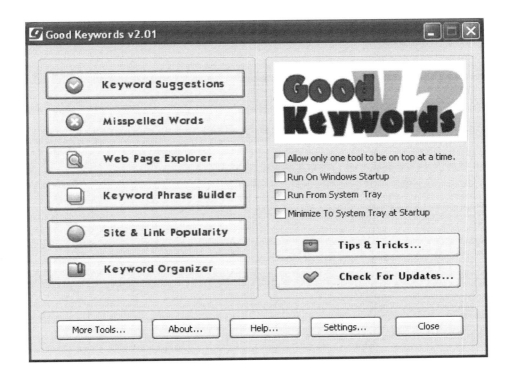

For this part of the lesson, we will use only one feature.

When you have time later, go ahead and 'play around' with this piece of software. You'll find it to be a very useful tool!

So go ahead and click on "Keyword Suggestions." (Refer to the image below, it should look like that)

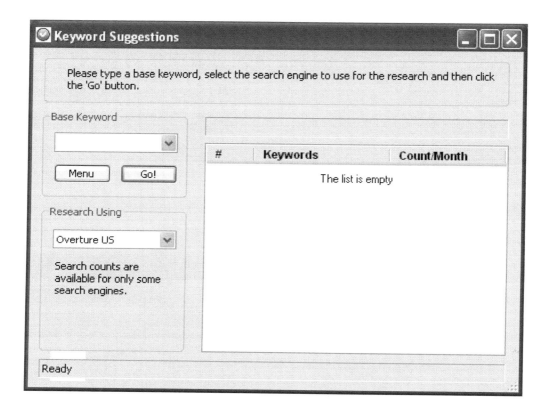

In this example, since my niche was **saltwater fish** - I typed that where it says 'Base Keyword.' To get an idea of what I'm explaining to you, please refer to the image below.

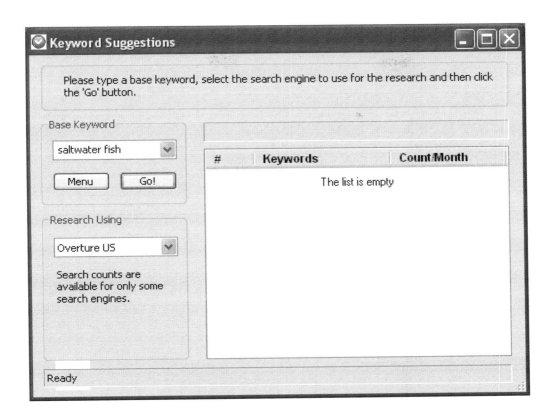

Click on the "Go!" button, wait several seconds, and the following similar results will appear in the program (please refer to the image below):

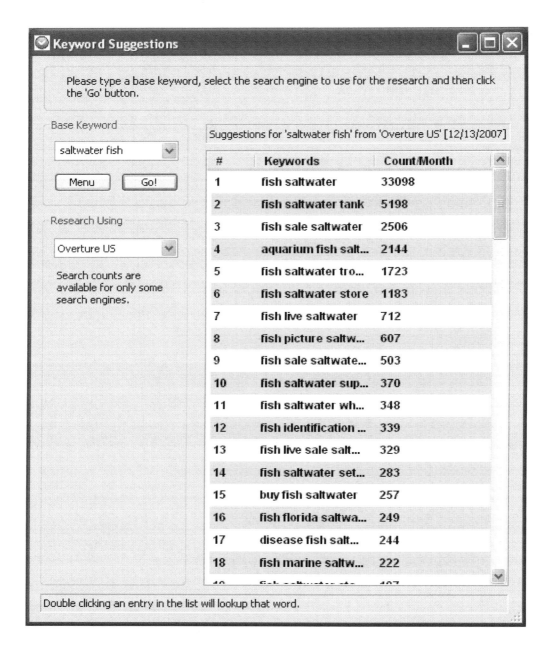

After reviewing the results, I decided that the number count was adequate enough to be a market people were interested in.

At this point, I'm sure you are asking:

"What does the search count need to be at to satisfy the 1ˢᵗ qualifier?"

Ah ha . . . Good question! ☺ This is subjective really, and can vary from niche to niche. In my opinion though, you should have about 30,000 counts for the Base Keyword.

Meets Requirement

Niche Sourcing Qualifier #1 . . . . ✔

Step 3: I 'measured up' my chosen niche with my **2ⁿᵈ Qualifier:**

2)   People must be spending money in this area of the market.

Since saltwater fish was my hobby, I didn't have to research too much since I pretty much was familiar with everything related to it.

I knew a lot of money was being spent in this type of market - because I was spending it! ☹

For example, purchasing fish can range from $7.00 to $120.00, that's for a typical average fish you can get in any tropical fish store. The cost for hard to get fish are obviously a 'bit more' expensive.

Purchasing equipment (this is the most expensive part of the hobby as far as up-front cost are concerned) is expensive, but unfortunately necessary.

Obviously you need the aquarium. This will 'set you back a ways.' Since this is saltwater, the tank size tends to be larger because saltwater fish require more 'living space' than freshwater fish. Then there is filtration equipment, test kits, quarantine tanks, lighting equipment (can be very expensive depending on what kind of livestock you are maintaining such as corals), RO/RI water equipment, and YOUR Electric Bill - to name just a few items!!

This is just the Short List . . . !

Yikes!

You can enter a saltwater fish store and by the time you leave, spend up to and past $1,000.00 easily - if you are just getting started!

So, as you can see from the niche I chose, you need to make sure that the people in your target market will spend 'some' money, willingly!

If individuals are not willing to spend the money, or have no desire or interest in buying anything - it's probably not a good choice!

To expand on this **2nd Qualifier**, if the individuals who are associated with your niche are passionate about it - then they will be more willing to spend money on it! ☺ So, it comes down to the willingness of spending money without too much 'arm twisting!'

In order to make a profit - money has to be spent and a willingness to part with the money cannot be an obstacle!

Meets Requirement

Niche Sourcing Qualifier #2 . . . . ✔

On to the next Qualifier . . .

Step 4: I 'measured up' my chosen niche with my 3rd Qualifier:

3)   There must be at least some competition existing in the marketplace for this product.

If there is competition in the marketplace, then it's safe to assume that it would be a beneficial market to enter - money is being spent.

You've probably heard it many times before! Well - you are going to hear it once again . . . ! I may have even mentioned it previously . . . I'm a big believer in not re-inventing the wheel!

I guarantee you'll hear this again and again - why? Because it's a FACT!

You are going to see many items in the market that are similar - they may differ just a bit because of a slight change or a different method was introduced or its got a different 'twist' to it.

If you discover a niche that has no competition it's probably because of the following reasons:

i.   The niche is too small - not enough people interested, or . . .

ii.   It's readily available and as a result no one is willing to spend money on it!

You'll want to look for two types of competition, those who may have a similar product to you and those who cater to the same general niche.

There is an advantage to seeking out this competition, mainly because this can be used as initial research for potential Joint Venture partners! ☺ So, keep this in mind - it is very important and will prove to be very advantageous to know down the road.

It wasn't hard to find my competition. After a bit of searching in the search engines, I found a plentiful supply of it . . . literally hundreds of sites but not updated regularly (so I saw the need to provide up-to-date information, for a market that is constantly changing)!

I also found many, many forums that a large group in the hobby tended to congregate. This is a simple trademark or tell-sign that indicates the individuals in that hobby are passionate about it!

Why?

Because they are spending time asking questions, providing answers and generally providing information in these tight knit communities.

Meets Requirement

✔

Niche Sourcing Qualifier #3 . . . .

O.k., on to the next Qualifier . . .

Step 5: I 'measured up' my chosen niche with my 4ᵗʰ Qualifier:

4)   The product you've chosen must have a long-term sustainability in the market.

Best case scenario, our goal is to find a product that will continue to grow as time goes on. But everything in this world seems to 'run out' sooner or later.

My goal and yours, is to try to find a product that has growth potential. The obvious reason for this, there is no profit if there is no product! ☹

When I analyzed my niche, I found that there was certainly potential for it to grow. From the early ages (I mean a long, long time ago), individuals enjoyed watching fish. Even more so today, the popularity of keeping fish, tropical fish, saltwater fish and reef - has grown, due mostly to technology improving.

With the introduction of global warming, reefs throughout the world are being threatened and this can be potentially disastrous. However, groups of saltwater fish and reef keeping hobbyists have been learning to 'home grow' their fish and corals, so hat less are taken from the pristine ocean areas.

Besides that, this is also a growing industry throughout the world!

So even with the worst-case scenario, this specific niche has the potential to grow as time goes on!

Meets Requirement

✔

Niche Sourcing Qualifier #4 . . . .

Now, this leads us to the last Qualifier . . .

Step 6: I 'measured up' my chosen niche with my 5th Qualifier:

5) Decide whether you will enjoy your choice if you decide to develop it as a business.

I'm a firm believer that you try to find something you are good at, that you are an expert at, or that you have a passion for!

Now, you may hear this from many business oriented individuals. However, I don't think it's emphasized enough!

I'm going to assume that most people who read this book such as yourself, have a regular day-to-day occupation. Perhaps even a few readers have two!

The point I'm trying to make is that if your occupation is part of your overall life picture because I'm sure you have other responsibilities that include paying off debt, paying for a house, an apartment, taking care of your family, you have children - the list could easily go on and on - when do you have time to run a business!?

Well, that's where having an interest in, an expertise in or more importantly a passion for something comes into play.

With all that we do each and every day, it's hard to keep up with just the normal routine let alone anything extra along the way.

So you need to have a strong desire and passion to make sure you do more than the normal routine.

You need to be able to wake up every morning with the same passion and zeal you had the day before.

You need to have the will to tell yourself that your effort will be worth it.

If you cannot motivate yourself to be successful, then you need someone to show you how. If you can't do that or not willing to do that, your chances of success become very slim.

'Stuff' gets in the way of our lives everyday. We procrastinate and we simply 'put things off' to the next day. This pattern turns into a habit and before you know it another year has gone by without any progress! ☹

Well, your mindset should be solidly against this way of thinking!

To be successful, to have a good life, to have and enjoy the nice things in your life, your business mindset should be founded on a solid foundation of passion and desire. Otherwise, you are going to slip back into the normal life of 'just getting by.' ☹

Now, having said that, it's certainly not a requirement to have a passion for something you do. Many people are extremely successful at things but they may not necessarily have a passion for that specific area.

You should not limit yourself to concentrating your efforts at just stuff you like, have a passion for or are an expert at - not enough to go around!

Your goal as a business person is to 'spread your wings' so that you give yourself the opportunity of growing into other markets.

Ultimately, your success is going to come down to one thing - DESIRE! Do YOU want it bad enough? If you have the proper mindset of desire - you are capable of doing anything you put your mind to - you are the one making the decision - that responsibility is yours.

Success requires a proper mindset conditioning. Once you can accept that - you'll find it a whole lot easier to understand and a clearer path to success will grow larger and larger! ☺

Meets Requirement

Niche Sourcing Qualifier #5 . . . . ✔

1.4   Brainstorm Ideas.

If you're struggling to get ideas for your niche marketing business, try brainstorming ideas to identify your niche and hone in on your approach to tap it. The focus of your ideas is the clincher for your business. A business is made or broken by its degree of strategic focus. Your idea, the idea that helps you select your niche market and your plans to target the niche, they determine what type of business you build, what products you sell, who your customers are, how you approach them, how you market your business, and how you brand it in the beginning and in the future.

So what's the best way to brainstorm your ideas when so much is expected of them? One of the best ways to hone in on your planning is to develop a mindmap that let's you both expand and focus your thoughts for the business.

To show you how well mindmaps can work in this case, why don't you take a look at a couple samples that have been developed to demonstrate the type of thing you should end up with. You'll be able to visualize things more clearly by using these excellent resources. The first addresses the main questions you'll need to consider as you draw your mindmap to plan your business such as: "Where are you now?" and "Where do you want to be in the future?"

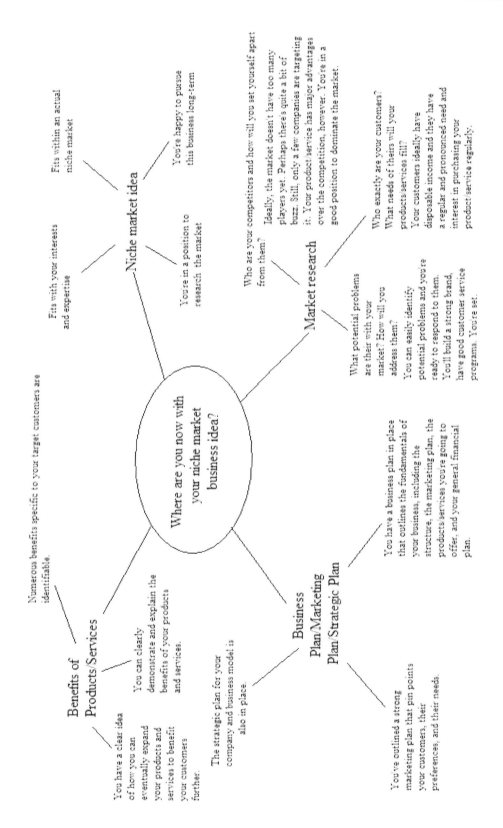

Where are you now with your niche market business idea?

Niche market idea
- Fits within an actual niche market
- You're happy to pursue this business long-term
- Fits with your interests and expertise
- You're in a position to research the market

Market research
- Who are your competitors and how will you set yourself apart from them? Ideally, the market doesn't have too many players yet. Perhaps there's quite a bit of buzz. Still, only a few companies are targeting it. Your product/service has major advantages over the competition, however. You're in a good position to dominate the market.
- Who exactly are your customers? What needs of theirs will your products/services fill? Your customers ideally have a regular and pronounced need and interest in purchasing your product/service regularly.
- What potential problems are their with your market? How will you address them? You can easily identify potential problems and you're ready to respond to them. You'll build a strong brand, have good customer service programs. You're set.

Benefits of Products/Services
- Numerous benefits specific to your target customers are identifiable.
- You can clearly demonstrate and explain the benefits of your products and services.
- You have a clear idea of how you can eventually expand your products and services to benefit your customers further.

Business Plan/Marketing Plan/Strategic Plan
- The strategic plan for your company and business model is also in place.
- You have a business plan in place that outlines the fundamentals of your business, including the structure, the marketing plan, the products/services you're going to offer, and your general financial plan.
- You've outlined a strong marketing plan that pin points your customers, their preferences, and their needs.

The second mind map looks at some of the hot niche markets and offers some ideas about how they can be tapped.

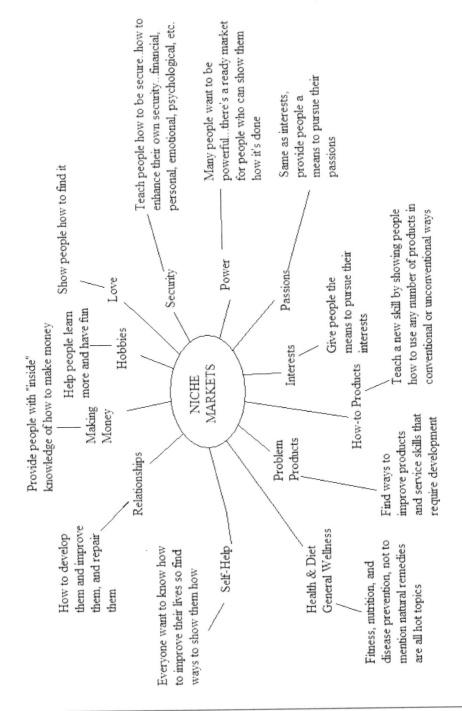

1.5   Analyze the Online and Offline Marketability.

Companies conduct market analysis to secure a better understanding of their immediate business environment. For the vast majority of successful businesses, online and offline marketability analysis is a main step in the development of a marketing plan. Generally, the first step involves conducting market research. Effective market research involves the gathering of information. Often the information is gathered from a variety of sources. Sources generally include direct mail, telemarketing, focus groups, and online surveys.

The second step is general market analysis. This process centers upon the critical review and organization of relevant data collected. The objective is to present the data in a manner that it can be used to make reasoned strategic marketing decisions.

In his book, *What Every Manager Needs to Know About Marketing*, David J. Frieman pointed out: "Just as one would not build a house on sand, one should never undertake a marketing program that is not built on a firm foundation of market knowledge . . . It is remarkable and alarming how little managers of businesses really know about their markets and the other elements of their outside environments."

A successful market analysis effort involves collecting information on everything from industry trends to major competitors and their strategies. It involves a comprehensive review of the channels of distribution, and characteristics of current and potential customers.

Overall, market analysis is the crucial stage in the development of a marketing plan. Of the identified marketing segments, the company can select whichever particular area it wants to target.

In their review of *Marketing: Mastering Your Small Business*, Gloria Green and Jeffrey Williams argue the following: "Small businesses that identify the needs of specific target markets - existing and potential customers who are the focus of marketing efforts - and work to satisfy those needs are more effective marketers."

The best way to undertake market analysis is in stages. The first stage should involve a broad study of your industry and the second, or the final stage, should offer a very specific or narrow definition of the company's customers, the target market.

The more information you can draw together about your market, the better.

To focus your market research, try to collect information to answer the following questions:

1) Who are the primary decision makers and purchasers in my market?

2) What are their main motivating factors?

3) When and where do my customers tend to buy?

You need to understand how your customers make their purchasing decisions. When you understand this, you are in a position to influence their decisions.

As you conduct your market research, you might decide to assess demographic features such as age, gender, income level, educational background, financial situation, marital status, household size, and ethnic or religious background. This information might well help you develop a stronger and more accurate profile of your customers.

However, your market analysis should also demonstrate why your chosen target market is more favorable than other segments. Since you're concentrating on a niche, you will be investing resources in marketing to your target market only. You must be very sure that the limitations you set on your marketing are valid.

Market research has a wide application, though.

"Once we understand the phenomena that underlie the behavior of our markets, we can assess our strengths and weaknesses relative to those phenomena. External threats and opportunities need to be carefully examined so that we can apply our strengths to areas with high potential and avoid major environmental pitfalls. Finally, we must link the resulting diagnosis to our corporate capabilities, strategies, and constraints in order to ensure a good fit between our marketing strategy and major corporate goals and objectives," said Glen L. Urban and Steven H. Star their book *Advanced Marketing Strategy*.

1.6   Determine Its Profitability.

How can you really determine profitability of your company before you actually take the plunge and launch your business? A number of crucial steps must be taken well before you accept any financial risk with your business.

You absolutely must weigh up the costs of your business and set that information against the minimum projections of what you can expect to make in the business over a given period. A year is generally a good time frame.

So what kind of expenses are you going to have that relate to your business?

Here's a general list of fees you might have to consider with some notes about how and when they might apply to you.

1. **Auction Site Fees:** If you decide to auction products online, which for many individuals is a very lucrative business, you'll nonetheless need to look out for internet auction service fees. Usually, the deal is that you pay a fee for listing your item for sale. You might also pay a final value fee as a percentage of the selling price when the item is actually sold. Depending on the other features you use to enhance your auctions such as bold text, highlighting, gift icons - it may require you to pay a few extra bucks here and there. The best advice on monitoring these expenses: if you're items are priced under $25 or just selling for under that price, consider very carefully what you're paying as overheads, so mind your budget.

2. **Credit Card Fees:** Most online merchants, indeed, most merchants, will attest to the benefits of accepting credit card payments from your customers. However, be wary about the size of your business and its relative income. Online services such as PayPal, Bidpay.com, and CCNow are just a few of the many services that allow anyone to accept credit cards and electronic check payments without having to sign up for a merchant account, which, unless you're doing a lot of business, is too costly to be worth while. Obviously, third-party payment processors like PayPal don't offer an entirely free service. You can expect to pay a percentage of each transaction, but it is free to transfer your cash by direct deposit to your bank account and the fees applied against each transaction tend to amount to a very small percentage anyways.

3. **Inventory Costs:** These are an often overlooked or underestimated expense. When you are thinking about the overall profitability of your business, you must consider the cost of the items you're selling. Inventory cost should also include reference to the cost of shipping an item plus any applicable taxes or handling fees payable on items. Your objective is obviously to keep such fees at a minimum - so investigate your options as fully as possible.

4. **Shipping Supplies:** It doesn't matter whether you're planning on using the US Postal Service or UPS to ship your items, you have to watch out for shipping supply costs as a potentially draining overhead to most any business. It will definitely add up if you are going to ship tangible products. The postal service and UPS actually offer free shipping supplies if you sign up for particular shipping services. You can also get free shipping supplies for priority and express mail packages from the post office. Your only problem may be persuading your customers to use this shipping method rather than First Class, Parcel Post, or even Media Mail. Regardless of your customers' preference, you must always look to recover the cost of boxes, envelopes, padding, and any other package items, such as labels, in your shipping fee.

5. **Postage and Shipping Expenses:** You must be aware of what it costs you to ship your products to your customers. There can be no getting around it. I cannot emphasize enough that if you decide to ship tangible products, you need to take into account the extra expenses you will incur. Also, look out for special service costs such as delivery confirmation and insurance.

6. **Auction Management Services:** Tools and services are available that will improve your ability to manage a larger volume of auction items in less time. You need to consider costs to maintain your records - ever important for monitoring your income and watching your taxes - and track listings and manage your inventory. For most of these services, you can expect to pay a flat fee.

7. **Interest and Finance Charges:** As your business expands, you're more likely to have to consider these types of charges and you will want to monitor the extent to which they dig into your income. Interest could very well be the interest on your credit cards or loans you use to finance your business.

8. **Special Equipment Fees:** Most businesses require you to invest in at least a few items of equipment. You may need a top-of-the-line computer, a digital camera, or even a scanner.

9. **Internet Service Provider Fees:** You are likely to end up paying for an ISP fee regardless of whether or not you need the internet for your business. However, you do need to consider the type of service you require. You may need to ask yourself whether an expensive broadband service is required, or whether a $9.95/month for dial-up is viable or not.

10. **Bank Charges:** You should have a separate bank account for your business expenses to operate the costs associated with maintaining a separate account. I'll explain more about this later on in the book but it's extremely important that you keep your personal accounts separate from your business accounts.

11. **Office Supplies:** Everything from paper, printing supplies, pens, folders, paper clips, envelopes, and even the odd pencil. Don't forget that all of these cost money and you must add up the cost of these items and reckon them against your income.

12. **Web Site Fees:** You don't necessarily need your own website or e-store (however, I highly recommend you do), but many of the most successful online businesses and even the most successful offline businesses will have an online presence. You will have to consider the cost of a domain name, hosting service, and subscription service for a website, if you decide to launch one. You would also need to consider the cost of designing the site, whether you design it yourself using a template or hire a professional. Again, I will review many of these aspects of your business in more detail later on in the book.

13. **Legal and Business Expenses:** Forming a separate legal entity for your business is always a good idea, but it does cost money, including the cost of legal forms, filing fees, and lawyer fees.

14. **Professional Services:** As your business expands, you'll probably benefit from a lawyer and an accountant to help you keep track of the technicalities that will affect your business.

15. **Taxes:** These will become quite significant as your business grows but taxes vary considerably depending on the type of business you have and even in terms of where it is maintained.

In terms of all of these expenses, you should be sure to add up every consideration and be aware of the price. Weigh everything up in terms of your income.

1.7 Study Your Competition.

As you embark upon your business, targeting a niche based on your hobby or your interest, be sure to learn as much as you can about the industry in which you're looking to operate. Regardless of how much you think you know about your product, your service, or your industry, you do not know everything. Remember, you're targeting a niche market - it's a very specific market you're looking at, which means information is your key - you must get as much information as you can about your competitors, their product or service, price, location, promotion, management, and financial position.

Recognize your limitations in the context of your competitors. If your company is first in quality, your competition may be better at general marketing or advertising campaigns. Experience your competition. What do I mean by that? Purchase some of their products and see what you may be competing with. Be aware of your industry and of the business!

Of course, against your own business weaknesses and the strengths of your competitors, you should also look out for the weaknesses of your competitors. Conduct a critical examination of their business structure and their offerings to customers. Consider that the most effective way to evaluate a competitive service is to pose as a customer or as I mentioned earlier, BECOME a customer! You can, for example, call one of your competitors and ask for job rates, delivery schedules, terms of payment, discount policies, warranties and guarantees. You can then evaluate your experience; from the point you make initial contact to the conclusion of the service. You can also talk with the customers and suppliers of your competitor.

By weighing up the strengths and weaknesses of your business and your competitors, you can determine your vulnerable spots; based on your examination and critical review, you'll be sure what you need to improve or compensate your customers for.

1.8   Resources That Will Benefit Your Research.

We've outlined in this chapter a whole host of issues that you must research to establish an effective business model and, ultimately, an effective business. However, it's not just your competitors you must research. You must undertake detailed reviews of the industries in which you intend to operate. This requires you to access specialist information.

You may save yourself time not visiting your local library however it would behoove you to actually spend some quality time scouring the shelves of your library. In actuality, you may likely find an enormous amount of useful information that will educate you sufficiently on the points of business most pressing. After you've developed a good foundation of knowledge, start focusing your energy on exploring your ideas online. Search for keywords (write yourself a list) and see what you come across. Online forums are a fantastic start. You may want to look for books online from specialist providers. You may even be able to find a library, probably online, that offers a host of specialist information on your industry and more.

Eric's Top 10 "Niche Sourcing Methods"

1. "Keyword + forum"

2. "SoYouWanna.com"

3. "Lycos Top 50"

4. "Hot Selling products on Ebay.com"

5. "Hot Selling products on Amazon.com"

6. "Hot Selling products on ebooks.com"

7. "eHow.com"

8. "Press Release Sites"

9. "Technorati.com"

10. "Google Zeitgeist"

Eric's Top 10 "Niche Sourcing Method" #1 "Keyword + forum"

The first test to judge if you have a good niche is to find out if there is a demand for it. To satisfy this requirement, your niche research should begin with a search on google.com.

So where do you look or what should you type to find out if there is a demand for something?

➢ Follow the crowd! ☺

➢ Where are people gathering and talking about the hottest topic?

Yep, start your search in the forums!

Why?

This is where you'll find the 'CROWD', it's where people are gathering together talking about the hottest topic related to their topic! ☺

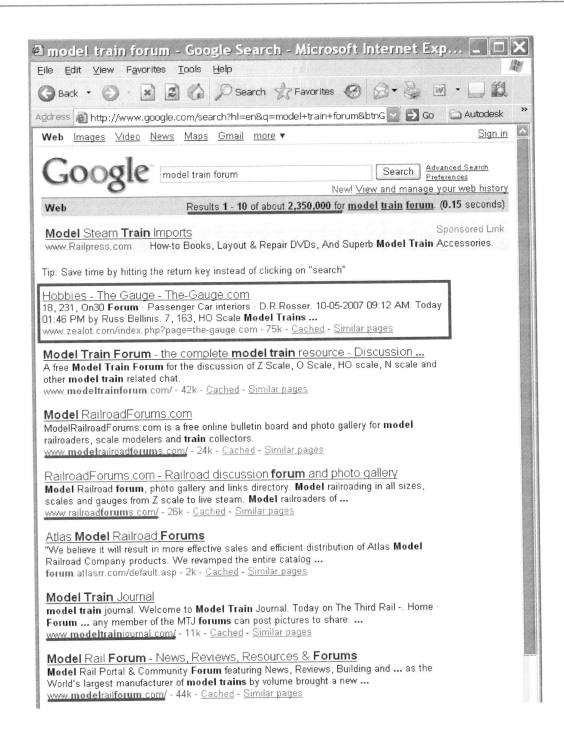

This will work in any search engine, not just Google - see example above.

Format: "Keyword + forum".

Substitute "Keyword" with your niche topic you've decided to research.

So let's say your niche topic is . . . model train, then

Type (in a search engine of your choice): "model train forum" (without quotation marks)

If the topic you have chosen is "hot", it'll be obvious simply by what results appear in your search query.

After your initial search, you'll want to get more specific and find what topics are being talked about most.

How?

Click on one of the forums listed in the search you did and start browsing. Look for topics and threads that have the most views and replies.

As you can imagine, the possibilities on finding something are limited to your imagination! ☺

Eric's Top 10 "Niche Sourcing Method" #2 "SoYouWanna.com"

Website: http://www.soyouwanna.com

After you've browsed this site and gotten a feel for this it, you'll realize that there are dozens of info-product ideas here! This is an excellent idea generator - so take advantage of it!

The site splits all the topics into specific categories. Each of the topics includes a summary as well as a step-by-step review.

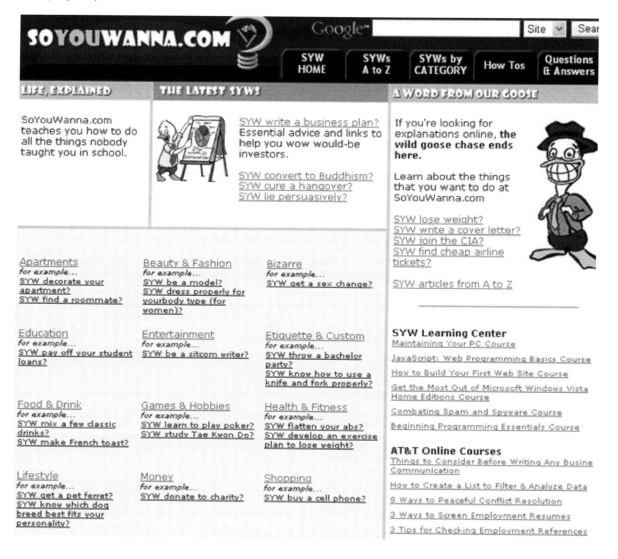

Some of the categories include the following:

- Bizarre
- Beauty and Fashion
- Education
- Entertainment
- Etiquette and Custom
- Food and Drink
- Games and Hobbies
- Health and Fitness
- Lifestyle
- Money
- Shopping
- Sports
- Technology
- Travel
- Work,
- etc.

Let me be clear on something here . . . we are using different methods to finding good niches, but the information we find could be protected by copyright.

As with any website you visit, you should not copy the information you find word for word. Many of the sites that I may suggest to you are idea generators, to get your mind thinking, to brainstorm. Once you have the ideas, the information you decide to put down on paper should just flow without any barriers! The purpose of much of these 'exercises', is to help you with finding an in demand, profitable niche with growth potential! ☺

For example, here is an example how you can use this valuable tool:

Under the category 'Money': the topic "SoYouWanna pay off your student loans?"

To decide if this a high demand topic, do a search on it's main subject.
[Main Subject "loan, student loan": 52,000+ searches]

This has good potential. ☺

Here is another example:

Under the category 'Health and Fitness': "SoYouWanna cure your insomnia?"
[Main Subject "insomnia": 52,000+ searches]

Eric's Top 10 "Niche Sourcing Method" #3 "Lycos Top 50"

Website: http://50.lycos.com

This is a good site to find out what the latest trends are and what the hot topics are. Once you find something, you can further your research into more specific sub-topics (niches). You'll discover that using this site will encourage your thought processes and you'll be open to new ideas.

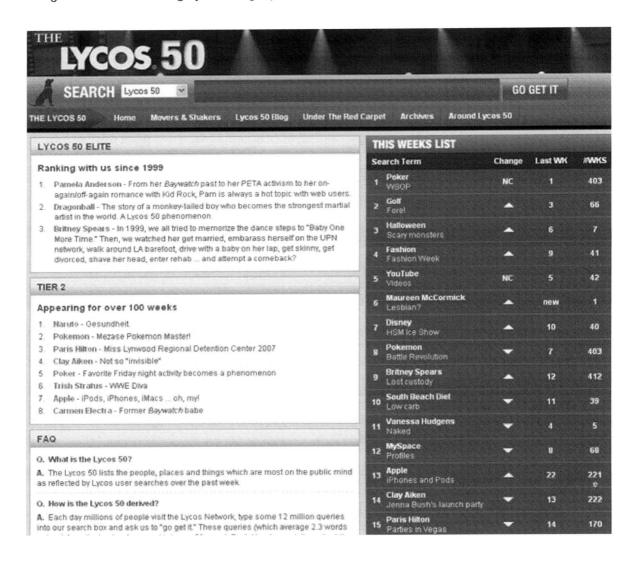

Eric's Top 10 "Niche Sourcing Method" #4 "Hot Selling products on Ebay.com"

Website: http://listings.ebay.com

Here you'll find a selection of categories with an extensive list of popular sub-categories (niches).

Accessories, Parts (292062)
Bluetooth Wireless Accessories (10007)
Cell Phones (47242)
Smartphones (1260)
PDAs & Pocket PCs (7124)
Phone & SIM Cards (3390)
Wholesale & Large Lots (1397)
See all Cell Phones & PDAs categories...

Clothing, Shoes & Accessories (2274507)
Costumes & Reenactment Attire (158563)
Cultural & Ethnic Clothing (854)
Dancewear & Dance Shoes (7910)
Infants & Toddlers (185318)
Boys (54569)
Girls (113671)
Men's Accessories (96425)
Men's Clothing (321454)
Men's Shoes (84756)
Uniforms (11797)
Unisex Clothing, Shoes & Accs (5109)
Wedding Apparel (34414)
Women's Accessories, Handbags (205360)
Women's Clothing (709210)
Women's Shoes (218428)
Vintage (60756)
Wholesale, Large & Small Lots (6913)
See all Clothing, Shoes & Accessories categories...

Coins & Paper Money (206896)
Coins: US (104502)
Coins: Canada (11192)
Bullion (13844)
Coins: Ancient (5755)
Coins: World (29772)
Exonumia (9174)
Paper Money: US (10276)
Paper Money: World (14923)
Publications & Supplies (4090)
Scripophily (3368)
See all Coins & Paper Money categories...

Entertainment Memorabilia (195901)
Autographs-Original (18697)
Autographs-Reprints (11269)
Movie Memorabilia (64191)
Music Memorabilia (74063)
Television Memorabilia (16336)
Theater Memorabilia (2804)
Video Game Memorabilia (684)
Other Memorabilia (7857)
See all Entertainment Memorabilia categories...

Gift Certificates (9553)

Health & Beauty (344776)
Bath & Body (23712)
Coupons (1286)
Dietary Supplements, Nutrition (14509)
Fragrances (67738)
Hair Care (23814)
Hair Removal (7873)
Health Care (11847)
Makeup (68287)
Nail (10829)
Massage (4753)
Medical, Special Needs (13463)
Natural Therapies (6675)
Oral Care (4049)
Over-the-Counter Medicine (2355)
Skin Care (52639)
Tanning Beds, Lamps (523)
Tattoos, Body Art (7256)
Vision Care (8510)
Weight Management (10284)
Wholesale Lots (2073)
Other Health & Beauty Items (2301)
See all Health & Beauty categories...

Home & Garden (698581)
Bath (21165)
Bedding (54360)
Building & Hardware (23565)
Dining & Bar (30914)
Electrical & Solar (3106)
Food & Wine (19812)
Furniture (29429)
Gardening & Plants (53808)

Wholesale Lots (546)
See all Sports Mem, Cards & Fan Shop categories...

Stamps (149732)
United States (40088)
Australia (3090)
Canada (11267)
Br. Comm. Other (10496)
UK (Great Britain) (4467)
Africa (1660)
Asia (9854)
Europe (34567)
Latin America (5045)
Middle East (3140)
Publications & Supplies (1271)
Topical & Specialty (10804)
Worldwide (13983)
See all Stamps categories...

Tickets (53697)
Event Tickets (50253)
Experiences (1472)
Other Items (1972)

VERY HOT !!

Toys & Hobbies (677855)
Action Figures (97964)
Beanbag Plush, Beanie Babies (14131)
Building Toys (15096)
Classic Toys (6675)
Diecast, Toy Vehicles (112493)
Educational (6664)
Electronic, Battery, Wind-Up (6158)
Fast Food, Cereal Premiums (5821)
Games (54818)
Model RR, Trains (58963)
Models, Kits (40991)
Outdoor Toys, Structures (5388)
Pretend Play, Preschool (27031)
Puzzles (10431)
Radio Control (49441)
Robots, Monsters, Space Toys (3469)
Slot Cars (8484)
Stuffed Animals (18505)
Toy Soldiers (6340)
Trading Card Games (43872)
TV, Movie, Character Toys (66582)
Vintage, Antique Toys (14466)

The number in parentheses indicates the number of listings for that category/niche. The more listings - the more popular the niche is.

Don't stop there! Each of the sub-categories has their own sub-niches, so you can narrow down your search to something more specific.

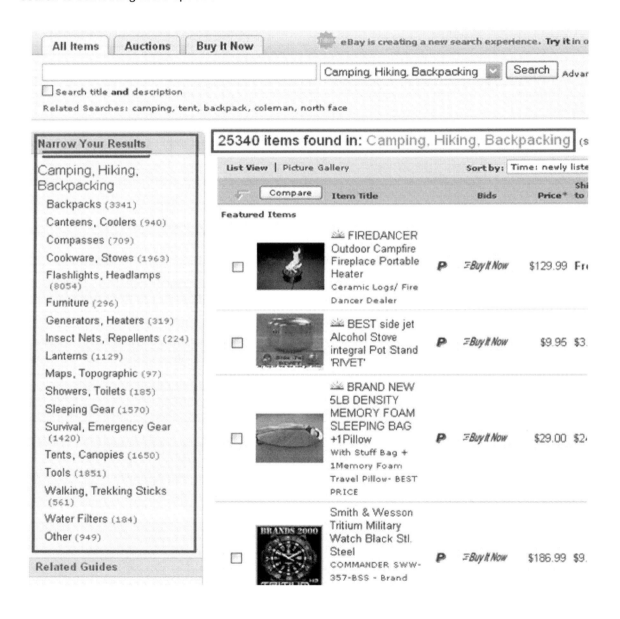

Your goal should be to find something that is manageable, small enough so that you can dominate it. Once you accomplish this, you find your next niche and dominate that. Soon, you will realize that you now have multiple streams of income! ☺

If you decide that you'd like to focus in on tangible items (ex. electronics, action figures, books, etc.), you can purchase items from wholesalers at rock-bottom prices and turn around by selling them at retail. A considerable profit can be made if you decide to go this route.

> All you will need is a list of legitimate wholesalers who you can buy from and who've got as many products as you can imagine . . . ! Follow closely as I'll show you! ☺

I strongly suggest that you look no further than **Worldwide Brands**, they have the largest database of businesses that sell just about anything, at rock-bottom wholesaler prices!

You can read more about how **Worldwide Brands** can help you find products that sell by visiting their website: http://www.onesource.nichesourcing.com.

I first discovered this incredible resource 6 years ago and have used it ever since!

There are other businesses that claim to offer the same info - but **Worldwide Brands** is hands-down, the best there is, it's "the cream that rises to the top!" ☺

These guys have developed the best source of wholesale products anywhere, it's called OneSource and it's "The World's Only Complete Product Sourcing Solution." It's a one-time fee, lifetime membership to your very own market research staff who will work for your business every day! You pay for it once - no monthly fees, and in return you get access to millions of products, thousands of brands and guaranteed to work with true wholesalers. Along with that, **Worldwide Brands** continually adds to their database every single business day to guarantee the most current suppliers and products are on hand.

Eric's Top 10 "Niche Sourcing Method" #5 "Hot Selling products on Amazon.com"

Website: http://www.Amazon.com

Since Amazon.com is one of the most heavily used sites on the internet, you will find an enormous

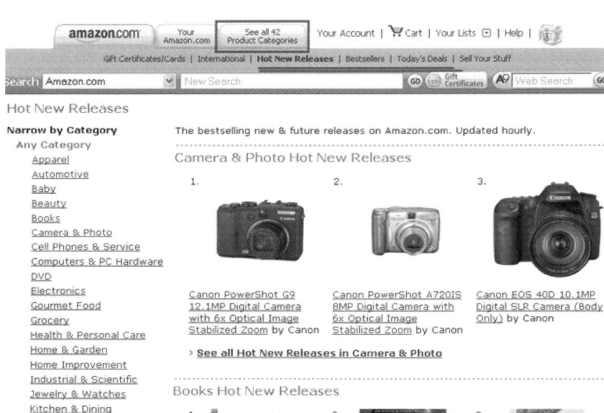

Hot New Releases

Narrow by Category

Any Category
Apparel
Automotive
Baby
Beauty
Books
Camera & Photo
Cell Phones & Service
Computers & PC Hardware
DVD
Electronics
Gourmet Food
Grocery
Health & Personal Care
Home & Garden
Home Improvement
Industrial & Scientific
Jewelry & Watches
Kitchen & Dining
MP3 Downloads
Music
Musical Instruments
Office Products
Patio, Lawn & Garden
Software
Sports & Outdoors
Toys
Unbox Video
Video
Video Games

The bestselling new & future releases on Amazon.com. Updated hourly.

Camera & Photo Hot New Releases

1.

2.

3.

Canon PowerShot G9 12.1MP Digital Camera with 6x Optical Image Stabilized Zoom by Canon

Canon PowerShot A720IS 8MP Digital Camera with 6x Optical Image Stabilized Zoom by Canon

Canon EOS 40D 10.1MP Digital SLR Camera (Body Only) by Canon

› **See all Hot New Releases in Camera & Photo**

Books Hot New Releases

1.

2.

3.

Deceptively Delicious: Simple Secrets to Get Your Kids Eating Good Food by Jessica Seinfeld

I Am America (And So Can You!) by Stephen Colbert

Love in the Time of Cholera (Oprah's Book Club) by Gabriel Garcia Marquez

variety of products that people are purchasing every hour of the day, every day of the year. As a result you will find that Amazon.com is a "treasure drove" of niche sourcing ideas.

Bestsellers

Narrow by Category

Any Category
 Apparel
 Automotive
 Baby
 Beauty
 Books
 Camera & Photo
 Cell Phones & Service
 Computers & PC Hardware
 DVD
 Electronics
 Gourmet Food
 Grocery
 Health & Personal Care
 Home & Garden
 Home Improvement
 Industrial & Scientific
 Jewelry & Watches
 Kitchen & Dining
 MP3 Downloads
 Magazines
 Music
 Musical Instruments
 Office Products
 Patio, Lawn & Garden
 Software
 Sports & Outdoors
 Toys
 Unbox Video
 Video
 Video Games

More to Explore
Movers & Shakers
Hot New Releases

The most popular items on Amazon.com. Updated hourly.

Books Bestsellers

1.

Deceptively Delicious: Simple Secrets to Get Your Kids Eating Good Food by Jessica Seinfeld

2.

Eat, Pray, Love: One Woman's Search for Everything Across Italy, India and Indonesia by Elizabeth Gilbert

3.

Clapton: The Autobiog by Eric Clapton

> **See all bestsellers in Books**

Electronics Bestsellers

1.

Canon PowerShot SD1000 7.1MP Digital Elph Camera with 3x Optical Zoom (Silver) by Canon

2.

Garmin Nuvi 350 Pocket Vehicle GPS Navigator with Maps for North America by Garmin

3.

HDMI 2M (6 Feet) Sup High Resolution Cable I DVI Gear

> **See all bestsellers in Electronics**

DVD Bestsellers

1.

2.

3.

After surfing over to Amazon.com, you can start your researching into sub-niches by using the linked tabs at the top of the site such as: "See all 42 Product Categories", "Hot New Releases", and "Bestsellers".

As you continue searching, pay attention to the categories on your left. By doing this, you will be able to narrow down your search to sub-categories (sub-niches). Make sure you check out the extra sub-categories you see on the left such as "Movers and Shakers".

Eric's Top 10 "Niche Sourcing Method" #6 "Hot Selling products on ebooks.com"

Website: http://www.ebooks.com

Here you can use the menu on the left as well as the "Choose a category" pull down tab, to search for popular subjects. This site is a great place to find hot niches where there is a demand. Check out the current best sellers and browse the lists to find other topics that people want to read about.

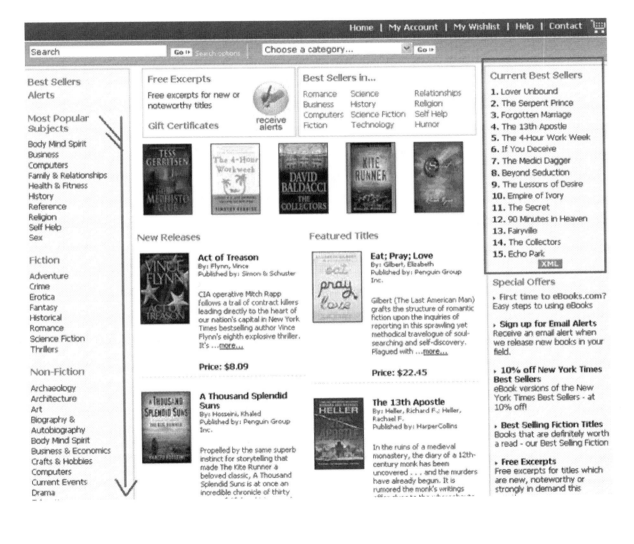

Eric's Top 10 "Niche Sourcing Method" #7 "eHow.com"

Website: http://www.ehow.com

If you are having problems thinking of product ideas look no further than this extensive database of instructional articles that explain how to do just about anything! The site contains over 70,000 written

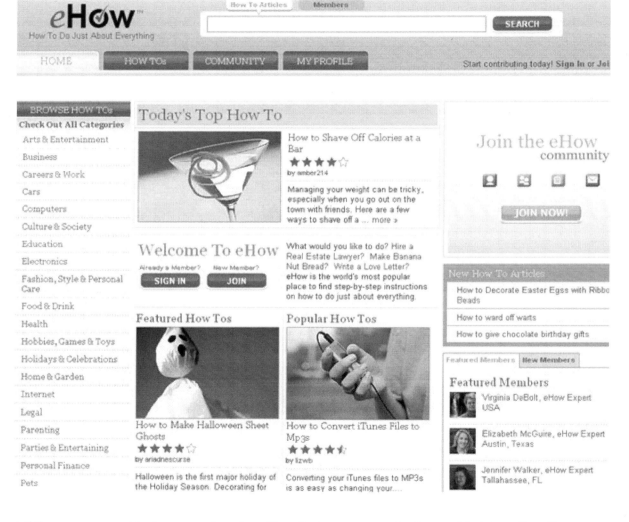

articles on every subject you can imagine. The site has easy navigation and is interactive. You can even sign up and share your knowledge with others by commenting on the articles and interacting with other site members.

To search for a niche you can use the linked categories on the top left side of the site. When you scroll down the page you will notice a couple other useful tools. There will be a box down towards the right labeled "Popular Categories" and a box down towards the left labeled "Top 10 eHows". These categories will have thousands of useful ideas that you can choose from.

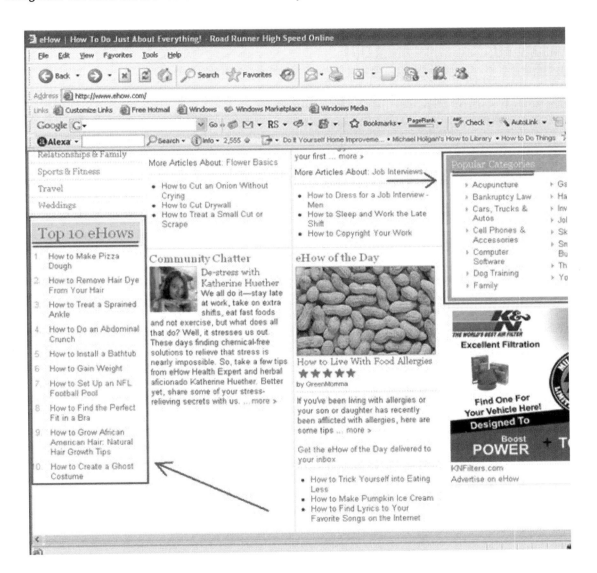

Eric's Top 10 "Niche Sourcing Method" #8 "Press Release Sites"

Website: http://www.imnewswatch.com

Press releases, when used correctly, provide a wealth of information. By being vigilant and keeping your research uncomplicated but thorough, pay attention to trends that tend to appear time after time

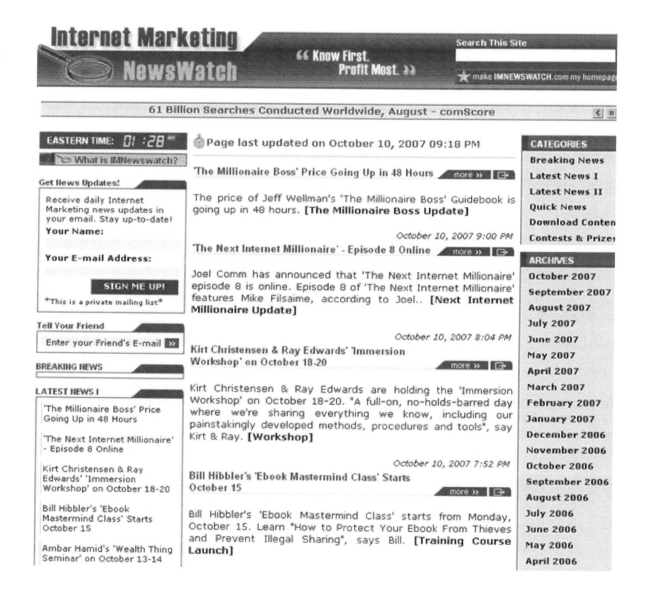

Your job is to notice these topics and subjects that tend to repeat themselves, its usually material that can be used to benefit others. PR sites are like databases made up of offline and or online news/ publications websites, blogs, ezines, etc.

There are hundreds of different sites that host the latest news. I'll summarize two sites that I find to be extremely useful but I'll also provide you with a comprehensive list of other PR sites that are both free or that will cost you.

First, there is "Internet Marketing NewsWatch" at http://www.imnewswatch.com.

You'll find everything that there is to know concerning Internet Marketing. It'll keep you well informed and up-to-date on relevant news from the industry, the individuals of the trade, their services and products and everything in between - By far the best PR site in the internet marketing industry.

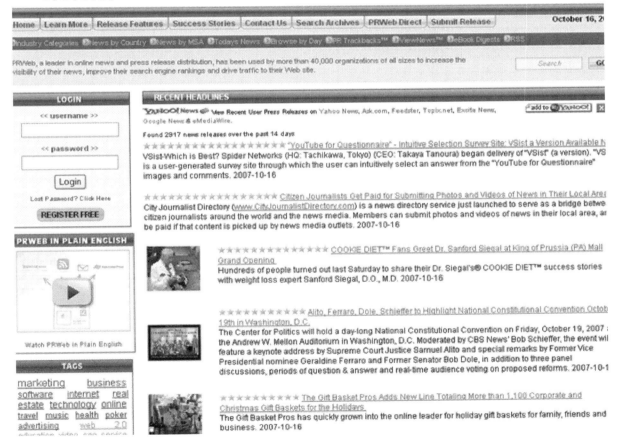

Everything other than internet marketing turn to PRWeb: http://www.prweb.com. They have been at the forefront of online news and the distribution of press releases. They've been used by tens of thousands of businesses to increase their visibility in the marketplace as well.

PRWeb was originally developed to help small businesses communicate their news to the public through the use of the internet. It was PRWeb that encouraged companies to communicate directly to their customers, their prospects and media, doing so by means of electronics.

Here is a list of other Free Press Release sites you can use for your research:

http://www.1888PressRelease.com
http://www.24-7PressRelease.com
http://www.AddPR.com
http://www.ClickPress.com
http://www.Click2Newsites.com
http://www.ECommWire.com
http://www.E-xl.com
http://www.Express-Press-Release.com
http://www.FreePressRelease.com
http://www.FreePressReleaseServices.com
http://www.Free-Press-Release-Center.info
http://www.Free-News-Release.com
http://www.Free-Press-Release.com
http://www.FreePressReleases.co.uk
http://www.i-Newswire.com
http://www.Media-Press-Release.com
http://www.NewswireToday.com
http://www.PR.com
http://www.PR9.net
http://www.PRbot.com
http://www.PR-Inside.com
http://www.PRbuzz.com
http://www.Press.ArriveNet.com
http://www.Press-Base.com
http://www.Press-Releases.Blogspot.com
http://www.Press-Service.net
http://www.PressAbout.com
http://www.PressBox.co.uk
http://www.PressMethod.com
http://www.Press-World.com
http://www.PressWorld.com
http://www.PressZoom.com
http://www.PRfree.com
http://www.PRleap.com
http://www.PRlog.com
http://www.PRNewswireDirect.com
http://www.PRurgent.com
http://www.PRzoom.com
http://www.TheOpenPress.com

Here is a small list of Paid Press Release Services:

http://www.EnewsRelease.com
http://www.InternetNewsBureau.com
http://www.MarketWire.com
http://www.MediaMap.com
http://www.Send2Press.com
http://www.URLWire.com

Eric's Top 10 "Niche Sourcing Method" #9 "Technorati.com"

Website: http://www.technorati.com

This is a great site to help you with your brainstorming. By using this tool, you will be able to easily reach the conclusion if it's a researchable niche to work with or not and if there will be plenty of

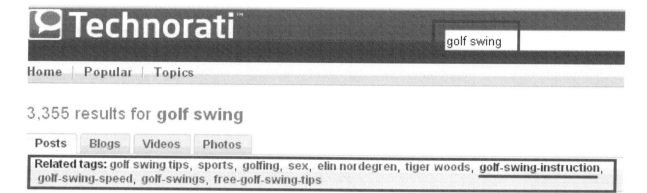

 Technorati™

golf swing

Home | Popular | Topics

3,355 results for **golf swing**

Posts | Blogs | Videos | Photos

Related tags: golf swing tips, sports, golfing, sex, elin nordegren, tiger woods, golf-swing-instruction, golf-swing-speed, golf-swings, free-golf-swing-tips

 Is It Just Me Or?...Knuckleheads of the Week

[Icon]Is it just me or... Should Manny Ramirez learn to read the freakin' scoreboard? ... winner of knucklehead of the week. The good news is he can use that **swing** on the **golf** course next week

20 minutes ago by **breport** in **Bleacher Report** · Authority: 200

 Crazy Capcom!

If you've been a longtime reader of buttonmashing, you'll note that there is a lot of love for the ... mus from Street Fighter 2 will be used, plus remixed versions of all those tunes. Wii Love **Golf** From the Everybody's **Golf** team

58 minutes ago by **rice75** in **buttonmashing.com** · Authority: 62

Usefulness

permalink | bookmark Random Thoughts posted 10/16/07 [my mood: Pensive] Random thoughts. I□m sitting on top of a pub in a corner office. Everyone can see me. I□m right smack in the middle of this town and its New Urbanism development.

6 hours ago by **Fijufic** in **The Inner Circle** · Authority: 13

 Michigan high school athletic director goes "Southwest Airlines" on school's Girls' Golf Team

material to work from. For example, let's say you type in "golf swing" in the search box, refer to the screen shots for visualization.

Results of your query will be shown and will include several options to choose from that will increase your chances of finding something you are looking for.

The first thing you will notice is a result number, in this case there are 3,355 results for "golf swing".

15 results for golf-swing-instruction

| Posts | Blogs | Videos | Photos |

Learn To Stack And Tilt Your Golf Swing - Part 1

I'll bet your wondering what the heck is a stack and tilt **golf swing** right? ... Have you ever heard it before? If you have, you most likely read about it in the **Golf** Digest Magazine. In the past few months they've had quite a bit of coverage on it, as well as strong responses ...

9 days ago in **Golf Instruction Online - for swing, putting, schools and Videos** · Authority: 9

Why Don't Golfers Improve

The USGA states handicaps for amateur golfers have not gone down in 20 years! Wow! With all the technology golfers aren't improving? How can that be? Why is this happening? There are many reasons why golfers don't improve! Could be as simple as poor fundamentals. Lack of practice. Inadequate equipment.

29 days ago in **Golf Instruction Online - for swing, putting, schools and Videos** · Authority: 9

Golf Instruction Books To Improve Your Golf Swing

There are a ton of **golf instruction** books on the market, by all the big name teachers, but what I've found is they have forgotten how it is to be an average hack golfer. For those

37 days ago in **Golf Instruction Online - for swing, putting, schools and Videos** · Authority: 9

Learn to play golf holidays Malaga - Professional Golf Lessons Spain

Offers information on how to learn to play **golf** during your **golf** holiday in Malaga Spain ... **golf Golf Swing**

61 days ago in **MyProgs - find new software, keep your program list online** · Authority: 45

Online Golf Instruction Tips, Lessons & Videos

Do you want ONE resource you can turn to, to improve your **golf swing** and game the quickest? No driving or time away from your schedule. I'm talking about at YOUR convenience! Whenever and wherever you choose, it's up to you!

80 days ago in **Golf Instruction Online - for swing, putting, schools and Videos** · Authority: 9

These results are referenced from 4 different categories - Posts, Blogs, Videos, and Photos, you'll have access to each of these sources.

You can find additional information from within the 'Related Tags' box. However, don't be surprised if you get results that have nothing to do with your search! This happens - so simply ignore that stuff!

Technorati

golf swing

Home | Popular | Topics

Videos about golf swing

Posts | Blogs | **Videos** | Photos

Related tags: golf swing tips, sports, golfing, sex, elin nordegren, tiger woods, golf-swing-instruction, golf-swing-speed, golf-swings, free-golf-swing-tips

How to swing a golf club like Tiger Woods
212 days ago by VideoJug

Charles Barkley Golf Sw
440 days ago by philwashington

Golf Swing Analysis
226 days ago by pgampro

Tiger Woods golf swing dynamics
392 days ago by cquinto

Tiger Woods Golf Swing
536 days ago by eatgolf

The Basic Golf Swing
189 days ago by leftbette

Fixing Charles Barkley's golf swing
192 days ago by apeacock

Golf Instruction - Use of in the Golf Swing
370 days ago by mfbrow

By taking these steps you are actually making progress towards finding a niche - and it will be specific.

Pay attention to the search results, you could even use some of the words that resulted from your search as keywords.

So after your initial search of "golf swing", you can further your search by honing-in on sub-niches by clicking on "golf-swing-instruction." This will create further results that are more specific to what you chose. Again, I've provided screen shots for your visualization.

You will find that Technorati is invaluable as you will be able to quickly realize if there will be enough material to use for your research.

By using all of the categories such as the Posts, Blogs, Videos, and Photos, and using a methodical process of narrowing in on your sub-niche, you'll find that you may have more than enough material to work from to research your idea.

Eric's Top 10 "Niche Sourcing Method" #10 "Google Zeitgeist"

Website: http://www.google.com/press/zeitgeist.html

This resource can help you find if there is a good market or not before you create your product.

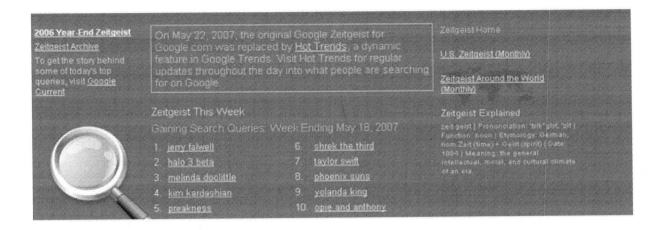

Google Zeitgeist is a database of the hottest search trends targeted within the US market as well as around the world.

The database is basically made up of the search results that have been generated over a period of time such as the week, month, or annually. The results are gathered through Google, and as a result it's based on millions of searches that are being conducted.

These statistics are converted from an extremely enormous source and results in revealing trends within the US and in other countries throughout the world. For example, it'll find the searches that have gained the most popularity or it'll find the most top searched queries.

It's like getting a snapshot of what the human population may be interested in or are asking about at the time. Google Zeitgeist is even archived back a couple of years, so your research can expand into looking for patters that seem to appear over time.

You can choose whichever category you'd like to zero-in on your specific niche idea.

The previous **"10 Niche Sourcing Methods"** are not the 'be all', 'end all' list to finding a niche! This is what has worked extremely well for me in the past and why I've labeled it as: **"Eric's 10 Niche Sourcing Methods".** These are simply a few examples that can be used to benefit your research.

However, I'm going to make it even easier for you . . . by listing another 118 resources to benefit your research!

Yikes . . . ! You heard right . . . ! I'm going to literally hand you the "Bible" to Niche Sourcing.

However, there is a catch! You have to actually use some of these resources - the **"Eric's 10 Niche Sourcing Methods"** above or the additional methods that will be provided. You will NOT get results if you do not take action. The more you put in, the more you'll get out!

💡 Tips & Suggestions:

The 118 additional niche sourcing methods can be found at the end of this book under the heading 'Additional Resources'.

This is the most extensive list of Niche Sourcing Methods ever assembled; therefore there is no excuse for anyone that thinks that they cannot find an idea that has the potential to make a profit!

Follow These Action Steps:

- Identify your niche!

- Research, research, research!

  - Internet

  - Library

  - Bookstore

- Conduct 'brainstorm' or 'brain-dump' sessions.

- Analyze the online/offline marketability of your choices.

- Determine the profitability of your niche choices.

- Study your potential competition.

- Use and act upon the **"Niche Sourcing Methods"** just discussed to find your niche.

Chapter 2
'Shooting blanks'? Choose From 9 Effective Business Models

2.1 Affiliate Marketing.

Like in the traditional businesses in which you recruit "associates" to sell your products for a commission, you can have "affiliates" on the net selling your products through their websites for a commission. Or, if you're clever, you can become the affiliate for other companies and earn a sizeable commission for selling their product.

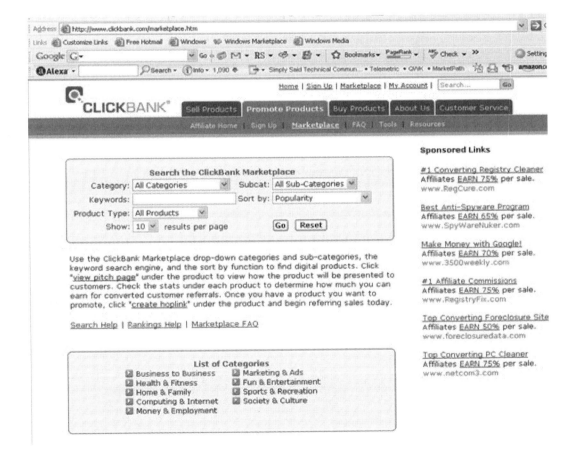

Affiliate marketing is a good place to start if you don't have a product yet. It can also provide a valuable foundation from which to learn marketing as well as any future products you decide to develop.

A good resource to begin your research for affiliate products is the Clickbank Directory, a.k.a. the Clickbank Marketplace:

http://www.clickbank.com/marketplace.htm

Most if not all of products listed in this directory offer the choice of joining their respective affiliate programs.

To sign up as an affiliate: http://www.clickbank.com/affiliateAccountSignup.htm

To get into affiliate marketing, you need to gather information about products and services from a range of service providers. Preferably, you'll need a website and you need to make that website attractive to the right customers.

In most cases, you may not even need your own website. In order to promote the product, all you'll need is an affiliate link that you could easily integrate within a signature, which you could use by inserting at the bottom of your emails that you send out to your friends. The affiliate link you will promote will directly refer the potential customer to the sales page of the product you are recommending as an affiliate. Obviously, if you have your own website, you can integrate the affiliate links within the site. There are many more available options to take advantage though if you have your own site to promote from rather than using just the email signature.

If you decide to develop your own site, a potential customer may visit your website and see a product or service that they like and as a result will click on a specific product or service link. If the link that is clicked on is an affiliate link, then the potential customer is then routed to the provider's website. The customer can choose to make a purchase and if a sale is made it is tracked.

This "routing" is tracked and you, the owner of the website from where the link originated, receive a "credit", commonly referred to as a commission. The commission can be as low as 5% (similar to what amazon.com offers) to 20% of the sale and in most cases 50% to even as high as 100% depending upon the nature of the products, the parent company, the business relationship you've established with the provider or the product pricing. However, the most common affiliate payout is around 50% of the product being sold.

2.2   Ebay/Auction Store.

An increasingly important online business venue is, as most have heard by now, the online auction site, Ebay. Membership to this site allows you to post information about items you have to sell. You can set a price and pay additional fees if you desire to market your product. As people search by keywords for items like yours, your product is brought up on the search result pages.

I've mentioned the fees associated with a service like this, but you don't generally pay anything (except fees for additional features you decide to use) unless your product sells. With a bit of work, you have a viable business model presented to you by Ebay or any one of the other auction sites listed below:

1. **Auction Universe** (http://www.auctionuniverse.com) - A great all-around auction site, second to Ebay but nonetheless very useful.

2. **Ebay** (http://www.ebay.com) - Arguably the most popular auction site on the net. This is a great place to sell anything, including niche market products.

3. **First Action** (http://www.firstauction.com) - This is a newer auction site. The First Auction is positioning itself as a serious rival of eBay and Ubid.

4. **OnSale** (http://www.onsale.com) - This site lets you browse, bid, and buy, using a live Internet auction of new, refurbished, and closeout goods.

5. **Yahoo! Auctions** (http://www.auctions.yahoo.com) - Yahoo offers twelve main auction categories for you to buy or sell whatever you want or have.

2.3 Drop Shipping

This is another viable business model, particularly suited to online businesses and niche marketing. Drop shipping or wholesale purchasing provides an ideal way for many individuals to sell products. In this model, you are purchasing products that people want to buy at a lower price from the manufacturer or wholesaler - thus keeping your costs down - then selling them at a higher mark up price. The benefit to you could easily be a generous and tidy profit.

The cool thing, and which is perhaps the most beneficial thing in drop shipping, is not having to deal with the inventory or shipping details yourself! Your time is extremely valuable, so freeing it up from extra tasks will give you the opportunity of doing other important things that will help your bottom line! ☺

When you drop ship products, you are taking orders from your customer on your retail site, than sending an order to wholesaler for that purchase paying the supplier at the set purchase price. The wholesaler then drop ships the product directly to your customer. You make your profit in the markup of the product to the customer.

Many people confuse this with being a middleman situation. This part of the supplier chain has been in existence for many years and is very legit.

In general, Manufacturers make the product. They sell their product or license their product to factory authorized wholesale distributors who handle the logistics of warehousing and shipping the products.

Retailers (including you as an online retailer) will purchase product from wholesalers in bulk quantities and resell it to the end consumer. When you're drop shipping a product, you're purchasing from the wholesaler in individual quantities instead of bulk quantities and the wholesaler sends the product straight to your customer instead of direct to you.

What you need to be careful about are the fake wholesalers, otherwise know as middleman, who pretend to be wholesalers and just take from your bottom line by selling you product that they "say" is wholesale when it is not true wholesale.

You have a variety of avenues to buy and sell products. You may develop a website to promote products that others want to buy. You can also sell your products to the appropriate consumers. Drop shipping is available to help you sell products through mail order as well.

To make any money at wholesaling, you need to purchase and sell products that people want. Of course research will help you. With a program such as eBay, the research is easy.

First, you must find a product that sells well. Take the time to research the right products. In my experience, I've found the following resource to be an excellent tool to discovering what is selling really well:

Useful resource: http://product-index.ebay.com/best_selling_1.html

Once you've decided what to sell, you will need to track down factory authorized wholesalers or manufacturers that will work with you as an online retailer. Once again, I'll recommend the one source that'll aid you in your search. You don't have to look anywhere else other than Chris Malta's site at: http://www.worldwidebrands.com where you will get the most complete, up-to-date information on distributors and wholesalers. This is the most extensive resource available that I highly recommend you look at! ☺ It's one of the most reputable sites I know of in this area - bar none!

Most people who put some effort into promoting their products do well at selling them. Don't forget that you can also make your own product. Recognize that there's plenty of money to be made out there and you're well on your way.

2.4   Private Label, Resell & Master Resell Rights.

Master resell rights, private label rights, and resell rights also present a great business model for those interested in running online businesses. Of course, if you don't know what these terms mean you can find yourself confused. There has not always been adequate information about these types of business models until recently, as there is a bunch of hype right now concerning them.

Why?

They can become instant money generators for you! You are basically purchasing the rights to these products and you therefore become the owner of it and as a result you make all the profits from it - at 100%! That's pretty cool huh!? ☺

There are three basic types of resell rights relevant to online businesses. They are master resell rights, resell rights, and private label rights. Master resell rights holders can pass on master resell rights to buyers. Resell rights allow you to sell the product to an end user.

Private label rights offer the most flexibility. They allow you to customize the product and come with source files for you to edit. Packages let you attach your name to the product as the creator and they are the closest thing to having your own product.

All three types of rights allow you to sell a product and keep 100% of the profit. Affiliates and internet marketers are quick to praise resell right products to give you complete control over.

By selling these products, you will be in control of processing your own orders and handling your own customer service. In terms of resell rights, you can find a wide selection of niche eBooks offering a variety of rights. Most packages come with their own set of sales letters and graphics. All of these make selling a breeze! ☺

If you want to purchase resell rights, there are several cost effective ways to go about it. With a little bit of research, you can pick up dozens of products for under $40. It's also possible to join a resell rights club or sign up for reseller service to provide brand new products to sell on a monthly basis.

Purchasing rights can also be expensive - since you are actually buying an already completed product.

You must do the proper research before you purchase rights to products. See how many other businesses are also selling this product. You don't want to end up spending a bunch of money on a product that is already being sold by 100 other people! If you feel there are too many being sold, then the market has been saturated or may be far too competitive to get in to.

Still kind of confused? Then download **Resell-Rights-101**, a free 5 page report written by Aurelius Tjin at: http://www.nichesourcing.com/reports/Resell-Rights-101.pdf. Aurelius does a fantastic job explaining this lucrative business model.

2.5   Paid Surveys.

Marketing research firms have paid consumers to participate in surveys for many years. Most of the research is undertaken by focus groups. The web offers a more efficient way to collect data and so many firms are conducting legit, online paid surveys, and other types of paid, online marketing research.

Some sites even offer payment in cash to take surveys. Some pay well in cash. Others offer payment in the form of goods, such as vouchers and service coupons. The reason to consider paid survey sights, however, is that if anyone is making a living from these things, they tend to be the middleman. The middleman, in other words, is the person who owns the website that offers to pay people for the surveys. So, it may not be as flexible and the profit potential is less. However, if you approach it properly, it can have great potential!

Of course, if you decide to turn paid surveys into your online business, you need to be prepared to solicit marketing partners and research a very complex and somewhat shady industry!

It's not uncommon to hear how many paid survey companies are not legit! ☹ Actually, this is probably very true and why some individuals don't bother with this business model. However, this is not all true. But don't let that discourage you! There are a few good sites out there that provide legitimate services and most important - you DO get paid.

There are also different types of surveys you can choose from doing such as focus groups, online survey, secret shopping, or phone surveys.

If you decide you'd like to do surveys, I highly recommend Survey Scout, it's very reputable and you can choose from 450 marketing companies willing to pay you for your opinions! You can read more about them by visiting their website at: http://www.SurveyScout.com.

2.6   E-courses.

One of the products you can easily sell is the e-course. The term e-Course is short for electronic course. You can offer one specific type or several on your website with very little trouble, few overheads, and a potentially high profit margin.

You can offer e-Courses via a website but you can also offer them via e-mail. Once you have a mailing list of existing, repeat, and potential customers, you can develop a series of marketing material and be prepared to send out your e-Courses to paying customers.

Why don't you download Jimmy Brown's free report entitled "How To Create An e-Course In Only One Day: A Simple and Profitable System ANYONE Can Use To Quickly Create An Email Mini-Course"?

It's an excellent resource! ☺

Here you go: http://www.nichesourcing.com/reports/design-ecourse-in-1-day.pdf.

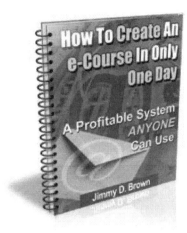

In this report, you'll learn how you can, in ONE day, create an e-Course that can provide passive profits for years to come - (and you don't even have to write it yourself!).

One of the most obvious benefits to this is that it can all be automated through the use of autoresponders, a feature that most web hosts offer as part of their hosting package - I'll explain more about this later in the book! ☺

2.7   Teleseminars and Webinars.

This is another form of online tutoring. Teleseminars offer a great way to engage with people in real time and the opportunities for this method of learning are as lucrative as opportunities to offer e-Courses. As with e-Courses, you can easily offer teleseminars via a website of your own or using a service that lets you chat with your paying customers.

This technique being used to teach is becoming more and more common. It's a powerful business tool for both the online and offline marketing crowd, but certainly in no way limited to that niche. Most if not all businesses, whether they are in marketing or not, are using these techniques to grow. The implementation of teleseminars and webinars has made it possible to teach groups of people, from 2 participants to literally thousands, by phone or by the internet, no matter where they are in the world!

A teleseminar is the simpler of the methods as its simply listening to someone over the phone line. The only requirement is that you need a phone. However, in the case of the webinar, it becomes a bit more complicated. You still use the phone but it also requires interaction through an internet connection via a computer. It actually becomes a better learning tool as more of your senses are being used; hear, see, participate! ☺

There is a big benefit to using teleseminars and or webinars as a foundation for your product because it can be perceived as having a higher value than an eBook. Where you could sell an eBook for $47.00 you could sell for $97.00, $147.00, or even $197.00 by simply making it available in this format.

Prior to conducting your teleseminar, you should make sure that you develop an outline of what you will be covering and I strongly suggest you consider whether you need a partner to help you with providing content, keeping on topic, or simply as the interviewer. Taking on a teleseminar without this could seriously hamper your efforts to teach and produce a quality product.

In order for you to get a better understanding of this extremely beneficial technique, it's best explained by Doug Champigny.

You can download Doug's free 10-page report entitled "The Champigny Guide To Webinars and Teleseminars" here:

http://www.nichesourcing.com/reports/Tele-and-Webinars.pdf.

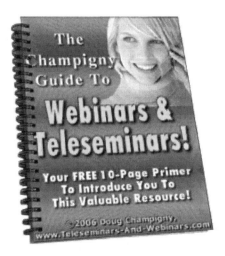

This brief report will give you a basic understanding of how the teleseminar and webinars work and how you can use these techniques to benefit your business!

2.8   Video Tutorials.

When you want - and when you are ready to go hi-tech, you can always educate people online using video tutorials. This method, as in the case of the previously mentioned formats, allows you to create a highly perceived product. The advantage to using the video format is that pretty much every niche uses video tutorials as an instructional tool.

There is really nothing that can take the place of live instruction, the 'classroom' in person education, except this format - which literally substitutes for the real thing!

So - isn't it hard to create video presentations?

No - not really . . . all you'll need is something that will record your 'material' which will either be a recording of yourself or a recording of something off your computer. You'll have to decide what type of 'recorder' you will use depending on how you present your material.

Basically, you have two alternatives on recording your product. If you wish to develop a product that teaches people how to upload files from your computer to your host - you will need a screen capture program.

If you are creating a product that requires physical demonstrations, you will need to use a camcorder to record the video and audio presentations.

Recording screen captures on your computer may sound complicated but its not! ☺ As a matter of fact, I'll recommend something to you that's even FREE and it does all the recordings for you, both screen capture and audio.

It's called Camtasia (and it is FREE at the time this book was printed) and you can download it here: http://www.download.techsmith.com/camtasiastudio/enu/312/camtasiaf.exe

Then you can get your software key by filling in this form: http://www.techsmith.com/camtasia/pcpls.asp

2.9   Blogging.

One of the most popular ways to communicate online is blogging. A blog is basically an online journal. You can find blogs for yourself and blogs that inform you about the goings on of the business world. There are many blog resources that will give you the opportunity of hosting with them at no charge. Wordpress.com and Blogger.com are very good. If I were to recommend the best service, I'd go with Wordpress.com - a very powerful program that can be hosted for free or hosted on your own website. If you do not have a blog, surf on over to: http://www.wordpress.com and sign up for a free account. This is actually a great way to go if you do not have your own website, you can set up your own blog and declare that you now have your own site!

There are however, several ways to make money with blogs. You can use advertising programs to gain money from your site. One of the best methods is to use contextual ads using programs such as Google AdSense. Another popular program is BlogAds.

New additions incude Chitika's eMiniMalls and CrispAds, Text Link Ads, Adgenta, Azoogle Ads, Intelli Txt, Peak Click, DoubleClickTribal Fusion, Adbrite, Clicksor, Industry Brains, AdHearUs, Kanoodle, AVN, Pheedo, Adknowledge, YesAdvertising, RevenuePilotTextAds, SearchFeed, Target Point, Bidvertiser, Fastclick Value Click and OneMonkey. Wow! That was a mouthful . . . , so much to choose from and the possibility of making money increases.

As you may have noticed, I haven't provided links to the additional programs listed above. However, doing a simple word search of the specific program you choose in any search engine will result in finding its url.

RSS Advertising and sponsorship are also available via an array of advertising programs. A quick web search will generally bring up the information you need to get started. When your blog has some traffic, there are larger affiliate programs you can target, such as Amazon.com and Linkshare.com.

Digital assets are also being used by an increasing numbers of bloggers. Generally, digital assets include eBooks, e-Courses, and teleseminars, which are also being offered via blogs.

Promoting affiliate programs from your blog is not your only alternative. If you decide to develop or simply sell someone else's product, you can promote it from your blog.

You can also create your blog as a review guide - pointing out what's good and bad on any physical product, piece of software or other informational product.

I recommend that you check out http://www.nicheblog.nichesourcing.com if you'd like to learn more about how to use your blog as a money-maker on autopilot! ☺

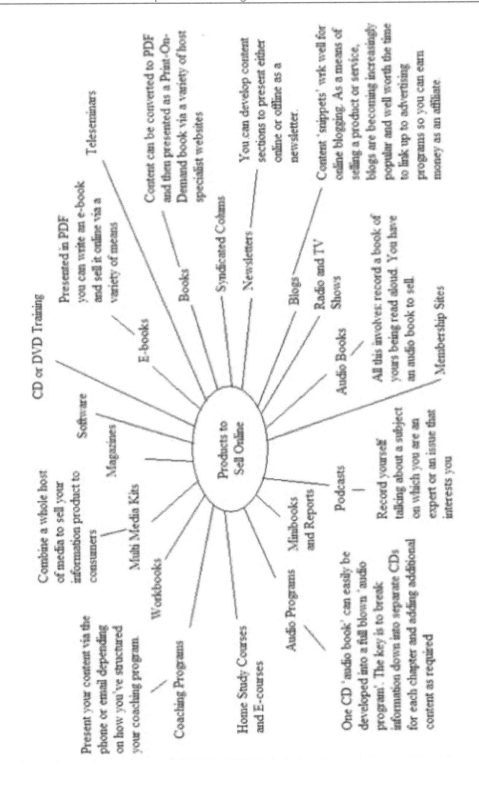

Follow These Action Steps:

- Undecided on a niche? Review, research, study and decide on one of these business models:

  - Affiliate Marketing

    - Clickbank Marketplace: http://www.clickbank.com/marketplace.htm

    - To sign up: http://www.clickbank.com/affiliateAccountSignup.htm

  - Ebay/Auction stores

    - **Auction Universe** (http://www.auctionuniverse.com)

    - **Ebay** (http://www.ebay.com)

    - **First Action** (http://www.firstauction.com)

    - **Yahoo! Auctions** (http://www.auctions.yahoo.com)

  - Drop Shipping

    - http://www.worldwidebrands.com

  - Private Label Rights - Complimentary (Free!!) Video Tutorials & Training Manuals

    - http://www.plrsecretsexposed.com

  - Resell Rights - Complimentary (Free!!) Video Tutorials & Training Manuals

    - http://www.ResellRightsForNewbies.com

  - Master Resell Rights - 200 Complimentary (Free!!) Master Resell Rights Products

    - http://www.resellrightspack.com

  - Paid Surveys

    - http://www.SurveyScout.com

  - E-courses - Complimentary (Free!!) 12-Week Internet Marketing e-course!

    - http://www.im-course.com

- Teleseminars

  - http://www.teleseminarsecrets.com

- Video Tutorials

  - http://www.internet-audio-video.com

- Blogging

  - http://www.wordpress.com (Sign up for free, it's also strongly recommended, you have the choice of hosting your account on your domain)

  - http://www.blogger.com (Sign up free, similar to Wordpress in that you have the choice of hosting your account on your domain.)

Chapter 3
Decision Time – Choose the Niche You Want to Focus On

3.1   Choose and Focus on 1 Niche (Area or Model) first.

Case Study One:

As a boy in the 1960's, Lawrence Livermore was an avid collector of rock-and-roll long-playing albums. At basement parties, he always brought his wide collection of recordings from the Chess label and others featuring the bands of the British Invasion. On a trip to the west coast from his home in Pennsylvania, two interesting things happened on the same weekend.

First, on a visit to a garage sale in the San Joaquin valley, he discovered copies of Herman's Hermits first American release. Livermore identified the rare album immediately, along with a program and uncollected ticket from the Monterrey Pop festival.

He bought the above items for a total of $17. The following day, he flew to Las Vegas, where he had a hamburger and coke at the Hard Rock Hotel and Casino. After striking up a conversation with the restaurant manager, he described and then sold the just-purchased materials in a framed display for $225. The cost of the frame was $45, leaving Lawrence with a profit of $163, or almost 300%, with a holding time of a single day. Lawrence knew he was on to something. He played twenty minutes of roulette, keying on the number "17" (the price in dollars of the original material). He won an additional $48 with this method, and took a walk to the Mirage to consider all he'd learned! ☺

Case Study Two:

Marge Sampson loved San Francisco. She loved the rich history, loved the beatnik cafes of North Beach, the hidden delights of Chinatown and the vibrant traffic around Fisherman's Wharf.

Best of all she loved the honky-tonk atmosphere in Haight Ashbury. Two weeks after losing her job as an Administrative Assistant, the 24 year old took a position as a guide on a tour bus. Two weeks after that, she began to write her own tour book: "A Midwesterner's Guide to the City by The Bay."

For two months Marge collected anecdotes from other tour guides. Between shifts she would race to the public library and scour the shelves for stories of old "San Fran." Within two more months, Marge had placed three articles in national magazines (two airline mags and "Cigar Aficionado").

Fortified with her new "press book" (copies of her published articles and also a promotional piece which referenced her work and how the Tour Bus Company had prepared to advertise her route as well), she attended the National Book Fair, held that year in Phoenix.

A national publisher, eager to introduce a new series of guide books by young writers, gave her a contract to prepare an entire guidebook, titled, "An Insider's Guide to the City by The Bay". The five thousand dollar advance against future royalties gave Marge the operating capital to buy a printer and promote her own tours on her day off!

Within an additional 2 years, she had made several deals with local merchants to stop at their tourist shops (one was for Guatamalan rucksacks, another at the Gap shop in Haight-Ashbury).

By working two tours for her new company on her day off, she soon saved almost $20,000. Re-investing in her business, and with the help of substantial bank financing, she bought a larger tour bus, and began running tours at night as well as on her days off.

One development in particular helped her during her second year. It was then that she forged a strategic alliance with the organizers of the Gay and Lesbian Mardi Gras Celebration. By including a discount coupon for a special tour in the standard registration packet, Marge doubled her business that February.

Flush with success, a similar coupon arrangement with the organizers of the City's Leather and Fetish Festival did almost as well. Contacts she developed at the local hotels during these two party weekends led to a "bounty program" which she instituted with first one, then several of the local hotel concierges.

Two years, four months, and 24 days after she first began work as a tour guide, Marge sold her new business to Gray Line Tours for 1.4 million dollars ($140,000 cash, and the rest on a deferred payment basis).

On Halloween she threw herself a massive party in the Mission District, and by Thanksgiving she had moved to Seattle, where she began the whole process over again.

Case Study Three:

Janis Gillette dropped out of college after her freshman year, with little desire to return. She worked the summer pulling soft ice-cream on the boardwalk at Virginia Beach. Late in July, the Lollapalooza tour came through and she had her photograph taken with Liz Phair.

When Janis posted a copy of the photo at the booth, sales jumped 20%. On a whim, the shop began to sell copies of Phair's second album, "Exile in Guyville." Sales of ice cream jumped an additional twenty percent! When the manager took off the first weekend in August for his sister's wedding, Janis really got her chance to shine. She arrived early Saturday morning, made certain that the stand was swept and cleaned, and she cued up the collection of Liz Phair CD's which made up the foundation of the daily soundtrack at the soft ice-cream stand.

That weekend the stand did record-setting business! The owner was so pleased with what Janis had achieved that he set her up with her own stand at the other end of the boardwalk!

Two weeks later, to celebrate the Labor Day end of season, Janis printed up special commemorative T-shirts, and promoted a special "Liz Swirl", a large soft ice cream for only $1 (vanilla only). Again the stand did record business, and, not incidentally, made record profits. The owner invited her to operate a stand he had in Hollywood Florida for the winter season, but Janis had other plans. She stayed in Virginia Beach, established a web-site to sell the remaining commemorative T-shirts, and planned her attack for the following year.

The niche market you choose to focus upon must represent your interests and expertise as well as represent a relatively untapped need of your customer base. It's best to start small and expand your business as success comes your way, as you can well infer from the case studies provided in this section.

3.2   Learn It & Master It.

Our three case studies illustrate the significance of knowing your market and being prepared to concentrate your efforts on one enterprise, seizing opportunities that present themselves, and looking for means to apply what you learn at each stage.

To achieve a successful niche marketing business, you must be prepared not only to concentrate on one niche market, you must be prepared to learn as much as you can and apply what you learn to become a master of your market.

If you opt to write an eBook on a given subject and look to sell it online - the same applies to the development of an e-Course, teleseminar series, or even a video seminar or blog series - you must be prepared to become an expert on the subject on which you write.

If you look to sell a product or service, you must acquaint yourself with your potential customers and know the value to them of what you are selling.

When it comes to market research, you must examine the success of niche websites. You need to be aware of three elements: your page impressions, your click through rate (CTR), and the cost-per-click (CPC) for advertisements displayed on your websites.

Traffic-generating strategies allow you to manipulate your page impressions and CTR is controlled through careful and reasonable ad placement and page design features. All of these are elements that you must master by reviewing and studying your competitors. Even if you plan to operate offline, you can still apply a similar model to these three to determine the best approach for operating your business. You should monitor the number of leads you attract to your business, the number of leads you attract per advertising method, and the cost of your advertising methods divided by the number of converted customers.

3.3   Use As a Template for Your Next Niche (Area or Model).

"So where do I start . . . ?" You ask yourself, "How do I start . . . ?"

The best place to start is at the beginning, with what you know. Your first business idea, your first effort at targeting a niche market, should rely upon basic and sound principles. There should be an established need and little competition in your chosen area. Develop a form of business deemed appropriate by the results of your market research. Examine customer preferences and consider your competition. You have a range of options available to you. You can't - and shouldn't try to do everything at once, but you can choose a single business model - a blog, an e-book - and stick with it.

As you follow through with your first business idea you should also make notes about your model and your approach in general. How did you approach the customers? How effective was your business overall?

You should look at a host of other issues in some depth as well:

1. Did you develop a business plan, a marketing plan, and a strategic plan as suggested here? Did you follow through on your plans? How effective was your planning overall?

2. How did you conduct your market research? How effective was your research?

3. How did you advertise your business? How successful was your advertising campaign?

4. What type of customer service did you provide? What was the overall satisfaction rating of your business?

5. Of your business model as a whole, would you say it was successful? What, if anything, would you do to improve the model?

When you can answer these questions fully, it is time to sit down and think about developing a template. A template is basically a business model or outline that is transferable from one business venture to another. The more effective a template you have - the more transferable - the more businesses you can launch and successfully run, with any target niche market.

Follow These Action Steps:

- Choose your niche!

  - By now you should have completed a reasonable amount of research that you are confident enough to choose your specific niche.

    - Let me give you an example of how it's done. This is one of several niche sites that I decided to build after I realized its potential. If you do the proper research you will see the benefits. First, I began with something I liked and have a passion for. If you are lucky, you will find something that will fill these requirements. I developed my product from a hobby that I knew others in this same hobby were also very passionate about (extremely important!). This makes it an easier crowd to sell to! After I found that niche, I developed a content-based website that included an opt-in form (extremely important!) to develop potential customers interested in the topic.

- Then I narrowed in on a sub-niche of the original niche that I started with to get targeted and less competitive. You want to be the big fish in the small pond! ☺ Or if you cannot become the big fish, than concentrate your efforts in providing something unique so that you can attract your customers away from your competition. To add to this, your goal is to be able to do something better or provide a superior product than your competition. After I discovered my sub-niche I then developed a product that catered to this sub-niche.

- Don't make the mistake of choosing 2 or 3 different niches! You must choose ONE Niche and then stick with it!

- Concentrate by putting all your effort into 1 niche at a time! Once you've capitalized and profited from one niche, go to the next! Use your last successful project as a template so that it'll be easier to do the next! Before you know it, you'll be selling 5 to 10 different products and probably thinking of doing it full time! (Goodbye **J.O.B.**!)

  - I was fortunate to not have to put too much effort into "testing the water", to see if there was enough interest in the topic. If you are lucky, you may not have to over extend yourself in your content-based site. If that's the case, you'll be able to put most of your effort into developing your product. Through my research, I found that I could capitalize on the Saltwater Fish hobby! So I developed a content-based site: http://www.saltwaterfishpets.com.

Added the all important opt-in form and continued to add quality content to encourage more subscribers to sign up and to keep my current subscribers happy with new information. By keeping the doors of communication open to my readers, I was able to establish what questions they needed answers to. This is how I developed my product - I basically answered their questions! ☺

I'll get into more details as to how I managed the development of my product later, and how I was able to persuade other people to most of the work (developing the product content) for me - FOR FREE! ☺ So keep on reading!

- Learn it, live it, breathe it, & master it!

- Think & plan steps ahead; mold the niche you've chosen as a template so that you can make your products even better.

Chapter 4
Purchase Your Virtual Storefront

4.1 Advantages of a Virtual Storefront vs. a Physical Storefront.

Well, websites are useful but there's actually just one very important reason to have one for your business - in this day and age, you are expected to have one! There's really no getting around this. The idea of a virtual storefront versus a physical storefront is pretty novel at the moment. A physical store front is a huge financial liability for the company. It can't be open 24/7 without requiring staff paid around the clock. It can only attract a limited population of customers and very few will come afar. At best, the majority of your customers will come to your store during normal business hours.

With the Internet available in almost every community in the world, you're expected to have a website accessible to both web surfers and established prospects looking to find out more about your business, your products, and services. The chances are, if you pay attention to your virtual storefront, you'll be in demand around the clock!

The following functions of the website will help you establish and further define your purpose.

1. **Position yourself to be found where customers are searching** - Key word optimization and meta tagging are essential for the success of your website. Invest in professional web-design and search engine optimization help if you need to.

2. **Sell more** - To make greater profits you need more customers - new and repeat customers - and the internet is one great tool to reach out to people at minimum cost!

3. **Make it more convenient for your buyers** - It is cost effective, fast, and simple for prospective customer to visit your website instead of driving to your physical location!

4. **Beat the competition** - Your customer is loaded with choices. Even though a customer may be interested in your business, it's easy for him/her to choose another company over you if reaching out to you proves too difficult.

5. **Improve your advertising efficiency** - You may spend hundreds of dollars advertising your business; in newspapers, magazines, radio or T.V. If you want to make your advertising efficient, start exploring your Internet-based marketing options. The internet lets you improve your leads and sales conversions while also cutting back on costs.

6. **Put your business on autopilot past normal working hours** - It is very important that your customer can reach you when they want to. On the web you can make information about your products and services available around the clock. A website means constant presence for you and your product.

7. **Cut costs while expanding your influence** - In traditional business strategies, expansion involves opening up new offices. Not only do you need to invest in real estate, you will incur huge overheads! Expansion can be a major drawback. With a website, however, your business has no physical restrictions; it can be accessed by potential customers anywhere in the world. You don't need multiple office locations just to reach your customers. Everything is streamlined! ☺

8. **One world; one address** - Marketing material looks jumbled when there are five or six physical addresses, three or four telephone numbers, and a couple of fax lines for the company. Online businesses need only advertise one address: yourname@yourcompany.com. It's stylish, ergonomic, and a damn site cheaper when you're charged for your ad at a per word rate!

9. **It's** business@light.speed - Searching for information over the net couldn't be any easier. When you come across a business website, you can request a service or product quote via e-mail and receive the quote within minutes to your mailbox. In this day and age, you need to keep up to stay ahead.

10. **No more Chinese Whispers!** - Everyone reads your message, as you wrote it. Thanks to websites, there's no more chance of getting the wires crossed about what your company does (unless of course someone hacks your site). For the most part, you are in control of what your website conveys.

11. **Stop worrying about the "Right Location"** - Your website is your one and only location and building the perfect website is a lot cheaper than renovating an office space! The better your website, the better the impression you make, and the more sales you will make! However, some customers are interested only in the quality of your products and the service they get. But the rule of thumb, your website will be making the first impression. First impressions are lasting impressions!

12. **Help democratizes the business world** - everyone can have a great website. Small businesses are equal to the giants in the online world!

13. **Update easily** - Add, modify, edit, and delete content or update info on latest products or services at almost no cost, done in a matter of few minutes, at anytime and anywhere!

14. **Foster two-way communication** - You can request feedback from your clients or start a message board so your customers can communicate about your products and services.

15. **Provide customer service online** - Tell your customers about new product features, how to use your products, and how to troubleshoot most problems. You can also have a help center for your customers to login to, in order to resolve small troubles with the product all by themselves.

To sell products to customers anywhere in the world, it is critical for businesses to have an uncluttered yet simple, easy to use functional website. For the most part, it only needs to be a 4-5 page website (we call these mini-websites). It really does give teeth to your basic Internet marketing efforts, not to mention the fact it helps you make a splash in the virtual world.

4.2   Decide on & purchase a domain name.

Your "Universal Resource Locator" or URL should match your business name in terms of what it communicates. Also like your business name, if possible, it should tell a word or two about your business values and area of focus. Keywords associated with your business should appear in the name, if at all possible, and the URL must be easy to spell and remember. Your customers have to type the name into their web browser when then want to visit your site.

You may want to check whether the URL you're planning to have is available or not. There are many, many websites that let you know the availability of a particular name along with its domain (.com, .net, .biz etc). A useful place to start in finding and purchasing good domain name would be at any one of the following sites:

- ✓   DomainOrb.com - http://www.DomainOrb.com

- ✓   GoDaddy.com - http://www.GoDaddy.com

- ✓   Domain.com - http://www.Domain.com

URLs can be registered for a minimum of one year and then you need to renew your registration after the end of the period you paid for. Urls can also be registered for up to 2, 3, 5 or 10 year periods. Registering over a longer period will in fact be less expensive in the long run!

Here are a few additional points to consider:

a. Your Domain Name Should Be (in most cases) Your Website Name.

This seems obvious enough but many people make the mistake of giving their website a different name from their domain name. Naming a site after its domain name is important, however. When people think of your website, they'll think of its name. If your business name is also your URL, your potential customers will automatically know where to go.

b. Should You Use Generic Names Or Brand Name Domains?

A number of people think that your domain name really must have some generic name. However, most people don't go looking for products by their generic name. If you're looking for a car or a book, you're unlikely to type "cars" or "books" into the search engine. That would be too broad a search - right? You're more likely to have a car brand in mind, like "Toyota" or a book title or subject, like "books on business".

The name that you use to advertise your product or combination thereof is the name that you will want for your domain. After all, your brand name is the first thing that people will type and search for with their browser. It is also the easiest thing for them to remember.

c. Long or Short Domain Names?

Domain names can run up to 67 characters. You can, therefore, avoid obscure names and generally write out the full title of your business.

Many people disagree, however, about whether a long or short domain name is better.

Shorter domain names are easier to remember, easier to type and far less susceptible to mistakes. However, a longer domain name is easier on the human memory.

Long domain names with your site keywords fare better in a number of search engines.

d. Should you use a hyphenated name?

Many users are used to typing things like freecpluspluscompilers.com but not free-c-plus-plus-compilers.com. Also, when people recommend your site to their friends verbally, having hyphens in your domain name leads to more potential errors than when the name does not contain hyphens.

One advantage is that search engines can distinguish your keywords better and thus return your site more prominently in search results for those keywords occurring in your domain name.

To hyphenate or not to hyphenate; it really depends on the nature of your business.

e. .com, .net, .org, .info, .name?

Just about every website owner wonders what domain ending they should use. Should they use ".com", undoubtedly the most common. If that's not available, is ".net", ".org" or other country-specific top level domains (TLDs) like .de, .nu, or .sg best?

If your business caters to a local community, it makes sense to get a country-specific domain. A local domain lets people in your home country know that they're dealing with a local entity.

A business can also benefit from an international audience. In reality, .tv, .org, and .net are perfectly acceptable domain names. You should decide whether it is more important to have the perfect domain name or a .com domain at the possible expense of your perfect domain name.

Your first choice should go with what's most common and what people will automatically think of first, pick a .com (best case scenario). If you think about it, when you think of a domain - you usually think of a .com first.

4.3   Decide where you want to host your domain.

Most of us think that websites exist on the web, end of discussion. The web, however, exists on a network of computers. The content of your website is stored in a computer from where it can be accessed by Internet users. It doesn't exist in thin air. Host computers are, however, very special; they are called "servers". To have a website, you need to pay to have your content on a server.

There are, however, many companies that offer hosting services. A quick Google search will bring you to a heap of choices! The next question: how do you go about choosing a server?

Below is a list of parameters you should use as a guide in choosing your hosting company:

1. **Money:** You'll be surprised after comparing a few web-hosting companies in terms of overall price versus value. There's likely to be a huge difference. You'll probably see a range of $8.95 per month to around $49.95 per month to well over $100 per month! The best value for your money will be in the range of $24.95 per month.

2. **Storage Space:** Particularly if you're going in for a large website, you need to be sure that that your web hosting company can give you enough space. You also need to check that they can handle a sudden surge of traffic to your site. The last thing you want is a website that shuts down as a result of high bandwidth, when a mass of visitors - or potential customers - come your way!

3. **Technical Support:** You need your website to be up all the time, so you may want to verify the track record of the company. Be sure that your host company also provides good backend support. You'll want to know that if you have technical issues, that you'll be able to get help quickly. Response time should be quick, efficient and courteous.

4. **Host Multiple Domains:** Your goal should be to use a host that will give you the capability of hosting several domain names under one account for one cost. Better value for your money and less administrative hassle when you only have to login to your account to manage a multiple number of domains/websites.

5. **Security:** Your web hosting company should also demonstrate sufficient security arrangements. There are few things worse than having your website hacked!

   Here are a couple hosts I've had success with:

   ✓ Thirdsphere - http://www.Thirdsphere.com

   ✓ IPower - http://www.iPower.com

   ✓ 1and1 - http://www.1and1.com

At a minimum, the company you've decided to host your domain/websites on should have the following:

- **Host multiple domains on one account** - this is convenient for you and can save you a lot of money and administrative hassle!

- **Large storage space** (500mb+ storage, minimum) - particularly if you want to have a lot of pages, images, audio files or even large download files for your customers.

- **Large bandwidth** (unlimited) - this will assure that you will not have problems when your site gets a lot of traffic.

- **FTP accounts** - these type of accounts let you manage the content of your website.

- **Email accounts** (unlimited) - extremely invaluable, you can never have too many.

- **Databases** (unlimited) - many programs and pieces of software that you may purchase in the future to increase the profitability of your company need databases to operate correctly, so you gain a major advantage by having this capability.

- **Sub-domains** (unlimited) - naturally, you'll want to expand your site, so you should ensure you have access to unlimited sub-domains to enhance your main domain.

Comparison Chart of Hosting Plans			
Features	**Thirdsphere**	**1and1**	**Ipower**
Monthly Fee	$24.95	$2.99-$19.99	$4.95
Host Domains	5	1	1
Storage Space	500MB	300GB	300GB
Bandwidth	30GB	3,000GB	3,000GB
FTP accounts	Yes	50	Yes
Email Account	Unlimited	4,000	2,500
Databases	Unlimited	100	25
Subdomains	Unlimited	600	?
Site Statistics	Yes	Yes	Yes
Autoresponders	Unlimited	Yes	2500
Webmail	Yes	Yes	Yes
CGI-bin	Yes	Yes	Yes
Ecommerce	Yes	Yes	Yes
Back-up	Yes	Yes	Yes
Additional Info	Click Here to www.thirdsphere.com	Click Here to www.1and1.com	Click Here to www.ipower.com

- **Autoresponders** - a very effective method of communicating with your customers and generating sales. Autoresponders can be problematic to create without the availability of special programs, so check to see if your host site offers something to make this important marketing process easier.

- **Site Statistics** - you definitely want to know who visits your site and when, your host should provide these statistics in an easy to interpret format.

- **Webmail** - as with e-mail accounts, you never know when you're going to need a webmail feature to stay in contact with your customers when you travel away from home.

- **E-commerce capability** - everything from shopping carts to checkout processes are covered under the term e-commerce. Since you are more than likely to want to make money from your site, you really should be sure that you can go about it in a straightforward way.

- **Cgi-bin** - this is a bit of technical jargon for common gateway interface, which is a standard protocol for presenting external application software on a website.

- **Forum capability** - these are a great means of establishing communication with customers and encouraging word-of-mouth marketing.

- **Ability to install other third-party software** - you never know when you might need a feature like this, particularly if you are offering products online, such as brand name products and e-books.

4.4   Set up Mini-merchant accounts

The Internet is a vehicle for the payment of goods and services. It's been used since the mid-1980s but it took off only recently in the 1990s when more online commercial applications and services were being developed.

The option of paying over the Internet was only available to businesses with specialized "merchant" bank accounts. The bank accounts were designed to accept credit cards, debit cards, gift cards, and other forms of payment cards and a "payment gateway" was used to hook into both the customer's account - credit, or debit - and the merchant's account. The gateway verified information, transferred requests, and authorized payments in real time.

The payment gateway thus became the equivalent of the physical point of sale (POS) terminal at the checkout in your average store.

Merchant Accounts and Payment Gateways are central to all online payments. Whether you are using a third party provider like PayPal or you've set up your own merchant facilities; whether you are physically aware of them or not, to accept payments online over the Internet these components will always be there, one way or another.

Some of the better known Payment Gateway providers are:

- Authorize.net

- Verisign

- Plug 'n' Pay

- LinkPoint

In the beginning, when Payment Gateways were first introduced, only credit cards were accepted as forms of online payments. Nowadays, however, many different forms of payment are processed online through the gateways. The following methods are commonly used:

- Credit Cards

- Debit Cards

- eChecks

Among these, PayPal is a special type of account from which money can be taken to pay for goods and services. The payee who opts to use a PayPal account already maintains a PayPal account. They have already deposited funds into their account and they are then able to pay for goods and services. Using their PayPal account, assuming of course that the seller allows PayPal payments, the payee is able to make a payment by simply disclosing their PayPal information.

PayPal began as a payment medium through which purchasers on eBay could deposit and then spend funds. At one time, PayPal was the only option for individuals who did not have credit cards. It is now considered a payment method in its own right and is widely supported as such. It is a measure of the program's success.

The process payment transaction is secure; information is transmitted between both the customer and your website and between your website and the customer and merchant accounts. The information is valuable. Often it is private information about your customer's transaction. It needs to be difficult for hackers to intercept and read.

Secure Socket Layer (SSL) Certificates are a good security measure to impose. These certificates work through a combination of programs and encryption/decryption routines that exist on the web hosting computer and in browser programs like Internet Explorer, Netscape, Firefox and other browsers.

Some of the better known SSL Certificate providers are:

- Verisign

- Thawte

- InstantSSL

- Entrust

- Baltimore

Although establishing a merchant account is relatively easy nowadays, many situations still emerge in which a merchant account either cannot be obtained or simply does not suit the purpose of the business. Sometimes it costs too much to setup and operate a SSL Certificate and is not cost effective for a business. Although you still need to make your online transactions secure, an alternative is to use a 3rd party payment processor, this will get the same thing accomplished in a less expensive process.

A third party payment processor has its own merchant account and payment gateway. It allows other individuals and companies to process transactions without having to sign up for their own merchant account. Virtually anyone can sign up to use these processors and the third party processor company makes its money by taking a slice of each transaction processed. As your sales increase a merchant account will generally become the more cost effective path. However, it is quite common and appropriate for a business to start off using a third party processor and, when sales volumes increase, to move to a merchant account and gateway.

The best known third party payment processor is, of course, PayPal. It is both a method of payment for customers that have a PayPal account AND a third party payment processor for accepting payments made using credit cards, debit cards, eChecks, and, of course, PayPal customer accounts.

There are many other third party payments processors. Here is a list of 3rd party processors that I'd recommend if you choose to start off with this method (most, by the way, are free to sign up to):

- ✓ PayPal - http://www.PayPal.com

- ✓ ClickBank - http://www.clickbank.com/affiliateAccountSignup.htm

- ✓ 2Checkout - http://www.2Checkout.com

- ✓ PayDotCom.com - http://www.PayDotCom.com

- ✓ Google Checkout - http://www.GoogleCheckout.com

4.5 Set up a Full-service merchant account with your bank/business account.

A true merchant account can only be obtained for a business, not an individual. The business owner is, however, responsible for the account. They are the designated merchant. In this case it would be you as the business owner, or someone you designate.

The business owner is responsible for developing their own payment gateway. This is not included with the merchant account. Most true merchant accounts are established directly with Visa or Mastercard. It requires more paperwork to establish an account with either American Express or Discover Card.

A major advantage of having your own merchant account directly with processors like Visa and Mastercard: you are in total control. You can process large volumes of sales, add your own personal touch to your checkout pages on your website, what's called an application programming interface (API). You can also build up a professional but personalized look and image on your customer's statements of purchase.

However, what's most beneficial to having your own merchant account is being able to get your cash from the purchases made, deposited directly into your business account the same day! You want it to be PAYDAY everyday - right?

A merchant account is a great way to market your business because your name - and often your name only - goes on most of the paperwork and pages associated with the purchasing of your products.

When a company has a true merchant account, they can also use a separate processing gateway, negotiating their own rates for purchases, and generally establishing their own protocol for every sale.

One major draw back of getting your own merchant account, particularly for individuals and many small business owners, is the credit check. All of the true merchant accounts require applicants to undergo a credit check. The check is generally against the business entity. With low volume business or bad credit - both of which are more common among small businesses - the merchant may not be eligible for the account. True merchant accounts are not for personal use. A high-risk business, generally identified as such by the credit check, is charged a higher rate. Depending on the background and financial standing of the business, some are also required to sign onto multi-year contracts before their account is approved.

A true merchant account is one of those online payment decisions that you have to live with if you go for it. That said, many businesses definitely benefit from having true merchant accounts. More than this, many businesses actually need true merchant accounts to make the most of online sales.

The following are some good full-service merchant account:

- ✓ Authorize.net - http://www.authorizenet.com

- ✓ Verisign - http://www.verisign.com

- ✓ iPower Pay - http://www.ipowerpay.com

The first thing most merchants think of when they hear the term, credit card, they know that they need some form of account to accept credit cards online. They need a merchant account with a payment gateway.

For the following situations, a true merchant account is perfect:

- **To process large volumes of sales**

- **To keep total control over a business account**

- **To maintain a transparent checkout**

- **To establish a professional image**

A true merchant account is perfect for business with large volumes of sales that need to process a lot of transactions. True merchant accounts do have some additional fees compared to third-party providers of accounts. On balance, however, large volume merchants pay less with true merchant accounts. With a large volume to process, merchants get good discount rate when they maintain their own account. The discount rate with third-party providers can be as high as 6% per transaction, with an additional transaction fee of one dollar applying in most cases. A true merchant account offers rates less than half of what most third-party providers offer. As a merchant's transaction volume rises, the amount of money you save by having your own true merchant account actually increases.

If you decide that your business could benefit from this option, there is 1 merchant I'd highly recommend you use: Authorize.net. I've had nothing but good to say about this company! ☺

A very large volume merchant easily clears the threshold for a true merchant account, it is by far a superior option for online payment processing. For big online businesses, a true merchant account tends to be the very best option.

Follow These Action Steps:

- Establish your virtual storefront.

- Decide on and purchase your domain.

    - **DomainOrb** - http://www.DomainOrb.com (Highly recommended)

- Decide on where to host your domain.

    - **Thirdsphere** - http://www.Thirdsphere.com (Highly recommended)

- Set up your mini-merchant account. Choose from any of the following options (Or sign up to all of them!):

    - **Paypal** - http://www.PayPal.com.com

    - **2Checkout** - http://www.2Checkout.com

- **Clickbank** - http://www.clickbank.com/affiliateAccountSignup.htm

- **PayDotCom.com** - http://www.PayDotCom.com

- Set up your full-service merchant account.

    - **Authorize.net** - http://www.authorizenet.com (Highly recommended).

PHASE 2:

Creating The Product

Chapter 5
Choosing Product Format/Package

Before you start thinking about how to package your product, you really need to think about what you're packaging. The success of your business will depend largely on one specific phase in this creation process. You need to focus on developing the CONTENT! How you develop the content will ultimately determine the outcome of what you are offering or contributing to your specific niche, so in this chapter, we'll take a look at some of the specifics.

5.1   Electronic Book (PDF or EXE).

Nowadays, it's very easy to select a topic for an eBook. All you need to do is a tiny bit of research to confirm the topic and away you go. People are so hungry for information these days - why else do you think Google is such a success? - All you need to do is feed them. Most people look to the Internet to quench their appetite, so you're already targeting the right spot to make your money.

So how do you go about choosing your eBook topic?

Number one, you should start by looking at what's going on around you. What goes on around you is very significant to determining what you can sell in an eBook. First of all, the information is easily accessible and engaging, and those around you will be full of ideas you can use. For example, if one of your friends has been traveling to exotic locations, you might consider developing a series of traveling books.

Similarly, you might find plenty to write about if someone in your family is expecting a child. Pregnancy and the first few years of child rearing are such a mystery, especially to expectant parents, there can never be enough books on the subject. Think about "What to Expect When You're Expecting . . ." This is one of only a few books on pregnancy you can use to get some good ideas should you decide to go for this one.

Of course, there are hundreds of ideas you can use. Brainstorm your ideas and you'll quickly find plenty to write about.

Number two, you need to start figuring out how to make your content engaging and unique. There are two elements to consider: the actual content and its presentation.

Ask yourself a few questions about the type of book you want to present:

- ✓ Do you want a lot of text or limited text supported by a lot of pictures?

- ✓ Do you intend to use a lot of pictures?

- ✓ Do you want to provide a how-to guide?

To refine some of your ideas, check out sites like Amazon.com, visit the groups at Yahoo.com and conduct a few Google searches to find out about your potential readers.

You can find hobbyists and niche groups by searching the web for "popular hobbies," "enthusiasts," or "what America is buying." You can search forums and discussion groups for hobbyists. People regularly talk with each other in forums, to share ideas with one another. They will often exchange testimonials for equipment, upcoming events, and even books. This should provide you with plenty of ideas for the content of your book.

Two common eBook formats are available. They are EXE and PDF. Both refer to a particular type of electronic file used for eBooks. One type has .exe after the filename. The other has .pdf. You, or if you choose a ghostwriter, may put your eBook draft in one of these formats, but probably more likely to start with a .doc file. Most ghostwriters use a program like Microsoft Word (MS Word). Unless you specify that you want your book delivered in PDF or EXE by your writer, you're likely to be responsible for converting the file. IF this proves the case, you can buy software that will make an EXE file, or you can purchase or use free software to convert the text to a PDF file.

Of the two, the PDF approach is by far the easiest to use for several reasons. First, PDF files are smaller. Buyers can download them faster. Secondly, PDF files are easy to read thanks to the free software that's available for both PC and Mac computers. Thirdly, PDF conversion software is not expensive and there are even free versions you can use. Most of the free versions work really well if all your eBook contains is text.

You can convert your eBook to PDF using one of Adobe's programs if you don't mind spending a bit of money. Most of the programs cost about $200. If your eBook contains animated film clips or other unusual features, an Abode program might be worthwhile.

On the other hand, you may prefer the EXE file. This can provide additional flexibility, graphic conversion, and other features. Most EXE converters or services do have an associated cost. The EXE files tend to be a bit more complicated to create, download, and read. But you can purchase eBook compilers that simplify this process. A drawback to using EXE files is they cannot be used on Mac computers because of an incompatibility issue. Since the majority of individuals who own computers use PC's, this may or may not be an issue for you.

A third option, of course, is the MS Word file. These are generally quite large. They take a while to download, and customers will still need to have a Word program to read the content. You could always put your book in .html format as well, but again, this format has a few disadvantages. The safest option by far is the PDF.

5.2   Software.

All over the internet, there are tools and guides for the development of software content. A lot of the tools are quite expensive. They'll set you back several thousand if you decide to buy. But at the very least, reading about some of the features offered by these programs should give you some ideas for the design of a viable software program.

The first question to ask yourself: what type of software do you want to develop?

You need, to answer this question, first to identify the need you want to fulfill. The same search methods may apply to your software content search as to your eBook content search. Check out Amazon.com, visit group message boards. Identify the need for software felt by a particular niche group. Writers, for example, are an obvious target for software and their needs are not all that complicated. First of all, you can search the web and find that a few sites are already offering software guides for book publishing, managing submissions to editors and agents, and article writing.

Another idea might be to develop a series of software templates for the development of websites. A little research will quickly point out how popular website are, how almost everyone wants one.

Of course, you can always develop software for the purpose of recreation, too. Games are as popular as ever nowadays. If you have a great idea for a game, you can certainly develop it into a valuable money making idea with the help of a software developer.

5.3   Blogs.

The great thing about blogs is that they are free-form and, it's like having your own website. You can write about anything you want. You can adorn your blog entries with pictures, photographs, sketches - anything you like. But how do you develop content that people will invest money in? Well, you have a few options to make money with a blog. First of all, you can use a blog as a marketing tool to sell other products. This is probably the easiest way to make money as a blogger. The second method you might consider: advertising. Become an affiliate marketer and earn money by having your blog readers follow your links through to products and services offered by vendors.

This is fantastic way to establish a good foundation if you wish to try your hand at affiliate marketing at a low, low cost! ☺

Blog content must match your purpose. Although it may be creative and freeform, it should also be carefully designed to solicit your readers to spend money. If you aren't confident in your ability to sell in this manner, then a skilled writer will certainly be able to assist you. Here is an inexpensive resource that could help you with 'bloggin to the bank': http://www.nicheblog.nichesourcing.com.

5.4   Video.

Check out YouTube for ideas on the types of videos that everyone likes to watch online. Almost without exception, people like videos that make them laugh. As a general rule, even if you're dealing with a potentially mundane and serious subject, you should try and inject at least a bit of humor to entice viewers!

A professional script writer should be able to help you develop the kind of content that will win viewers over. As with eBooks, blogs, and software, a skilled writer will be able to take a concept and turn it into a moneymaking proposition.

Second to humor, of course, is the provision of new, even controversial information. Controversy generally gets people talking, for example: Michael Moore! The word of mouth is a very important marketing tool in the real world, it is no less important in the virtual world! Word of mouth amounts to back links. Back links basically connect your video - or blog or website - to someone else's site. It's a form of free marketing and it's very effective. A skilled writer will be able to take an outline for your video and fill in the gaps. All you're likely to need then is a web cam ($40 - $70) or a basic video camera (about $200 - $300). Make your video according to your script, and you're well on your way.

If you need some inspiration to develop your video content, rent or buy a copy of the original Baby Einstein DVD. Even if you don't have kids (and if you do, you'll be amazed how much they love this), you can learn a lot watching the very simple presentation of images and the use of audio. The original creator of the series provided the voice for all of the English language segments, hiring native speakers to perform for the other language segments. Watch this video, which is very basic and yet very effective. You will be inspired and you'll have some great ideas to pass on to whomever you hire to work on your script. Wish to do it yourself then read: http://www.internet-audio-video.com.

5.5   Audio.

The most effective type of audio you can develop involves recording someone reading written material aloud. The best way to make money with audio is first to write a book on the subject of your choice, whether it's your hobby, something you're passionate about, or just something that inspires you. If you choose this option, read more about it here: http://www.internet-audio-video.com.

You or someone else with a good speaking voice can then read the book aloud and you can record the whole thing. Package the work nicely; point out how it can be useful. For example, people can listen to your book as they drive around, as they're walking around and as they go about their daily routine. Audio is a great way to learn, so it's very effective to offer audio content that educates.

5.6   Podcasts.

A podcast, despite the similarity in name, has nothing to do with Apple iPods. It's amazing how many people are confused by this. A podcast is basically an audio file that can be downloaded by someone browsing the web.

What makes the whole notion of the podcast all the more confusing: many people use the term podcast to refer to both audio and video content. An audio content is strictly speaking, your podcast. A vodcast is actually the video content. But virtually any internet term with "cast" at the end tends to indicate content that you can subscribe to and get on a regular basis.

So what type of content do you include in your podcast? The simple answer is anything along the lines of audio broadcasts, spoken word recordings, and musical pieces. These have been available on the Internet for years, but the recent combination of RSS (Really Simple Syndication) and audio files have made the process of accessing this material much simpler.

When you fit your site with an RSS feed, you can subscribe to content automatically. Just as you get a magazine delivered to your door, you get the new content via a notification in your RSS reader, followed by a wrapped audio recording inside an RSS enclosure (special XML code).

The RSS software recognizes the content and will download it automatically to a location that you specify on your hard drive.

Of course, you don't have to subscribe to everyone else's podcasts, although this is one way to generate attention to your site. Carefully selected material will always secure visitors. You can, on the other hand, develop your own podcast.

To get ideas for content, I recommend you check out the likes of Podcast.net (www.podcast.net) and Podcast Alley (www.podcastalley.com). Podcast.net is the more popular directory and it categorizes more than 18,000 links into Entertainment, Computers & Internet, News & Media, and Sports, to name but a few. You can also check out the podcasts according to how recent they are. This should give you some idea of the latest and greatest.

The best thing you can do for your podcast content is establish an outline for your episodes. When it comes to developing the content, one of the best sites is Podcast.com (www.podcast.com). This site offers general resources for podcasting, links to useful directories, help sites for podcasters, software for podcasting, and a podcasting gear room that shows you exactly what material you need to get started.

Podcasting is easily done with a minimal amount of equipment. All you really need is a computer and a microphone. Quality, however, may be an issue. Popping and crackling are common problems with audio produced using the cheapest available equipment. So, you need a computer microphone worth at least $40 to avoid the poor quality audio content.

5.7   Workbooks.

Now it's time to describe to you a few advanced packaging techniques. The following formats are extremely lucrative ways to package a product and are a mainstay for niche marketers. A few examples are provided for your benefit. These packages offer a very user-friendly form of interactive learning (Most of the images will have active links, so feel free to use them for your research.).

Copyright © 2008 http://www.ruthlesssecrets.com - All Rights Reserved

Workbooks can be a great way of teaching people about hobbies, interests, or very specific subject areas. Judicious insertion of a reply form within the workbook and you may very well secure a valuable set of future customers.

5.8   Home Study Courses.

A well-designed home study course can generate a "mother lode" of revenue, typically one to two hundred dollars per student. Interactive features are good. Plenty of reading material is generally helpful to really help students get to grips with the authorities on whatever subject you are addressing. Good packaging will be worth its weight in gold. At the end of the day, you can also offer courses online as e-courses, via e-mail, or as a printout correspondence course. The more options you offer your customers, the happier they'll be and as a by-product, your chances of increasing the value of your product will rise.

Above is the only course ever created that completely reveals the insider truth about getting rich in the Information Products Business!

In just a few moments, I'm going to reveal how you can be among a small handful of lucky individuals who can become privy to my step-by-step secrets to building an insane fortune from selling information.

I guarantee this is <u>unlike</u> anything you may have seen or read before! In fact, you're about to discover why almost all information marketers are DEAD <u>WRONG</u> about how to make *staggering profits* selling information products. And you'd better take advantage of this now because I don't plan to sell any more of these courses once this batch is done.

In other words, I'm <u>NOT</u> talking about chump change from just selling a few $29 ebooks so it takes forever just to make a buck or two. I'm talking about making <u>REAL</u> money selling high-demand, low-risk, high-profit information products. *Like...*

Copyright © 2008 http://www.marketingtips.com/tipsltr.html - All Rights Reserved

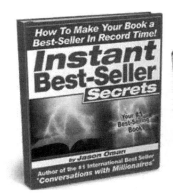

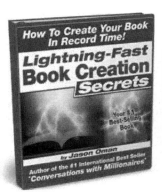

Copyright © 2007 http://www.jasonoman.com - All Rights Reserved

5.9   Membership Sites.

A membership site, either free or for nominal cost, will provide leads to hundreds of potential customers that can be approached with mass-marketed e-mails. Elance.com and Guru.com are examples of these but you can also check out the like of Questia.com, an online library, Britannica.com, an online encyclopedia, and a whole host of others. Paid membership sites are guaranteed income streams and have grown in popularity.

Learn more about this technique here: http://www.membershipmillionaire.com

5.10   Teleseminars.

A well-promoted, well-run teleseminar can add thousands to your bottom line. Equally important, your appearance on a teleseminar will enhance your reputation and increase your credibility as an expert in your field. Learn about this technique here: http://www.TeleseminarSecrets.com.

5.11   Syndicated Column.

Websites and newspapers always need fresh material. To develop a syndicated column, first place the column on a regular basis with either your local paper (free or sold) or with any regular publication for which you enjoy good access to the editor or publisher. If your column is well-received in one publication, you may be able to get national syndication. There are agencies that handle this multi-paper syndication (cartoonists rely heavily on this sort of agency) or you can work to develop the syndication yourself.

Be careful: Once you start working on getting additional outlets, you may not have any time or energy left to produce the material! Learn more here: http://www.syndicate.nichesourcing.com.

5.12   Multi-Media Packs.

These are usually more trouble and expensive to produce, proceed with caution. Multi-media packs often prove to be a quagmire, focus instead on products that stand on their own such as the packages shown below. If you are highly organized and you have a specific topic to discuss, this option can be a very beneficial income stream.

Copyright © 2008 http://www.milliondollarinternetpromotions.com - All Rights Reserved

However you decide to package your product, you need to be sure you are doing it right or better than someone else. To do this you will need to study your competition. One of your options is to actually purchase a product or two from your competition. Once you have an idea how they have packaged their products, you will get a better understanding of how to develop your own product. This also gives you the chance to put your own spin on it to make your product unique.

If you can assemble a package such as what you reviewed above as well as what you see below, you will be well on your way to branding yourself as an expert in your field.

"*Lucrative List Secrets*" System!

Here is EXACTLY what you'll get shipped to your door... You'll get my entire step-by-step system that I used to build a database of over 6 million double opt-in subscribers for me and my clients. It includes 17 video tutorials, audio tutorials, 148 page interactive workbook, 10 list building mastermind CDs, and much, much more!

*Above is the Lucrative List Secrets multimedia home study course. It's a complete A to Z Blueprint** on how to build your own highly profitable opt-in email list even if you have no money, no experience and no time...

Copyright © 2008 http://www.lucrativelistsecrets.com – All Rights Reserved

Copyright © 2008 http://www.marketingtips.com/pro-bootcamp/ - All Rights Reserved

Copyright © 2008 http://www.auctiontips.com/ebaycourse.html - All Rights Reserved

Copyright © 2008 http://www.rebelmillionaire.com - All Rights Reserved

5.13 Coaching Program.

For the customer with more money than time, a personal coaching program may be just what the doctor ordered. Charge heavily for this, for it is very time-consuming. However, this option can be extremely profitable if approached and developed properly. John is one of the best when it comes to copyrighting. He provides a service that is extremely valuable and he is really, really good at it! ☺

"Kick-Ass Advertising Secrets of the World's Smartest, Happiest & Wealthiest Online Marketers!"

How cool is this? The most respected (and most *ripped off*) copywriter alive is now offering you the same personalized, step-by-step help that other famous marketers *rely* on to kick Operation MoneySuck into high gear.

Best part: You can check everything out for FREE if you choose!

Howdy...

My name is John Carlton... and in just a moment, I will show you how to quickly, easily, and inexpensively *force* your Website or offline advertising to start generating *mind-blowing* new levels of profit and success...

...just as I have for vast numbers of *other* people, year after year after year.

And I will do this for you...

...no matter what kind of results you've been getting (or *not* getting) up to now... ...and no matter how much you currently *suck* at persuading people to buy.

If you've got the guts to **survive a brutally-honest business reality-check** that will SHOCK you to the roots of your soul , **you really can change your entire life**. Starting today.

"Have You Heard What Other Marketers Are Saying?"

"He doesn't just tell you how to do it... he don't just show you how to do it... he *involves* you so you learn his strategies, techniques, and the psychology of world-class copy."

Alex Mandossian

Created Millions In Profit
"John **has created millions in profit for us**. We pitted his ads and letters against big-city ad agencies, PR firms, and writers with lots of awards... and John slaughtered them all. He consistently hits 'home runs' for us -- a 20-to-1 return in profit is not unusual. He has saved our butts on several occasions."
Robert Pierce, President, Tactical Response Solutions

Copyright © 2007 http://www.marketingrebel.com - All Rights Reserved

Copyright © 2008 http://www.alexandriabrown.com - All Rights Reserved

Copyright © 2008 http://www.alexandriabrown.com - All Rights Reserved

Copyright © 2008 http://www.youchandoit.com - All Rights Reserved

5.14   Speaking Engagements.

Speaking engagements enhance credibility, provide a superb opportunity to make valuable contacts, and improve your overall poise and confidence. Experienced business advisers suggest you never turn down an invitation to speak. To pursue these opportunities in a proactive rather than re-active fashion, contact a local or national speaker's bureau that specializes in bookings of this sort.

In addition or as an alternative, you can speak to your local community organizations (church, temple, YM/YWCA, Shriners, Elks, Kiwanis, College, University, etc.) about scheduling a lecture on your subject. Most organizations of this sort will be happy to host you if you can provide the material and do some independent promotion towards delivering an audience. Use the human element: identify the decision-maker who can okay your plans for a lecture or seminar, then go for it! Nothing is more likely to jump-start your promising business than a couple of well-timed public speaking engagements. This can become an extremely lucrative way of making money! ☺

5.15   Radio Shows.

Like public speaking, radio is a good vehicle for gaining name recognition, promoting a web-site, and firming up your credentials as an expert in your field.

5.16   TV Shows.

Nothing will come anywhere close to increasing your name-recognition as even the briefest appearance on the "Idiot Box", the "Boob Tube", or the "Rectangular Hypnotist". For enhancing general name recognition, television ranks first, second and third (and probably fourth and fifth too!), with the other contenders still stumbling towards the finish line while television is being strewn with roses and having its picture taken in the Winner's Circle!

If you ever get a chance to be on television, accept (unless you're a fugitive and you're invited to appear on "America's Most Wanted")!

Follow These Action Steps:

- ⊘ Decide on how to package your product.

    - ▸ If this is your first time packaging a product, start off with some of the more simpler methods such as packaging your product in the following formats:

        - Electronic format such as PDF or EXE.

        - Software format.

        - Blog format - http://www.nicheblog.nichesourcing.com.

- Video format - http://www.internet-audio-video.com.

- Audio format - http://www.internet-audio-video.com.

- Podcast format - www.podcast.com.

► If you feel adventurous, you can package your product in any of the following formats:

- Workbooks.

- Home study courses.

- Membership sites.

- Teleseminars.

- Syndicated columns.

- Multi-media packs.

- Coaching programs.

- Speaking engagements.

- Radio shows.

- TV shows.

Tips & Suggestions:

If you decide to package your product in the EXE format, I'd highly recommend you think of choosing from the following options:

- ✓ The Internet Marketing Center's - eBookPro: http://www.ebookpro.com

- ✓ Armand Morin's - eBookGenerator: http://www.ebookGenerator.com

- ✓ Cyber Share Enterprises - eBook Edit Pro: http://www.ebookedit.com

Each of these pieces of software are similar in that they offer basically the same benefits. They differ mostly in their cost. This software converts HTML files into a single executable file that is similar to a web-browser. Once the book is compiled, it is extremely secure and offers a tremendous amount of flexibility. The software is flexible enough that you can integrate audio, video, flash, and much more. This results in an enjoyable interactive experience for readers.

Chapter 6
Create & Design Your Niche Product

6.1   Delivery Method.

You're probably going to need a website no matter what form your content takes. Websites are basically online business addresses. You'll need some web space to advertise your work, whether it's a book, a work book, a home study course, a podcast, or a TV show you're looking to promote. It's better to pay for your website and to buy your domain name too – it's just a lot more professional than if you chose to use a free option.

Next, you need to think about the most effective design for your web pages. You can outsource this if you prefer. Literally thousands of web designers are out there to lap up your business. Avoid paying too much though. Plenty of web design companies claim to be able to create websites that will really sell your work. For around $5000 they promise to get you on all the search engines, etc. This is almost always rubbish and empty promises. You can get a perfectly good website for as little as $150. If you pick your friends carefully, you can even get a website designed for free. Find someone who can write html code and you're set to go! ☺

Next you need to think about how you're going to deliver your content precisely. How are you going to deliver the content for sale? This assumes, of course, that you're selling a product, an eBook or a home study course. This assumes that you're looking to sell your podcast content or video content.

First, you need to think about how your customers are going to want to buy your content. You need to consider what information is available. Most of your buyers will want to pay by credit card.

You should also provide a mail box address so customers can send a check for your products. This also shows that you have a physical address and additionally will add to your credibility.

If you don't set up a merchant account to accept credit card payments, there are plenty of services that will accept customer's credit card information for you and send you the money. If you remember, this was discussed earlier. PayPal would be a good option.

The sooner you set up your payment information, the sooner your customers can buy.

Next you must upload the relevant information onto your web page about the content you're providing, your eBook or whatever else you intend to sell. You must upload whatever cover art you have, the content itself, a link to order and pay for the content, and finally, your sales letter.

To upload from your computer to the internet, you'll need an FTP program. Most web host services will provide you with necessary software and clear instructions on how to use it. If your service doesn't provide you with FTP help, you can purchase or use a free FTP program like www.ipswitch.com.

6.2   Compatibility Issues.

We've briefly touched upon the issues of compatibility relating to eBooks. The PDF format, as mentioned, is the most appropriate for eBooks simply because customers can read PDFS on their computers - Mac or PC - by downloading free software.

If you're developing a workbook or a home study course, you can also use PDF. This will be the most appropriate format for these as well.

What about videos and audio? Some of the most popular formats include .wma, .avi, .mpeg, and mjpeg.

The first good quality video clips were first featured in the opening scenes of computer games. They demanded extensive storage space, and they were available only on CD-ROM drives. Nowadays, most of the video clips, the Windows Media, the Real Video, and other players are fairly easy to access.

The H.261 standard is the classic and most appropriate format for videoconferences and video telephony. The format is generally transmitted via an ISDN network. H.261 makes the image quality adaptable to the bandwidth of the transmission line.

Unless you're offering only written material, you should try to offer your material in at least two common format types. This will ensure that most people can easily access your material without having to download or even, worse case scenario, buy a software program to access your work.

6.3   Profit Potential/Cost Effective.

When it comes to packaging your product, undoubtedly, you want to cut your expenses to a minimum and do all you can to increase your profit. While the precise methods for increasing profit and enhancing cost effectiveness will need to be determined on a case by case basis, there are a few basic principles to bear in mind.

First of all, when it comes to enhancing your profit potential, pricing is extremely important. Price and value are very significant concepts. One thing you must be aware of: it's better to price a product at $9.97. Why, you may wonder. Well, the human mind generally recognizes numbers, prices in particular, along the following lines: "nine dollars something . . ." The vast majority of your customers will recognize a price of $9.97 not as $5.50 but as $9-and-something. In this case, you might as well charge $9.97, $5.97 instead of $9.50, etc.

Second of all, remember that your customers love to think they are getting a bargain. You can take advantage of this by offering a few free additions to your product, perhaps some bonus products that will compliment yours or even a series of how-to eZines.

In terms of making a product that is cost effective, cutting unnecessary overheads is the key. This might seem too obvious to even mention here, but the key word is "unnecessary". You're targeting a niche market with your product.

The chances are, your customers will have a fairly sophisticated notion of value. At the least, they are unlikely to invest in a product that is unworthy of attention and devoid of value. It is necessary to spend money on developing good content, rich in information - useful information at that. It is not an unnecessary expense to hire a writer to develop your eBook, blog, or home study course. It's not an unnecessary expense to hire a software developer to develop your program; it's not an unnecessary expense to hire a graphic artist to provide cover art and even a website design that works.

You can, however, manage your expenses. Set a budget for your product development and stick to it. Don't spend on unnecessary website design and marketing. The best marketing is viral and you should be very cautious about the amounts you spend on advertising. It could surely get out of control if not monitored properly. Beyond that, the best way to manage your profit and your overheads - it really does bear repeating - set a budget and stick to it.

6.4   Choose Who Will Author/Develop Your Product?

Content is best left to the experts. However, perhaps you count yourself among this hallowed group. That said, there is no single reason why you should not, at least for your first product, outsource the work. At the end of the day, you're likely to have a lot of other elements to manage. During the course of this book, we've pointed out the need for a business plan, a marketing plan, and a strategic plan. You also need to plan your website and coordinate its development. The bottom line is this. You have a lot of work to do without worrying about spending probably about thirty or forty hours researching, producing, and refining the product you intend to sell!

The best advice from the experts is along these lines. Outsource the development of your first product, regardless of whether or not you want to do the work yourself. On your second project or perhaps your third, then you can do all of this work yourself.

6.5   D.I.Y. (Do-It-Yourself).

Despite the advice just shared above, let's think for a moment about what's involved in developing your own product without the help of a professional. If you're planning on developing written content - an eBook, an e-Course, a blog, a syndicated column, or even a series of newsletters or eZines - you will need to conduct extensive research. Depending on your market and your product, your local library and the regular search engines may prove adequate. On the other hand, you may need to sign up to one or other of the specialist research sites, such as Questia.com or Britanica.com.

Regarding the development of software, interactive features, audio, video, or even graphic features, you will probably need to invest in superior software. While this can be something of a drawback, if you plan to develop more than one product over time, your money won't be wasted.

6.6   Ask Experts in Your Niche.

One great way to develop the content for your product is to ask an expert to help you. This has a number of advantages you probably may not have thought of. First off, asking an expert to help you is a great way to flatter them. A second advantage to working with an expert: they are likely to have the content you need!

The best way to develop your content with the help of an expert is through an interview.

There are three reasons that most experts will be happy to help you for free:

1. It's flattering to be invited on the basis of expertise.

2. It's a chance for the expert to be published in a relatively easy form.

3. Some people just like to help.

Of course, not everyone will agree to your offer to be interviewed. The majority may but you could start with at least three or four experts on your list. However, a thorough interview process should include 10 or more individuals. This results in a broader range of experience that can be shared and furthermore adds additional value to your interview.

If you decide to interview experts, there are specific ways you can approach this option.

First, it's really unselfish to just ask someone you've never contacted or meet before to help you with something. In most cases, a prior working relationship is necessary in order to begin the process of building trust.

Ninety-nine percent of the time, when someone contacts me to help them with something, I use a very simple, quick and efficient filtering process.

4. If I don't recognize the individual contacting me, I can immediately tell if it's headed for the trash via my delete button. I'll quickly scan the message and if they are asking me for something - it's deleted.

5. If however the person trying to contact me introduces who he or she is, offers a kind compliment on my newsletter or website and perhaps even offers to share my site with his or her friends, I'll assign it a higher priority to come back to later and review.

6. After a more thorough review of the recent contact, there is a more probable chance that I will return the message and express my thanks for the compliments expressed.

7. This contact starts a process of establishing a 'working relationship' with me and begins the development of trust needed to sustain a two-way highway of communication.

8. Only after I'm sure of whom I'm 'talking' with will I be ready to consider helping or assisting someone. This usually requires a bit of correspondence before I'm comfortable and open for any future requests.

In my experience, I've found this to be extremely valuable to master. I literally applied the same principals that I used for myself when I contacted individuals that I had no prior contact with.

You should never use a template. Individuals can 'see' right through that, especially if you are contacting experienced individuals who regularly receive these kinds of requests every day!

You need to be unique, you need to be yourself!

To help you visualize and understand this process, take a look at some of the actual email messages I've sent in the past to establish the process of building trust with individuals I'd never had contact with before.

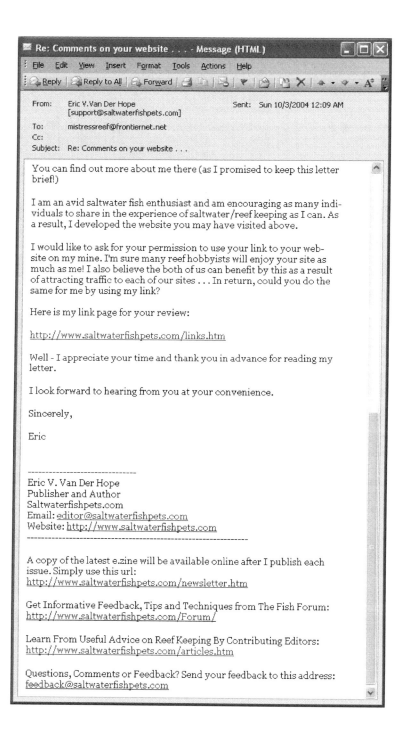

Re: Comments on your website . . . - Message (HTML)

File Edit View Insert Format Tools Actions Help

Reply | Reply to All | Forward | ... A⁺

From: Eric V. Van Der Hope   Sent: Sun 10/3/2004 12:09 AM
       [support@saltwaterfishpets.com]
To: mistressreef@frontiernet.net
Cc:
Subject: Re: Comments on your website . . .

You can find out more about me there (as I promised to keep this letter brief!)

I am an avid saltwater fish enthusiast and am encouraging as many individuals to share in the experience of saltwater/reef keeping as I can. As a result, I developed the website you may have visited above.

I would like to ask for your permission to use your link to your website on my mine. I'm sure many reef hobbyists will enjoy your site as much as me! I also believe the both of us can benefit by this as a result of attracting traffic to each of our sites . . . In return, could you do the same for me by using my link?

Here is my link page for your review:

http://www.saltwaterfishpets.com/links.htm

Well - I appreciate your time and thank you in advance for reading my letter.

I look forward to hearing from you at your convenience.

Sincerely,

Eric

Eric V. Van Der Hope
Publisher and Author
Saltwaterfishpets.com
Email: editor@saltwaterfishpets.com
Website: http://www.saltwaterfishpets.com

A copy of the latest e.zine will be available online after I publish each issue. Simply use this url:
http://www.saltwaterfishpets.com/newsletter.htm

Get Informative Feedback, Tips and Techniques from The Fish Forum:
http://www.saltwaterfishpets.com/Forum/

Learn From Useful Advice on Reef Keeping By Contributing Editors:
http://www.saltwaterfishpets.com/articles.htm

Questions, Comments or Feedback? Send your feedback to this address:
feedback@saltwaterfishpets.com

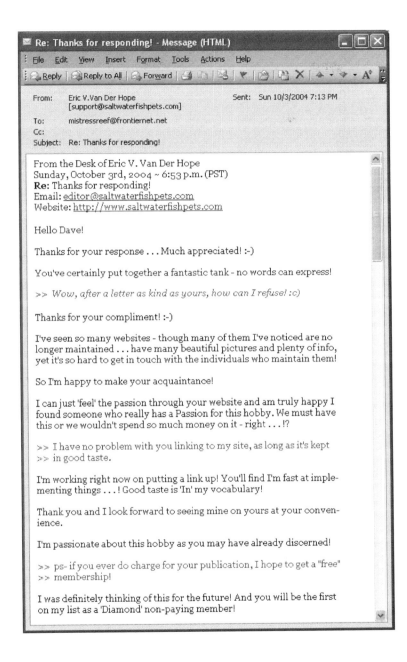

From the Desk of Eric V. Van Der Hope
Sunday, October 3rd, 2004 ~ 6:53 p.m. (PST)
Re: Thanks for responding!
Email: editor@saltwaterfishpets.com
Website: http://www.saltwaterfishpets.com

Hello Dave!

Thanks for your response . . . Much appreciated! :-)

You've certainly put together a fantastic tank - no words can express!

>> *Wow, after a letter as kind as yours, how can I refuse! :c)*

Thanks for your compliment! :-)

I've seen so many websites - though many of them I've noticed are no longer maintained . . . have many beautiful pictures and plenty of info, yet it's so hard to get in touch with the individuals who maintain them!

So I'm happy to make your acquaintance!

I can just 'feel' the passion through your website and am truly happy I found someone who really has a Passion for this hobby. We must have this or we wouldn't spend so much money on it - right . . . !?

>> I have no problem with you linking to my site, as long as it's kept
>> in good taste.

I'm working right now on putting a link up! You'll find I'm fast at implementing things . . . ! Good taste is 'In' my vocabulary!

Thank you and I look forward to seeing mine on yours at your convenience.

I'm passionate about this hobby as you may have already discerned!

>> ps- if you ever do charge for your publication, I hope to get a "free"
>> membership!

I was definitely thinking of this for the future! And you will be the first on my list as a 'Diamond' non-paying member!

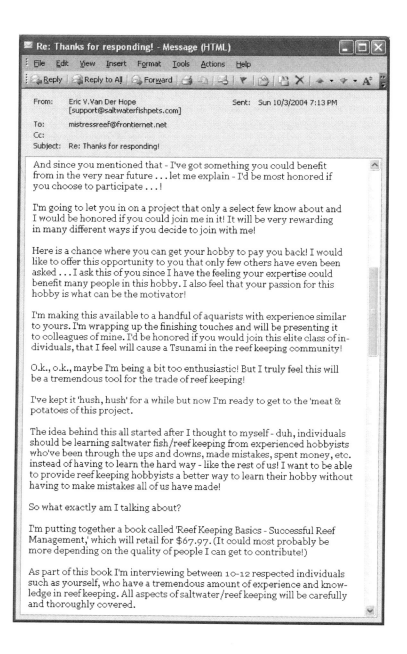

And since you mentioned that - I've got something you could benefit from in the very near future . . . let me explain - I'd be most honored if you choose to participate . . . !

I'm going to let you in on a project that only a select few know about and I would be honored if you could join me in it! It will be very rewarding in many different ways if you decide to join with me!

Here is a chance where you can get your hobby to pay you back! I would like to offer this opportunity to you that only few others have even been asked . . . I ask this of you since I have the feeling your expertise could benefit many people in this hobby. I also feel that your passion for this hobby is what can be the motivator!

I'm making this available to a handful of aquarists with experience similar to yours. I'm wrapping up the finishing touches and will be presenting it to colleagues of mine. I'd be honored if you would join this elite class of individuals, that I feel will cause a Tsunami in the reef keeping community!

O.k., o.k., maybe I'm being a bit too enthusiastic! But I truly feel this will be a tremendous tool for the trade of reef keeping!

I've kept it 'hush, hush' for a while but now I'm ready to get to the 'meat & potatoes of this project.

The idea behind this all started after I thought to myself - duh, individuals should be learning saltwater fish/reef keeping from experienced hobbyists who've been through the ups and downs, made mistakes, spent money, etc. instead of having to learn the hard way - like the rest of us! I want to be able to provide reef keeping hobbyists a better way to learn their hobby without having to make mistakes all of us have made!

So what exactly am I talking about?

I'm putting together a book called 'Reef Keeping Basics - Successful Reef Management,' which will retail for $67.97. (It could most probably be more depending on the quality of people I can get to contribute!)

As part of this book I'm interviewing between 10-12 respected individuals such as yourself, who have a tremendous amount of experience and knowledge in reef keeping. All aspects of saltwater/reef keeping will be carefully and thoroughly covered.

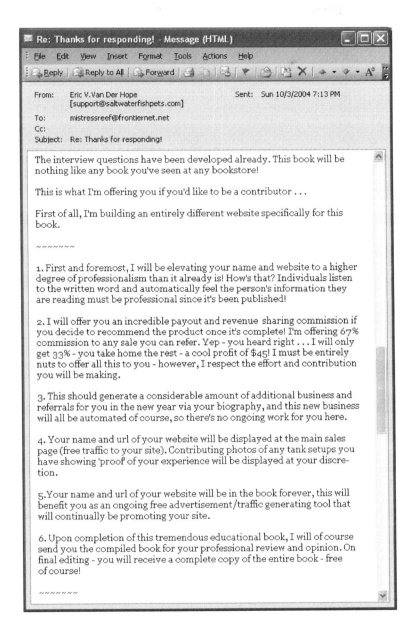

The interview questions have been developed already. This book will be nothing like any book you've seen at any bookstore!

This is what I'm offering you if you'd like to be a contributor . . .

First of all, I'm building an entirely different website specifically for this book.

~~~~~~~

1. First and foremost, I will be elevating your name and website to a higher degree of professionalism than it already is! How's that? Individuals listen to the written word and automatically feel the person's information they are reading must be professional since it's been published!

2. I will offer you an incredible payout and revenue sharing commission if you decide to recommend the product once it's complete! I'm offering 67% commission to any sale you can refer. Yep - you heard right . . . I will only get 33% - you take home the rest - a cool profit of $45! I must be entirely nuts to offer all this to you - however, I respect the effort and contribution you will be making.

3. This should generate a considerable amount of additional business and referrals for you in the new year via your biography, and this new business will all be automated of course, so there's no ongoing work for you here.

4. Your name and url of your website will be displayed at the main sales page (free traffic to your site). Contributing photos of any tank setups you have showing 'proof' of your experience will be displayed at your discretion.

5. Your name and url of your website will be in the book forever, this will benefit you as an ongoing free advertisement/traffic generating tool that will continually be promoting your site.

6. Upon completion of this tremendous educational book, I will of course send you the compiled book for your professional review and opinion. On final editing - you will receive a complete copy of the entire book - free of course!

~~~~~~~

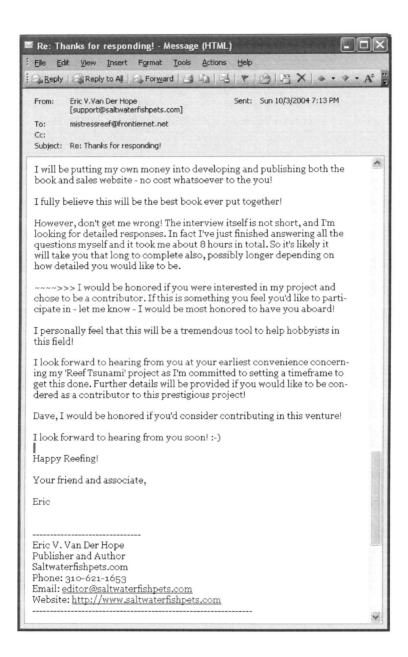

I will be putting my own money into developing and publishing both the book and sales website - no cost whatsoever to the you!

I fully believe this will be the best book ever put together!

However, don't get me wrong! The interview itself is not short, and I'm looking for detailed responses. In fact I've just finished answering all the questions myself and it took me about 8 hours in total. So it's likely it will take you that long to complete also, possibly longer depending on how detailed you would like to be.

~~~~>>> I would be honored if you were interested in my project and chose to be a contributor. If this is something you feel you'd like to parti- cipate in - let me know - I would be most honored to have you aboard!

I personally feel that this will be a tremendous tool to help hobbyists in this field!

I look forward to hearing from you at your earliest convenience concern- ing my 'Reef Tsunami' project as I'm committed to setting a timeframe to get this done. Further details will be provided if you would like to be con- dered as a contributor to this prestigious project!

Dave, I would be honored if you'd consider contributing in this venture!

I look forward to hearing from you soon! :-)

Happy Reefing!

Your friend and associate,

Eric

Eric V. Van Der Hope
Publisher and Author
Saltwaterfishpets.com
Phone: 310-621-1653
Email: editor@saltwaterfishpets.com
Website: http://www.saltwaterfishpets.com

Remember, not until you have established some sort of informal correspondence with each other should you attempt to request whatever it is that you have in mind.

If you decide to conduct an email interview, you need to develop an organized and logical series of interview questions that are designed to encourage detailed answers. Your goal is to not ask questions that will result in a simple 'Yes' or 'No' answer but detailed answers that have substance and worth their weight in gold!

In my book *'Reef Keeping Basics - Successful Reef Management'*, I interviewed 14 individuals and asked each of them approximately 56 questions.

		Section
Interview Four		
David Playfair	==>	Introduction
Getting Started	==>	~1~
Choosing Your Type of Reef Environment	==>	~2~
Essential Components		
Water	==>	~3~
Lighting	==>	~4~
Filtration Methods	==>	~5~
The Substrate	==>	~6~
Other Important Accessories		
Salt	==>	~7~
Test Equipment	==>	~8~
Specific Gravity Meter	==>	~9~
Tank Heater and Thermometer	==>	~10~
Powerheads and Wavemakers	==>	~11~
Quarantine Tank	==>	~12~
Important Supplemental Additives	==>	~13~
Feeding Fish, Corals, Anemones/other tank-mates	==>	~14~
Preventative Maintenance		
Algae Control	==>	~15~
Water Maintenance	==>	~16~
Purchasing Equipment Prior To Your First Tank Setup	==>	~17~
Important Tips/Suggestions	==>	~18~
Commonly Asked Questions	==>	~19~
Revealing Tips From Our Contributing Reef Enthusiasts	==>	~20~
A Call To Action - the 'Wrap Up'	==>	~21~
About You	==>	~22~

You will notice that I've included examples for you above and below on the general layout of how the interviews were organized in the book. The 56 or so questions were categorized under their respective subtopics and or categories. You will also notice the quality of the questions being asked, the resulting answers and an example of one of many colorful pictures shared throughout the book.

If you could sum up reefkeeping in 10 steps, what would they be? Briefly explain each step.

1 - Determine the size of the system you can afford to maintain (both financially and time wise)

2 - Allow flexibility in the design of the aquarium. You are sure to upgrade or replace equipment over time, and initial limitations will prohibit progress.

3 - Be wary of people who say their methods are the only ones that work. ESPECIALLY fish stores! A strong, established tank speaks more than those who talk big.

4 - Stay away from "magic potions" or unproven gadgetry! There are a lot of people out to make money from this hobby, and most of it is unnecessary.

5 - Use only top quality liverock to aquascape with, the dead stuff will stunt your system.

6 - Keep your hands out of the tank as much as possible. If you think that coral is unhappy where you put it, don't keep moving it around.

7 - Keep watch over your equipment, and make sure it's in top condition. If something goes wrong, you have a better chance of pulling through if the animals are healthy.

8 - The rock structure should be open and accessible to make cleaning easier.

9 - Don't muscle everything- you don't need the BRIGHTEST lights or the BIGGEST pumps.

10 - Learn to be in tune with your tank and understand its language.

What would be the Top 5 Areas our readers should concentrate on (add more if you feel is necessary), to increase their chances of success and to guarantee the smoothest transition into the reef-building hobby?

1 - Don't expect results overnight.

2 - Maintain your interest in the system and it's development.

Revealing Tips From Our Contributing Reef Enthusiasts

Back to
David's Intro ▲

If there were one or two secrets to successful reef keeping - what would they be?

I would have to say the biggest tip to be successful is to plan for the duration . . . The coolest part of a reef is watching it grow. Anyone can set up a tank for a day, but the talent lies with carrying it for the long-term. Don't get caught up in overcrowding corals or fish; be happy with what works for you.

Ricordea floridea "corner", and a "lost" feather duster worm hitchhiker.

This also includes practicing patience, and loosing the attitude that you can do it cheaper and better than everyone else. The other "big" one is consistency. The world is generally pretty stable, so providing a routine for your reef helps it to balance. A great example of this is feeding. Bacteria run the nitrogen cycle, and there are exactly enough to handle the load of the tank. When we feed the entire tank, we are also feeding the organisms that consume what's left over, and changes to these amounts will cause a "rollar coaster" effect with their populations, which can effect the entire food chain!

I also encouraged each of these individuals not only to share their answers in as much detail as possible but to include images of their progress of maintaining their own reef tanks. In this book, a picture or image is literally worth a 1000 words! What would be hard to express in words was easily expressed in the exquisite pictures provided by each of the interviewees. The finished product was an informative and extremely valuable resource for hobbyists. ☺

My book, *'Reef Keeping Basics'*, wasn't some cheap little book with simple answers but an enormous educational guide, containing over 345 digitally colorful images and 700+ pages of pure substance!

Check it out for yourself at: http://www.reefkeepingbasics.com.

By e-mail you do risk receiving short, stilted answers to your otherwise probing questions. As an alternative, you could conduct an interview either by phone or in person, as both such methods require one-to-one interaction. You may want to have the interview transcribed and then typed up. If the interview is particularly well organized and goes particularly well, you may be able to use the actual interview recording as the product. All that's required: you must ensure the interview is well organized and that the sound quality of the recording is good.

6.7   Outsourcing.

Even if you're developing a product on a subject on which you're a certified expert, you might want to outsource your work. Most likely, if you're considering outsourcing, you should think of hiring a writer. Perhaps, as an afterthought, you decide to hire an artist to design a front cover and provide some illustrations to pad out your book. You may want to decide to hire a professional to develop professional content for your video. Well, maybe not. You can make your video with only a webcam, but you might still need a writer to script your show.

Fortunately, outsourcing is pretty easy online and the process is pretty much the same, whether you need a writer or a tech professional to develop your video. When you hire for a writer, technically, you're hiring a ghostwriter. A ghostwriter is a writer who publishes under someone else's name. They write your book and hand over the rights to you as part of the service contract.

Ghostwriters are often hired by celebrities to write autobiographies when the celebrity doesn't have the talent to write a book themselves. Ghostwriters sometimes create works for well-known authors as well, such as Tom Clancy. The author's name alone will sell the books, no matter who actually wrote it. In a sense, you're going with the same notion. You're credentials - your expertise, your hobbies, or your passions - will sell your e-book even though someone else will write it for you.

The first step to outsourcing is to write up a project description and find a place to post it. Your top choices for posting your outsourcing project include:

- Elance.

- Guru.

- Rentacoder.

- Scriptlance.

These are four of a handful of sites that allow you to post your project description and invite professional service providers to bid on your projects. You will have to sign up to one or other of these sites to post your details but this step generally takes only a few minutes to complete. You will need to provide contact information and - although not necessarily immediately - you'll have to provide payment information.

Your project description should provide a brief overview of the project, give some indication of the time frame you have in mind, and provide information about how much you are willing to pay. For an e-book of about 80 to 100 pages, a good price is around $1000 to $1200. A budget like this will secure the services of a dedicated and competent ghostwriter. You may well find excellent talent for less, but the better you pay your writers, the more time and focus they can lend to your project.

Once your project details are posted, you'll start receiving bids from service providers. With each bid, you'll have access to the provider's profile. I strongly advise you to read through references, credentials, and reviews from past customers. You should also ask to see samples from service providers you short list for your project. Reviewing all of this information should give you a very clear idea about which of the writers you will be best able to work with on your project.

Select your writer (or other service provider depending on the particulars of the project you're outsourcing). The next step is to set up a formal contract and, in most cases, a Non Disclosure Agreement (NDA).

Provide your service provider with as much information you have available. Sit back and relax as they do their magic.

Follow These Action Steps:

- ✅ Decide on your delivery method.

- ✅ Choose your product designer/creator or author.

- ✅ D.I.Y. (Do It Yourself)

- ✅ Ask experts in your chosen niche.

  - ▶ Interviews.

- ✅ Outsourcing.

  - ▶ **Elance** - http://www.elance.com.

  - ▶ **Rentacoder** - http://www.rentacoder.com.

  - ▶ **Guru** - http://www.guru.com

  - ▶ **Scriptlance** - http://www.scriptlance.com.

PHASE 3:
Developing The Offer

Chapter 7
Designing Your Niche Website/Salesletter

7.1   Capture the Attention of the Visitor With A Powerful Headline.

Now that you have both your concept and your product planned out, it is necessary to address your marketing strategy in some detail. It should be prominent on the web page for your niche market product; yep - you are going to need a catchy sales letter!

You have two options with your design process: you need to decide if you want to design it yourself or to outsource this task.

If you are familiar with html and like doing your own design as well as have a knack for writing, the obvious choice would be to accomplish this task yourself.

However, if you don't have much knowledge in this area or you simply do not have the time, outsourcing will be your best option.

 Useful Tip:

If your decision is to outsource, you need to understand an extremely important issue. You need to make sure that your website designer is familiar with Direct Response Marketing. Otherwise, you'll end up getting a nice pretty website that will do nothing for you. Your website is your storefront – this will bring you your customers and ultimately make you money! So you need to tailor your website to getting the customer's attention as quickly and as efficiently as possible. So if you are going to use two different resources to handle your web design and copy, they have to be on the same page before you accept their final concept and or design.

There are a multitude of resources, tools or individuals that can make this task easier for you. I highly recommend the following options:

Since you will need several versions of your sales letter at a given time (for testing the response of your copy) and since you are going to need to update them and improve them regularly, **I'll review with you 12 of the most important aspects a good sales letter should be composed of.**

The first part of a sales letter really must grab the interest of the reader. When you go about writing your letter, you are assuming that the reader has at least clicked on to your web page or opened your envelope on purpose. You have only two or three seconds to hold their interest with your opening headline. This is the first thing your reader will look at. If it doesn't catch their attention in those two or three seconds, it's unlikely to catch it at all. People often sort their mail over the wastebasket so it's as dramatic as, say, "eat or be eaten", "kill or be killed". The salesletter is looked at in pretty much the same way! So your sales letter must pique the interest of your potential customer to such a degree that they just stop dead in their tracks. This is by far the most important aspect of your sales copy!

Shawn Casey 'pulls' you into his salesletter! Just take a look at the image below . . . good use of a main Heading as well as sub-heading. You can read and learn more by visiting his 'live' site by clicking on the image below.

There's a 94% Chance Your Online Business Is <u>NOT</u> Compliant.

"It Only Takes One Simple Word, One Missing Statement, One Innocent Mistake Or One Small Complaint To Completely Devastate You In The Blink Of An Eye!"

"Whether You Run A Website Or Not, You Run The Risk Of Not Only Paying Astronomical Legal Fees And Fines, But Also Being Criminally Prosecuted And <u>Going To Jail</u>."

Copyright © 2007 http://www.internetlawcompliance.com - All Rights Reserved

Your **headline** should be **big** and **bold**, **eye-catching** and **inspiring** one way or another. Don't be afraid to use shock tactics, it'll get you into the door!

Your **well-designed headline is the gold at the end of the rainbow!** You need a headline that will entice visitors to stay and look during their first visit.

These three types of headlines are proven motivators. People love to learn new things, they definitely love to learn things other people might not know (i.e. secrets), and they certainly are motivated by fear.

The goal of your main headline is to grab the visitor's attention, then the sub-headline should lead your visitor to progress through the rest of your salesletter.

I've provided a few examples of headlines that grab the attention of the visitor and or reader and ultimately leads them onto the rest of the salesletter. I cannot provide the full essence of these powerful headlines by simply showing samples of them within this book - you will learn better from reading them firsthand by visiting the 'live' sites by clicking on the images of each of the headlines below (or visit the website link that's been provided underneath each headline)!

The Confidential Files Of A Multi-Millionaire Marketer That <u>NO ONE</u> Was Ever Supposed To See...

"Kansas Man Breaks His 18 Years Of Silence To Teach You The <u>EXACT SAME SECRETS</u> He Used To Balloon His One-Man Basement Operation Into A $70 Million Company -- On A Shoestring Budget!"

Copyright © 2007 http://www.ruthlesssecrets.com - All Rights Reserved

Here Are 15 Reasons You Should Crawl Naked Over Glass To Get The Profit-Making Strategies In Ruthless Marketing System™:

Copyright © 2007 http://www.ruthlesssecrets.com - All Rights Reserved

"Who Else Wants To Be Spoonfed The Hottest Copywriting Secrets That Will Transform You Into A World-Class Copywriter Virtually <u>Overnight</u>?"

Copyright © 2007 http://www.milliondollarinternetpromotions.com - All Rights Reserved

"The 'No-Sweat, No-Brainer' Way To Generate Insanely Profitable Product Ideas That Are Guaranteed To Sell Like Gangbusters!"

Discover How You Can <u>Easily And Effortlessly</u> Crank Out Sizzling Hot Ideas For In-Demand Products... Every 60 Seconds!

Copyright © 2007 http://www.creativitysucks.com - All Rights Reserved

"A Revealing Look Into The Minds of 14 Dedicated Reef Keeping Hobbyists With A Combined Total of 110 Years Experience! Learn From Their Mistakes And Imitate Their Success !!"

Copyright © 2007 http://www.reefkeepingbasics.com - All Rights Reserved

"The Secret 'Jet Fuel' 1,000's of Internet Newbies Have Already Used to Generate Extra Income from the Internet -- Literally *Overnight*.

(Yes, Overnight! And I'll PROVE It to You...)"

Copyright © 2007 http://www.internetentrepreneurclub.com - All Rights Reserved

---

You've absolutely made the right decision to...

"Locate Secret 'Niche Money Holes' As Easily As Waving A Magic Wand!"

Discover Why Nearly Every Internet Marketer And His Dog Are Scrambling To Be The First To Harness The FULL Power Of This Astonishing "Ultimate Keyword Research Management Software"...The First Real Breakthrough In Keyword Research In Internet History!

Copyright © 2007 http://www.mortaltomillionaire.com - All Rights Reserved

---

Absolutely Ridiculous But True...

"How A Fractured Foot Can Result In A Massively Successful Internet Business That Spits Out Profits For You 24/7 On Auto-pilot, Even While You're Sleeping!"

(And How You Stand A Chance Of Having Your Online Empire Custom Built FOR You, If You Act Fast Enough!)

"You'll Want To Read This Letter Now As You'll Only Be Able To Do So For The Next 72 Hours..."

Copyright © 2007 http://www.mortaltomillionaire.com - All Rights Reserved

---

Attention Ezine Publishers!

Amazing Breakthrough In Ezine Publishing Technology Finally Makes It Possible For You To Bypass Harsh Censorship Laws And Deliver Your Ezine <u>DIRECT</u> To Your Subscriber's Desktop!

" Find Out Why So Many Ezine Publishers Are Scrambling To Be the <u>First</u> To Use This Astonishing Desktop Marketing Technology!" (And how this new technology puts the unfair advantage right at your fingertips...)

Are you ready to supercharge your online marketing and <u>slaughter</u> your competition with this monstrous marketing sledgehammer?

Copyright © 2007 http://www.mortaltomillionaire.com - All Rights Reserved

Special Report

"SHOCKING - A New Superfood That Can *Naturally* Double Your Energy, Dramatically Improves Your Mood, Reduce Feelings of Stress, Increases Your Libido And Triples Your Vitality In As <u>Little</u> As 3 Days!"

Imagine Tapping Into The Most Powerful New Super Food On Earth That Contains More Antioxidants, Youth Restoring, Anti Fatigue, Mental Clarity Boosting Nutrients Than Any Other Food Found Anywhere Ever (And Is Becoming The New Jealously-guarded Youth-retaining Secret In Hollywood)...

Read On to Discover The Real Truth Behind This Mysterious New Superfood Secret that Only 1 in 10,000 people will ever get to know about.

Copyright © 2007 http://www.mortaltomillionaire.com - All Rights Reserved

Even though we paid over $248,000 for this, I want you to have it risk free for the next 90 days...

"Discover how we recruited a sales force of OVER 70,000+ affiliates who sent us $3.2 Million in business last year alone!*

...PLUS, learn how you can get $1,000's in FREE advertising on high-traffic web sites... with ZERO risks or costs!"

Copyright © 2007 http://www.marketingtips.com/assoc/ - All Rights Reserved

7.2   Reveal the Dilemma.

Once you have the attention of your reader, thanks to your eye-catching title, you can hold their interest by explaining out precisely, that is, in no uncertain terms, the problem that you, with your product, are going to solve for them. Derek Gehl of the Internet Marketing Center does a fine job! Read below or click through to his site to see for yourself.

*** WARNING ***

If you choose the WRONG eBook software, **you could be at risk.**

First of all, NO OTHER so-called 'viral eBook solution' that I've seen to date offers the ability to **collect the contact information of every person who reads your eBook.**

This is a HUGE problem! If you can't follow up with potential sales leads, **you're losing $1,000's in future profits...** You MUST collect the first name, last name, and e-mail address of every person who reads your eBook.

Second, it's CRITICAL that when you capture this contact information, you **get permission** to send these sales leads e-mail in the future using an opt-in offer.

To keep your business SAFE, *eBook Pro 6.0* <u>automatically does this for you</u> by including this critical bit of opt-in text on your behalf...

PLUS, the software gives you the ability to carefully customize the opt-in message! So you can safely follow up with these sales leads, **without FEAR of spam complaints and law suits!**

Copyright © 2007 http://www.ebookpro.com - All Rights Reserved

A great way to address the problem is to insert a sentence like, "If you're like most people, you . . ." They either need, want, or think something. For example, "if you're like most people, you want the very best for your home . . ." A statement like this will hold your reader's attention. Already, they're thinking, "yeah, I do want the best for my home . . ."

Once you've hit the spot with a well-aimed dart at the heart of the problem, it's time to rub a little salt on the open wound! Make the problem sting! Remind the reader just how much of a problem they're faced with.

"If you're like most people, you value your home. Unfortunately, keeping your home in tip-top condition . . . well, it's expensive, isn't it!? Not only is it expensive, you don't often have a rock-solid guarantee that your handyman knows even the first thing about what you're paying them to do! Unless your Uncle Charlie happens to be in the trade, finding a good builder, plumber, or electrician is down to the luck of the draw."

In this scenario, you might be selling an eBook on "Finding A Reliable, Qualified Professional To Maintain Your Home . . ." or a home study course, "DIY For Homeowners".

7.3   Present the Solution.

Now it's time to introduce yourself and your product or service. Explain precisely what you're selling and why it is useful. How exactly can it be used?

Use your knowledge of the niche market to identify and explain - do so as always in no uncertain terms - the type of scenario in which your customer needs your product or service.

For example, you might introduce your product like this:

The Complete Guide To Copywriting – Your Realistic Route To Wealth

1. *The Complete Guide To Copywriting* is a simple, practical home study guide written with you, the home-based entrepreneur, in mind.

2. Based on my direct-response copywriting experience, it provides you with proven, step-by-step strategies and techniques designed to enable almost anyone to learn how to write effective sales letters.

3. Letters, moreover, which can generate response and earn you money on a consistent, long-term basis.

4. Here's my business philosophy – **I want to help you make money and enjoy a better lifestyle.**

Let me make something ELSE clear

If you're looking to make a fast buck from a 'can't-lose' bizopp product, with no effort involved on your part, then you've come to the wrong place. Please stop reading now.

- I am **not** promising you *'loadsamoney'* overnight
- I do **not** guarantee success, and
- I am **not** offering you a guaranteed *'get rich quick'* formula for becoming an *'instant millionaire'*

The Complete Guide To Copywriting won't guarantee enormous riches, or that you'll never fail or lose money ever again. That's just a load of rubbish, and I'd be insulting your intelligence to suggest otherwise.

Copyright © 2007 http://www.thecompleteguidetocopywriting.com - All Rights Reserved

If you noticed, Nick Wrathall's salesletter process is impeccable! If you just glanced at the example above - that's not enough! Click on the image above to visit his 'live' site to learn for yourself!

Manage 10,000 affiliates as easily 1 affiliate.

Once you've recruited all those affiliates, the last think you want is to suddenly find yourself bogged down with the job of taking care of them!

Sure, having to answer the odd question is no big deal when you only have a few dozen affiliates -- *but what happens when you have* _thousands_ *of affiliates?*

Since AssocTRAC is the same software I use to manage my own affiliate program, I've designed it to be **completely automated** AND **completely scalable**.

> **So it doesn't matter to AssocTRAC whether you have 10,000 affiliates... or just 10!**

... AssocTRAC has been built to automatically manage an unlimited number of different businesses and affiliates, so you don't need to spend your whole day tracking customers and who referred them.

It's all done for you so there's...

- **No paperwork,**
- **No manual calculations,**
- **No order tracking,**
- **No updating affiliates' information,**
- **No finding passwords for affiliates,**
- **And no writing checks.**

... Your affiliates sign up on a simple web form, and their information is **automatically entered into your database**.

There literally is **no limit to how quickly your business can grow!**

Copyright © 2007 http://www.marketingtips.com/assoctrac - All Rights Reserved

7.4   What Makes You the Expert?

Unfortunately, if your reader is still looking at your offer, they're going through their first phase of doubt. Everyone - even those who are offering worthless products - they all say that they can solve the problem! Your reader is getting skeptical. Before they get too skeptical and toss you, it's important to hit them right. Explain, in no uncertain terms, why you can be trusted.

List your credentials by providing information about your success stories (testimonials), prestigious companies, individuals who have bought your product or paid for your services or product, how long you've been in business and where you've made public appearances to discuss your expertise. You should also list and explain the significance of awards and recognition you've received. Doesn't take too much for John Carlton to show how he's qualified to help his customers!

I'll tell you this: I've taught many *stubborn idiots* how to follow **simple "sales maps"** that took them from humiliating failure to stunning success... almost *overnight*.

And I've shown shy, frightened entrepreneurs (who flunked English) how to **quickly produce kick-ass ads that *slaughtered* all competition.**

The key points are these:

✓ **I have *already* helped thousands of entrepreneurs and small biz owners get their marketing act together**, both on the Web and offline, in every different market you can think of...

✓ **I remain the ONLY world-class copywriter to offer both *personalized* mentoring... and also *do-it-yourself* "learn at home" options** (so you can master all the basic skills, no matter what your personal learning style is)...

✓ **And I offer you a complete, no-risk opportunity to see everything for *FREE*, if you choose**.

Boosted Sales 70% Online
*"Your headline suggestion for one of my web sites boosted sales by 70%! This equals an extra $3,000 every month... **from ONE simple change.** Thanks." **Terry Dean**, Internet Marketing Coach, New Castle, IN*

Who The Hell Is John Carlton?

After 25 years as a notoriously-successful (and outrageously high-paid) freelance copywriter and marketing consultant, John is firmly at the red-hot center of the marketing world, both online and offline.

His career arc is legendary: Partnering with **Gary Halbert** for a decade... being a "go-to" writer for the largest mailers in the world (including **Rodale**, where he currently has several controls)... pioneering online advertising tactics (*most* top Web marketers follow his early revolutionary blueprints)... and starring as the featured speaker at major marketing seminars, including: The infamous "Under-Achiever" event in Australia (with **Frank Kern** and **Ed Dale**)... **Armand Morin's** "Big Seminar" in Los Angeles... **Dan Kennedy's** "Copywriting Bootcamp" in Cleveland... **Carl Galletti's** "Information Marketing Seminar" in Las Vegas... **Lorrie Morgan-Ferraro's** "Marketing Bootcamp"... the "Tactic 7" blowout in San Francisco with **Harlan Kilstein** and **David Garfinkel**... and over 30 other mainline events.

John's own workshop seminars on copywriting and marketing *sell* out at $5,000 per attendee.

His podcasts, teleseminars and interviews are must-hear material for every serious marketer (including his online interviews for **Clayton Makepeace, AWAI, Michel Fortin, Bob Serling, Perry Marshall** and **Rich Schefren**, of "The Marketing Manifesto" fame).

More important: Even when John *isn't* at a seminar, other speakers frequently praise his teaching abilities, and defer to his expertise at crafting killer sales copy. He is a **central character** in the amazing explosion of online business, responsible for many innovations and famous for helping a host of top marketers get *started* with his brutal, real-world "kick ass" advice and *specific* advertising makeovers.

Copyright © 2007 http://www.marketingrebel.com - All Rights Reserved

Shawn Casey explains in simple terms how he is easily qualified to be in the 'driver's seat' to pass on his product or service.

You Can Be In Compliance In Less Than Just 60 Minutes From Now!

(And Without Paying Some High-Priced Lawyer to Boot!)

Is it really __THAT__ easy? Yes. But before I tell you how, you're probably wondering at this point who am I and why you should even listen to me.

Let me introduce myself. My name is Shawn Casey. As you might already know, I'm one of the top marketers of information products on the Internet.

My websites receive millions of visitors annually. Ranking.com and Alexa.com rank several of them in the very top echelon (0.01%) of sites worldwide. My sites include MiningGold.com and GoldAffiliateProgram.com — **among many others**.

I've sold over 85,000 copies of just one of my e-courses, "Mining Gold On the Internet: How To Make $1,000 In 15 Days!," to customers in 118 countries. I have *over 100,000 online customers* from the last few years.

But what you may not know is that I'm also an attorney.

Because I own and run an online business just like __YOU__, I've concentrated my efforts almost entirely on Internet law. So I personally understand the risks and requirements of running a website. That's why I've done all the research for you.

Copyright © 2007 http://www.internetlawcompliance.com - All Rights Reserved

Your reader/potential customer should really believe you've been there, done that. With any luck, they'll start to believe in you again.

7.5 Highlight the Benefits of Your Product.

Don't assume that your potential customers know the benefits of buying your product online versus going to their local bookstore or computer store. Once you've introduced yourself and your product, it's time to point out all of the most significant benefits of your product! It's extremely important you highlight the benefits of your product, NOT its features!

Let's see. If you're selling an eBook - basically anything online - you should mention that your customers get their product instantly. It's an instant download or they receive an email instantly with the download information. There's no risk of the product being damaged (if they backup their purchase). You never compromise the quality of the product; an eBook isn't subject to wear and tear!

You may also need to mention precisely that an eBook is basically an electronic book. A lot of people may be oblivious to this, surprising as it may sound to the computer savvy.

Once you've highlighted the benefits of your products, it's time to move on to the proof, as again your customers will be doubting your claims (don't take it personally, it's just the internal psychology of a sale). I've provide just a few samples on how John Carlton uses benefits on his site below. The images I've provided don't quite speak for themselves, so click on the images to get a 'live' example of how it's done!

 Flood your business with eager new customers
(no matter how dismal your efforts have been before)

> *Free Money!*
> *"Amazing! My web site conversion rate has nearly **DOUBLED**, just from what you've taught me. And guess what? Also following your advice, I tested a much higher price... and the conversion rate was not affected at all. **That's FREE MONEY without any extra work!** You were right, John." **Michael Norman**, UK*

✓ **Engorge your bank account with massive amounts of fresh cash** (no matter how broke you are now)...

> *One Tip, One New Car*
> *"On your advice, I edited my copy using your 'Action Verbs'. **This killer strategy ALONE allowed me to buy a new car (for cash) after the first campaign!** Dr. G.E. Nielsen, Wisconsin*

Copyright © 2007 http://www.marketingrebel.com - All Rights Reserved

✓ **Crush your competition** (even if you're competing against Attila the Hun)...

> ***"Worked So Good It Was Scary!"***
> *"Just finished a 1,000 trial mailing with new copy using Carlton's concepts. **Raked in $22,000 the first week**. It worked so good it was scary." **Dr. John M. La Tourrette**, OR*

✓ **And take almost ANY venture -- in ANY market -- from zero to breathtaking success** in the shortest time humanly possible.

And it doesn't matter whether you're on the Web, or in retail, or selling through direct response ads in magazines or in the mail.

> ***1,100% ROI With One Simple Idea***
> *"I put one simple idea I learned from John into action. The result was an immediate 1,100% return on my investment!" **Bill O'Connell***

Copyright © 2007 http://www.marketingrebel.com - All Rights Reserved

7.6   Highlight Customer Feedback / Testimonials.

To regain your customer's trust, you must bombard them with a bundle of well chosen pieces of evidence. Evidence includes quotes from people who have used your product or from people who know you and are willing to write something to confirm your efforts and that you are genuine. (Check out the examples below or simply visit the website links below!).

"Your Sales Copy Is Disgustingly Good!"

"I didn't know you. But since our first call together, I've taken some time to read the salesletters you wrote. They blew me away! I thought I knew every killer copywriter in the world... I didn't. Well, now I'm going to steal a lot of your ideas! They are truly that good. I mean that sincerely, since I don't pay compliments easily. Your copy is so good, it's disgustingly good. I have to grudgingly admit you are hands-down the best sales letter writer on the entire Internet."
— **Gary Halbert**
The Gary Halbert Letter

"Sold More Than Any Copywriter I Know!"

"Michel is the top copywriting on the Internet today. I believe he's the greatest Internet copywriter in the world. His copy has sold more products and services on the Internet than any other copywriter I know. When he speaks, you better listen."
—**David Garfinkel**
World Copywriting Institute

Partial Client List

Some of our clients or individuals with whom we worked include:

Yanik Silver	Neil Shearing	Corey Rudl
Armand Morin	Nitro Marketing	Jimmy D. Brown
Simon Grabowski	Mark Joyner	Ed Dale
Stephen Pierce	Miguel Alvarez	Craig Perrine
Jay Abraham	Kirt Christensen	Bill Hammond
Frank Kern	Terry Dean	Michael Kimble
Ryan Deiss	Ted Ciuba	Jason Potash
John Reese	Shawn Casey	David Garfinkel
Mike Filsaime	Gary Halbert	**And many more.**

Many clients are not just top, million-dollar marketers and Internet marketers, but also *fanatical testers*, too. Together, we've split-tested headlines, copy, offers, colors, layouts, closes, order forms, etc. We're also proud that some of our clients enjoyed record response rates as high as 7%, 11%, 18%, even 46%. Others have seen massive increases as high as 700% with our help.

You can also check out some copywriting samples. Or if you prefer, to read what others had to say about Michel Fortin, The Success Doctor, Inc. and its services, check out these testimonials.

Copyright © 2007 http://www.successdoctor.com - All Rights Reserved

"Made Over A Million Dollars In One Day!"

"A huge thank you to Michel for doing such a masterful job on writing the Traffic Secrets salesletter. He is the author of the biggest launch letter promoting the fastest selling 'how-to' course in the history of the web, grossing $1,080,496.37 in sales in less than 18 hours of its worldwide release."
— **John Reese**
Traffic Secrets

Copyright © 2007 http://www.successdoctor.com - All Rights Reserved

"Michael is one of the top copywriters in America if not the whole world! If you want to boost your business and add dollars to your bottom-line, he's definitely the guy you must listen to!"
— **Mike Litman**
The Mike Litman Show

Copyright © 2007 http://www.successdoctor.com - All Rights Reserved

"She makes $12,000 per month... from the Big Island of Hawaii!"

Melanie Boudar lost her job at the age of 50 when the company she worked for was bought out...

She hated the thought of starting over, working for a NEW company -- so she took a leap of faith and started a bed & breakfast on the Big Island of Hawaii!

Today, nearly **100% of her bookings come from her website...**

... And she's **making $12,000 per month** *(with $8,000 profit!).*

Letter from Melanie...

"I bought a copy of [your] "Insider Secrets To Marketing Your Business On The Internet" course... **The results were amazing!**

As soon as I opened my doors I began running a profit -- I was able to cover all of my expenses with my booking deposits.

I have no employees other than myself... [and] **my site brings in somewhere between $8,000-$12,000 a month.** Approximately $5,000 to $8,000 or 2/3 of that is pure profit.

It has the **potential to do about $16,000 per month**... and I've only been open for 6 months!

Running this business is exciting for me!"

Melanie Boudar
www.visitvolcano.com

Copyright © 2007 http://www.marketingtips.com/tipsltr.htm - All Rights Reserved

It's the nature of marketing that again - after you've presented all of your benefits, the reader/potential customer will again begin to doubt you. You have to, therefore, build you're credibility with testimonials, reviews, and even the contact information - as much as the reader/potential customer approves - so that you make a powerful statement about who you are and what you're doing.

7.7   Increase Value of Offer With Irresistible Bonuses.

At this point of your salesletter your readers are probably 90% convinced of the value of your product or service. They trust you enough to want what you are offering! That's good right? Yes, but they may still be a bit reluctant parting with their money . . .

This is where using bonuses, or as I'd like to refer to as - ethical bribes come into the salesletter process!

When you start offering bonuses to your product or service, you are offering them more value for what you are charging for. At this point, your reader/potential customer becomes less reluctant since there is actually more value being added to the original product or service, to the point where they are actually quite enthusiastic to pay for what you are offering! (I've provided an example of how Marlon Sanders uses his bonuses on his salespages. Notice he calls them bribes! Visit the website link below to see his 'live' site).

If You Order by Midnight, You'll Receive <u>10 Incredible Bribes</u>!

First, you'll notice there are several free bonuses or bribes that I'm NOT offering:

For example, I'm <u>NOT</u> offering reprint rights to a bunch of reports you can resell. Why am I not offering this? Because you know and I both know that **those reports are almost never commercially viable products**. If they were worth a lot, would people be giving them away? Would they really turn down the extra sales?

If you need products or reports to sell, you can create them in a few hours using my methods anyway.

I'm NOT going to send you a book filled with products you can buy at wholesale discounts and resell. That's crazy. You really think you're going to make any money off a laundry list of products? If you do, I have some land in Florida for you ... But if you're looking for a product to sell, in my course, I do tell you the one right way to get one.

I'm NOT giving you access to some secret forum where people without lives go to bicker and argue all the time and rarely exchange useful ideas.

But in my course **I do tell you several extremely useful places you can go for help** and as one of the bribes you do get access to my exclusive Players Club.

Copyright © 2007 http://www.amazingformula.com - All Rights Reserved

Here's What You're Going To Receive

BRIBE ONE: You'll receive my 31 page report entitled "How I Built A Successful Online Business From Scratch, With NO Experience and Very Little Money!"

This is a success story belonging to an average person who had a good idea and turned that into a successful online business.

BRIBE TWO: Special Report - "How To Accurately and Successfully Track Your Advertising Results!"

This BRIBE report reveals the hidden pitfalls in ad tracking systems and how they can be skewing your results.

Thought that latest promotion rocked? It may have... but then again the sales may have come from another promotion altogether!

If you can't accurately track your ad campaings, how are you going to know what worked and what didn't?

BRIBE THREE: ~~Three~~ FIVE step-by-step "Quick Start" videos.

These ~~three~~ FIVE videos (excerpts from my $997 Action Grid System) cover the following topics in depth, step by step:

Video #1: Setting up your online payment processing system (part 1)

Video #2: Setting up your online payment processing system (part 2)

Video #3: Setting up your online payment processing system (part 3)

BRIBE FOUR: A 30-day free trial of our "Ultimate Automation" service that lets you launch your own business in one hour.

At last there is a software program that does practically everything for you.

It keeps you from getting bogged down in technology and lets you focus on marketing your product and making money.

Copyright © 2007 http://www.amazingformula.com - All Rights Reserved

This new program:

1. Takes orders for you
2. Sends a series of follow up emails to customers
3. Signs up people to resell products for you
4. Tracks associate orders
5. Drops new associates in an autoresponder series
6. Gives you unlimited autoresponder sequences
7. Has built-in ad tracking software
8. Processes credit card orders in real time
9. Manages your mailing list for you
10. Sends out surveys and puts answers in a database
11. Much, much more
12. Allows you to move your whole business to a new ISP in a flash

Before this program, automating an entire business took weeks or months. You had to hire a programmer and so forth. It was tough to integrate autoresponders, your associate program, real time credit card processing, a list serve and a shopping cart.

This program does it all for you. Best of all, it'll cost you less than several sequential autoresponders. And it'll save you a ton of time in trying to put all these systems together.

You get a 30-day free trial to the service.

Copyright © 2007 http://www.amazingformula.com - All Rights Reserved

BRIBE FIVE: You'll receive a 30 minute audio recording from my "How to Get The Alligators Out of Your Pond" conference call.

Here are a few of the topics we'll be exploring on the 30 minute audio:

- Do You Have Alligators In Your Pond?
- Are 'Gators (In The Form of Bills) Biting At Your Toes?
- Do You Need To Make M*ney Sooner Rather Than Later?
- Are You Tired of Feeling Gullible?
- How To Get Out and Stay Out Of The Pond!
- What You Need To Know In Order To Become a Pond Builder
- What's The #1 Secret Of Getting Off To A Quick Start?
- How Do You Avoid The 3 Most Common Mistakes That People Make Getting Started On The Internet
- How to Avoid Listening To the "Songs of the Sirens" Which Usually Ends Up Being An Illusion That Leaves You Broke and Frustrated!
- What Is The Hidden Cause Of Gators In Your Pond That No One Really Understands?

You'll get instant access to the 30 minute audio conference recording.

BRIBE SIX: 13 page PDF transcript of the "How to Get The Alligators Out of Your Pond" 30 minute conference call.

You get instant access to the PDF transcript after ordering.

BRIBE SEVEN: 28 page "Secrets of Joint Ventures" magazine with step-by-step instructions on how to do joint ventures.

You get instant access to the magazine right after ordering.

Copyright © 2007 http://www.amazingformula.com - All Rights Reserved

BRIBE EIGHT: You're going to receive a 19 page PDF transcript of the "How to Grow and Promote Your Business" 30 minute conference call.

The topics discussed in the 19 page transcript:

- The Secrets Of Growing Any Business, Idea, Organization, Group, Company, City, Office, Government or Cause!
- How To Understand What It Is That Gets People To Respond To Your Offer And What Gets Results!

BRIBE NINE: Access to my exclusive "Players Only" web site.

This is for players... that is, for my customers who are aiming to make serious cash and ready to take action now, instead of sitting around dreaming. Players are the folks who make things happen.

You get a 7-month membership to the Players Club.

BRIBE TEN: Full color, beautifully illustrated 20 Page "Buzz Marketing" magazine.

In This Issue You Will Discover:

Introduction to Buzz Marketing:
An overview on how to get "buzz"

Spreading the Word: How to Get a Group of People Talking About Your Product Or Service.

Step-By-Step: Buzz Marketing Campaign How To's

Copyright © 2007 http://www.amazingformula.com - All Rights Reserved

As you can see, Marlon offers 10 free bonuses . . . and many other influential marketers offer just as many . . . this really creates an absolute MASSIVE amount of value to the product or service being offered!

So when is it time to say - enough is enough? Can you offer too many bonuses? Well, not really! I've read somewhere that some well know marketers actually encourage you to offer bonuses that will be worth 7 or 8 times that of your original product or service! Crazy huh!? Anyways, if you can't go that far, no problem! If you can offer 2 or 3 valuable bonuses - you'll be good to go!

7.8   Instill a Limited Supply or Time Offer.

Next on the list, you have to raise what we'll call the scarcity issue. Your offer should be limited. You need to imply or otherwise create a real sense of urgency.

An example of this could be: "But wait . . . this offer expires in 24 hours! Don't wait another minute to buy . . . you never know when you'll be hitting those Yellow Pages for a contractor . . . and playing pot luck with your home!!"

Here is another example of how to use a limited time or scarcity offer. There are many, many examples that I could provide here, however, I'm not going to as I'm sure you've probably seen your share of them!

Order Today and You'll Also Receive:

>> *Master Resell Rights*. When your order a copy of *"How To Become Wildly Successful Online"* you'll automatically receive FREE master reprint rights. Sell this course and keep every penny you earn...you'll receive a ready-made webpage template with salesletter just like this one.

>> *Free Bonus Report*. You'll also receive a FREE copy of the new report, "How To Be Successful In Everything." In this short report, Jimmy explains the 7 principles that will make you successful in EVERYTHING -- business, relationships, hobbies / sports, LIFE.

"Get How To Become Wildly Successful Online For Just ~~$19.97~~ ... $7.00!"
"Discover 2 Things That Will Change Your Online Business Forever... BUT, You've Got To Know Them And Do Them"

Your 72 Hour "Subscriber" Special Offer - Save $12.97 Today!!

Copyright © 2007 http://www.123webmarketing.com - All Rights Reserved

7.9   Offer a Rock-Solid Guarantee.

Your guarantee will be your real weapon against the doubters! The key to wielding it: keep things simple. Tell a couple of stories your customers can relate to about how your product is going to help them. Show them, plain and simple, with statistics that they can understand and relate to. Use straightforward language and terminologies that they are guaranteed to be familiar with. Now is not the time to go over their heads. I've provided a good example below!

Here's My Ironclad, 90-Day, 115% Satisfaction, Money-Back Guarantee

Go ahead and grab the Internet Law Compliance System kit, and the extra free $1,166.00 bonus package right now.

90 Day Money
Back Guarantee

Login the private members area, download everything, read through it at your own pace, and even **use the forms and tips** we provide.

Check out everything for 90 days. You can even have your lawyer check it out. If we have not delivered everything we promised and more, then I insist you email us and we'll *refund 100%* of your purchase price.

Now, I did say 115% satisfaction. What's the other 15%?

Here it is. I'm so confident in the value and quality of these resources, that I want you to keep **FREE** bonuses number 1, 2, 3, 4 and 5 — even if you request a refund!

Look at it as my way of saying "thanks for giving us a try." However, remember you will not be licensed to use our copyrighted documents after we have processed your refund.

Nevertheless, your happiness is really important to me.
You really have absolutely nothing to lose. Try it out for yourself and then decide. Secure your copy now.

Copyright © 2007 http://www.internetlawcompliance.com - All Rights Reserved

If you can, find quotes and citations from journals and leading experts in a relevant field about how your product or a product like yours is exactly what everyone should have! Now it's time to name drop, so mention clubs and organizations your customers may belong to or will be familiar with.

Bring everything down to the level of your customer and you are sure to win out with your guarantee. It's also a good idea to offer a 100% money back guarantee within a 30 day time frame, minimum, if the customer is not completely satisfied. Stand behind this and you will be offering a really excellent guarantee of quality.

7.10   Ask for the Order / Call-to-Action.

After a substantial build up it's time to ask your customer to act. It must tell precisely what you want your customer to do, whether it's "call x-xxx-xxx-xxxx" or "go to www.yourwebsitenamehere.com" or the most obvious "buy here now!" The following is a great example!

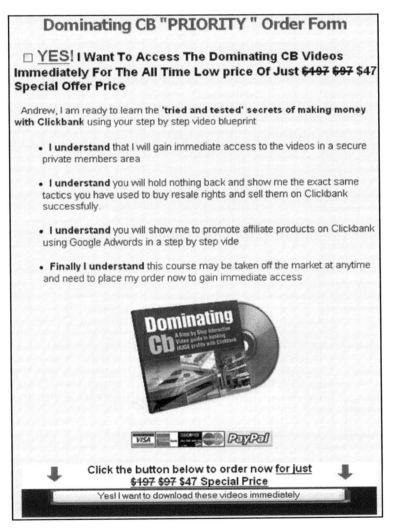

Copyright © 2007 http://www.dominatingcb.com - All Rights Reserved

Your next hook is the offer you make to your customer. The offer is basically your price, expressed as, for example, "it's only $9.97!" "Yours for only $9.97, the only book you'll EVER need to stay in control of your home repairs. Never get ripped off again. Just think how much you'll save!

The following images are excellent examples:

Copyright © 2007 http://www.listblueprint.info - All Rights Reserved

Here are more examples of how to ask for the order - quite simple really - just ask or demand it! There is no end to how this can be accomplished. As you may have noticed in your internet experience, there are many different ways to entice the customer to take action!

Copyright © 2007 http://www.averagejoemarketer.com - All Rights Reserved

Copyright © 2007 http://www.infoproductcreationexposed.com - All Rights Reserved

Here are more examples:

Copyright © 2007 http://www.hiddensalesproject.com - All Rights Reserved

Copyright © 2007 http://www.themarketingnightmare.com - All Rights Reserved

Here is another example on how to tell your customers precisely how you want them to take the order:

Let's Sum It Up...

You Spend:
Less Than Fourteen Bucks

Total Value of What You Get:
over $4,273

How To Collect Your Bonuses:

Step 1 Purchase the book, *Lucrative List Building.*

Step 2 Enter Your Purchase Information Below.

Just fill out the Bonus Gift Redemption Form below and if your information is valid we'll give you instant access to your bonuses - it's that easy!

☐ **Yes! I've purchased the book, now validate**

Copyright © 2007 http://www.lucrativelistbuilding.com/ - All Rights Reserved

---

And 1 more example (Phew!):

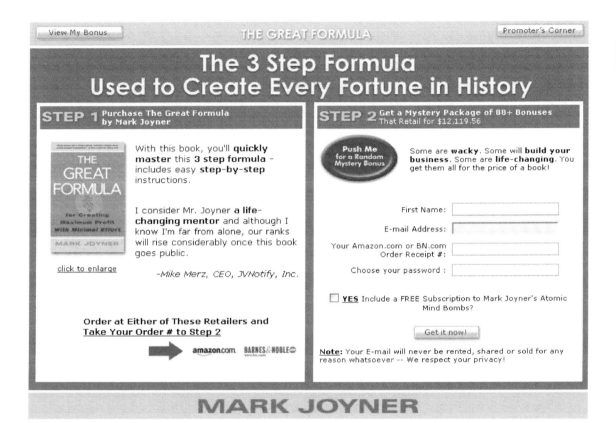

Copyright © 2007 http://www.thegreatformula.com - All Rights Reserved

7.11 Give a Warning.

You must follow up your call to action with another very deliberate and calculated effort. You must indicate to your reader yet again, that there is a particular need for them to act now. The need that you must present is a warning. Here's an example of how Jason Oman presents it:

This Is Easily Over $15,000 Dollars Worth Of Priceless Insider's Info, But You Won't Pay Anywhere NEAR That Much When You Jump On This Offer Today...

If you're serious about creating a book and becoming a best-selling author, you can save BIG right now by jumping on this opportunity right NOW!

Maximize your profit potential by getting access to all of these proven secrets for becoming a best-selling author in record time!

As a member of BestSellingAuthorSecrets.com, I want to give you the **best possible deal ever**... so I'm going to throw in something so valuable, you'd be crazy not to take me up on this offer.

Access To These Audios Is Worth Over $15,000.00 And You'll Get Access Right Now!

But Wait........

There's Even MORE...

Additional Bonus Gifts Below Just Added!

To make sure you get maximum value from these secrets and strategies, you'll also be getting the actual transcripts of these audios as well!

That way there's no chance of you missing even one of these absolutely golden secrets for becoming a best-selling author. (By the way, do you realize that once you're a best-selling author, that's something NO ONE can ever take away from you!?)

Copyright © 2007 http://www.bestsellingauthorsecrets.com - All Rights Reserved

Or, you could combine your call-to-action and warning similar to how Dan Lok does it (Also, read it for yourself by clicking on the image or visit the website link below it for a 'live' look):

BUT let's get one thing clear, right here and now:

- **DO NOT** order my program if you're just going to let it sit on your shelf and gather dust. If you ain't gonna use it - **don't buy it**!

- **DO NOT** order my program if you're only going to listen to one CD, and then send all the material back for a refund. I will be able to tell. If this is what you're thinking don't even bother. **This package is NOT for you**. Don't waste your time or mine. Instead go swim at the bottom of the ocean!

- Listen: I have no time to screw around with any person with a "refund mentality". If you're that type of person, get off this website. Get off my list. And get out of my life. Period!

  Go back to "Loser City" and clear the way for those with enough hustle to actually do something with the information.

  Also...

- **DO NOT** order any program if you will be forced to mortgage your house or "risk" your grocery money. If a few hundred dollars is out of your league at this moment in time - then sorry - *this information is not right for you right now.*

In fact the only people that should order any program for me... can quite honestly be summed up in one word:

PLAYER!

Man, if you ain't a player - then you ain't a buyer.

So... Are You In... Or Are You Gonna Sit On The Sidelines?

Copyright © 2007 http://www.instantwebprofitssystem.com - All Rights Reserved

7.12   Stop the Press - A Last Chance, Persuasive & Compelling Wrap-up. (the P.S!)

With your customers well reminded about why they need your products, it's time to make your closing offer. You should remind your customers of the value of your product, the extras you're offering, and the reasons that they should buy now rather than procrastinate!

P.S. **How much is protecting yourself**, your family, your business **AND** your freedom worth to you? Do you think it's worth a small investment of $99.95? Imagine the amount of *time*, *frustration*, *stress*, feelings of *overwhelm* — let alone the **massive amounts** of **research and legal fees** — you will save yourself.

P.P.S. Remember, ignorance of the law is **NO** excuse. The law doesn't care. The government doesn't care. The complaining party doesn't care. Innocence is not an excuse if you haven't complied with the law — because you're not innocent!

Click here to gain access the complete kit today. Please! Don't make the **horrible mistake** of thinking that the first time you get caught, you'll just get a polite warning. That's not the way the system works.

P.P.P.S. The FTC, or some other law enforcement or government agency, may have flagged your website and may be **watching YOU right now** — and you don't even know it! Or if you're new to the Internet, *why take needless risks?*

Copyright © 2007 http://www.internetlawcompliance.com - All Rights Reserved

Lesson 8 – Closes, Testimonials and P.S.'s

1. You've crafted your headline, you've written the body copy, you've made the offer – and they're ready to buy. Now it's time to **'close the sale'**.

In Lesson 8 of **The Copywriter's The Complete Guide To Copywriting, I'll reveal a series of proven closes** which will lock in your prospects and turn them from prospects into buyers (including the 'one-two' killer close which almost never fails.)

2. You'll also learn about **Testimonials,** and why they form such an important part of any sales letter.

You'll discover what makes a good Testimonial, how and when you should ask people for Testimonials, and exactly how I lay out a Testimonial in a sales letter.

3. And last but not least, **P.S.'s**

Another vital element of sales copy is the **P.S.** (which according to numerous split marketing tests, helps raise response rates by over 30%)

Copyright © 2007 http://www.thecompleteguidetocopywriting.com - All Rights Reserved

You'll notice that in both cases of the examples provided above and below, you are not limited to using 1 P.S. but you are encouraged to use a couple to even several more post scripts! You need to re-emphasize the benefits that will be experienced if your customer chooses to purchase the product or service. It's been researched that many people have purchased a product from simply reading the P.S.!

P.S. – Applying what you learn in *The Complete Guide To Copywriting* will make a huge difference to your business, increase your profits, save you valuable time and money, and provide you with a lifelong business skill you can use over and over again. You are under no obligation to us now or ever, and are fully covered by a 2-year double-guarantee. When you order today, you'll also receive two FREE Bonuses, yours to keep regardless. You therefore risk nothing by trying this. Order at once

P.P.S. – Nothing happens in anyone's business until the copy gets written. Once you have completed the Copywriter's *The Complete Guide To Copywriting*, you will have a powerful business-boosting skill you can use straight away. Order now.

P.P.P.S. – I'll never forget the day I left my last 'proper' job. As I closed the office door behind me for the last time, I was scared. I'd given up a well-paid job, I'd sweated blood to slide up the 'greasy pole', and now it was all over. No more security. No more regular pay-cheque. No more Christmas bonus, paid holidays or pension plan. What was I doing? Apart from the corporate world, I didn't know anything else. Was I throwing away a safe career? Was I making the right decision to train as a copywriter? **I needn't have worried.** You see, in layman's terms, **this stuff works**. The money is good, the demand is constant and through proper use of your new-found copywriting skills, you can provide a service of real value. Now if I hadn't taken this path, I DREAD to think what I'd be doing now. Doesn't bear thinking about. Please don't let this ever happen to you... Order *The Complete Guide To Copywriting* today.

Copyright © 2007 http://www.thecompleteguidetocopywriting.com - All Rights Reserved

Follow These Action Steps:

⊘ Develop your website/sales page by 'zeroing-in-on' the last 12 phases I just described, using the accompanying examples to assist you if you have difficulty understanding the idea you're trying to get across to your potential customer:

- ▶ **Capture the Attention of the Visitor With A Powerful Headline.**

- ▶ **Reveal the Dilemma.**

- ▶ **Present the Solution.**

- ▶ **What Makes You the Expert?**

- ▶ **Highlight the Benefits of Your Product.**

- ▶ **Highlight Customer Feedback / Testimonials.**

- ▶ **Increase Value of Offer With Irresistible Bonuses.**

- ▶ **Instill a Limited Supply or Time Offer.**

- ▶ **Offer a Rock-Solid Guarantee.**

- ▶ **Ask for the Order / Call-to-Action.**

- ▶ **Give a Warning.**

- ▶ **Stop the Press - A Last Chance, Persuasive & Compelling Wrap-up. (the P.S!)**

PHASE 4:

Creating The Back End Product

Chapter 8:
Create Your Profits Exponentially - Develop Your Back End

8.1   Up-Selling.

Few laypeople automatically know what the term 'Back End' is. However, I'm sure most individuals are more familiar with one of the characteristics of the 'Back End' method, that being the Up-sell. This is an excellent way to increase your profits. Businesses do it all the time. It's basically a sales technique for encouraging a consumer to purchase more expensive items, upgrades, or just more items than they originally intended to. At the end of the day, if the attempt is successful, you have a more profitable sale. If you've had the opportunity of purchasing a car, you know that the salesman is not finished with you when you've made the decision to buy the car, there is more to it to that, isn't there? The financing part of the process is an up-sell as well as the added features they want you to get. How about the extended warranty!? These are just some of the up-sell techniques used by the sales team.

Up-selling usually involves marketing more profitable services or products. When you go to a computer store, for example, most of the sales people on hand will try and up-sell. They'll definitely make sure you check out the more expensive brand of computer. They're guaranteed to try very hard to persuade you to buy a printer, print cartridges, cables, paper, and USB cables, whether you need them or not. They'll also try to offload the most expensive varieties.

Since you are ordering "Long Lost Sales Letters" today, I'm going to give you the **exclusive** opportunity to **upgrade to the "Long Lost Sales Letters" Gold Package**.

It includes **all 188 pages of "Long Lost Sales Letters" and the 4 incredible bonuses**...PLUS these extras:

Gold Bonus #1 "Long Lost Sales Letters - Volume II & III" ($299.00 Value)

Gold Bonus #2 "Long Lost Marketing Secrets" ($95.00 Value)

Four Long Lost Marketing Classics That Reveal The Secrets To Achieving Your Marketing and Advertising Success and Gain An Unfair Advantage

Answer these questions:

1. **"Do you need more customers?"**
2. **"Do you want those customers to spend more with you?"**
3. **"Do you want your customers to return over and over again?"**
4. **"Do you want them to refer their friends?"**

If you answered "yes" to any of these, then you'll find these four manuscripts are exactly what you've been looking for.

Copyright © 2007 http://www.longlostsalesletters.com - All Rights Reserved

Long Lost Marketing Manuscript #1: "Tested Sentences That Sell" by Elmer Wheeler

This long-forgotten classic manuscript from 1937 was the result of a huge study conducted by Wheeler who was commissioned by huge corporations to **test over 105,000 sentences on over 19,000,000 customers** to find out which "selling words and sentences" would make products sell like gangbusters.

You'll get 32 chapters of no-nonsense ideas and hot selling sentences that still work today. ANY business in ANY field can apply these proven power phrases to instantly decrease customer resistance and increase sales - either by selling in print or in person!

Long Lost Marketing Manuscript #2: "Scientific Advertising" by Claude Hopkins

You may have heard of Claude Hopkins. He's the guy that pioneered market testing; free samples; risk-free trials; coupons; "pre-emptive" strikes; and money-back guarantees. Ask every direct response marketer or advertiser and they will all mention this incredible resource.

David Ogilvy, who Time Magazine described as "the most sought-after wizard in the advertising business," had this to say about this book:

"Nobody, at any level, should be allowed to have anything to do with advertising until he has read this book seven times. It changed the course of my life." - **David Ogilvy, Marketing Legend**

Long Lost Marketing Manuscript #4: "72 Master Letters and What Made Them Pay" by A.W. Shaw

The author went to the trouble of analyzing over 5063 sales letters, and chose only 72 letters to feature in this book for one reason and one reason only - *these 72 achieved results...the only real measure of success in business.*

You'll go on a fascinating ride as each letter is dissected to uncover what elements made the readers of these 72 classics get off the couch, scramble to get their checkbooks and send in their money!

Copyright © 2007 http://www.longlostsalesletters.com - All Rights Reserved

Long Lost Marketing Manuscript #3: "The Psychology of Advertising" by Professor Walter Dill Scott

This little-known book was discovered in Max Sackheim's: "My First 60 Years in Advertising". Max Sackheim is the mail-order genius famous for the classic headline: **"Do You Make These Mistakes in English"** that ran un- challenged for over 40 years (a record that still remains unbeaten).

Here's what he says about this manuscript:

"The only book on advertising I read as a youth was written by Professor Walter Dill Scott of Northeastern University and was titled 'The Psychology of Advertising'. I still think it is one of the finest books ever written on the subject – and that his formula for successful advertising has never been surpassed."

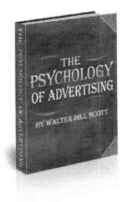

After learning that, we didn't need much convincing that we should read this book and find out all the secrets it held.

This book is an absolute treasure trove of psychological reasoning and insight into what makes people buy and respond to advertising.

Click Here To Upgrade To The Long Lost Sales Letters GOLD Package For Only $29.99 More If You Act Now >>

OR

Click Here If You Only Want To Order The Basic Version Of Long Lost Sales Letters WITHOUT The Additional $443.90 Worth of Gold Bonus Materials Listed Above

Copyright © 2007 http://www.longlostsalesletters.com - All Rights Reserved

A common and very successful technique for up-selling involves getting to know your customer's background and budget. With this information you can better understand what the particular person might need and what you can most easily persuade them that they need.

You should use the up-sell technique with products that will compliment your own. They don't necessarily have to be expensive either. Have a set of main products and a set of additional products, add-ons, if you will. These can be your items for up-selling.

Jeff Dedrick (of Hidden Sales Project) offers a very convincing up-sell that has incredible value: http://www.hiddensalesproject.com/platinum5.php, check it out, you'll see what I mean!

☐ **Yes!** Matt & Shawn, I want to attend Marketing Madness Live 2006! I realize that by signing up today I'll receive 3 full days of powerful training to take my business and income to the next level! PLUS I can bring one guest Free; PLUS I'll receive Matt & Shawn's Quick start CD; PLUS I get professionally recorded audios of the event. **A total value of over $844 for only $197 $97 (before Midnight on November 6th)**

Or

☐ **Yes!** Matt & Shawn, I'll take the entire 3 day Marketing Madness Live and all the bonuses listed above plus the "Git 'Er Done Workshop taking place Monday December 11th 2006. I realize this will be an intensive day of work and elbow grease where I can bring in my laptop and sit down with Matt & Shawn for an entire day to get all my questions answered plus a refresher on both Matt & Shawn's powerful systems for making money online! PLUS I can bring 1 Free guest. **A Priceless Value for only $594!** ($97 plus $497)

8.2   OTO (One Time Offer).

One Time Offers can be very compelling to many types of customers. Presented in the right way, these can do much to enhance your sales and, therefore, your profits. As we discussed in the context of your sales letter, it's important to inject a sense of urgency into the sales process.

Customers are notoriously fickle. They may want to buy something but if they are faced with obstacles, they can all too easily be put off. A sense of urgency, however, provides the incentives to overcome the obstacles, whatever they may be.

An OTO can be implemented as a last chance product offer before the primary sales page. "If you don't take the opportunity of purchasing this now, it'll never be offered again!"

A majority of marketers use this technique, by adding an irresistible offer that anybody could not possibly refuse! A good OTO will result in a substantial increase in profits for the product being sold!

8.3   Recommendations on additional training.

Depending on the precise type of niche market you're catering to, you may be able to increase your profits by making recommendations about additional training and courses.

There are at least two ways that such recommendations might lead to a jump in profit for you. First of all, you might develop the product that can provide them with the additional training they require. Second of all, and alternatively, you might sign up as an affiliate marketer for the companies that offer the training or studying options you're talking about. Make the recommendation and then direct your customer to where they can find the product. If you're argument is convincing and your affiliate's landing page is good, you will probably earn a nice little sum of money without incurring expenses.

8.4   Ecourse Lessons.

The more you can offer your customers, the better. eCourse lessons are always a sensible option when it comes to finding ways to increase the perceived value of your products and also to increase your profits. Why does this work? Well, you can add additional lessons to your eCourse. You can even develop just a few straightforward lessons to sell as individual items, follow-ups to your primary products.

It's taken over a year, and a team of eight people to complete.

You'll absolutely love this entry level eCourse. There is a HUGE amount of tried-and-tested information. You'll get an inside peek at many of the strategies mentioned in the Professional Training Program for way less than the $997 price tag.

If you're like me, you'll want to see the nuts and bolts, so you can know beyond a shadow of a doubt that you're getting everything you'll need to successfully attract clients using the internet.

Copyright © 2007 http://www.internetclients.net/ecoursetrial.htm - All Rights Reserved

By Jimmy D. Brown and Ryan Deiss

How to Create Best-Sellers Online

Generate Fortune and Fame With Your Own Runaway Hit Product

FREE SPECIAL REPORT

"Potential Best-Sellers List"

7 Hot Product Ideas That Are Destined To Become Best-Sellers Online

Have you always wanted to **CREATE and SELL** your own information product, but you just couldn't think of what to write about?

Are you motivated to succeed, but you just don't know where to start?

If so, then sign-up NOW to receive 7 DAILY "best-seller" product ideas. Who knows? The idea that finally gives you a "jump-start" may be buried somewhere in the list below...

- **DAY 01:** "How YOU Can Begin PROFITING From The FASTEST GROWING Niche Online"

- **DAY 02:** "One Of The BIGGEST PROBLEMS in America Can Produce YOUR Next Best-Seller"

- **DAY 03:** "How A STRUGGLING ECONOMY and a DISMAL FINANCIAL FUTURE Can Put Money Into YOUR Pocket"

- **DAY 04:** "What DIRT, TREES and HARDWOOD FLOORS Have To Do With Creating a Runaway Hit Information Product!"

- **DAY 05:** "How ANYONE Can Quickly and Easily Get Their Piece Of This BILLION-DOLLAR Pie!"

- **DAY 06:** "Fired ... Frustrated ... Fed Up - And Looking For YOUR New Product!"

- **DAY 07:** "TWO MILLION People Can't Be Wrong: Here's a Best-Seller If We've Ever Seen One!"

There's more great ideas in this FREE 7-day report than all the other info-product creation book combined. (And we're not even charging for it.) :o)

Best of success!

Jimmy D. Brown and Ryan Deiss

© Copyright 2003 **Jimmy D. Brown & Ryan Deiss.**

Copyright © 2007 Jimmy D. Brown & Ryan Deiss - All Rights Reserved

8.5 Extensive "How-to-Do-It" CD/DVD Training Products. (Multi-media packs).

Regardless of the product you start out with, you may well consider, down the line, the development of an extensive "How-to-Do-It" Training Product. If you take a quick look on Amazon.com, for example, you may notice how products are packaged together. You can develop one version, one course, and offer it in several different formats, including CD, DVD, and online.

That's right!... place your <u>order right now</u>, and you will get:

- ☑ The Full TMN Overview Video
- ☑ All 6 Course Module Videos
- ☑ All 6 Course Module Audios
- ☑ Complete Audio Transcripts
- ☑ *plus* Personal Worksheets

- *EVERYTHING* you need to ensure your online success for one low price!

Copyright © 2007 http://www.themarketingnightmare.com - All Rights Reserved

Copyright © 2007 http://www.hotmarketingvideos.com – All Rights Reserved

You can market such products with eBooks and other products, limiting your expenses and increasing your scope for sales.

8.6   Consulting.

If you offer eBooks, courses, and other material that is designed for educating and teaching people to achieve certain ends, you can attract a group of higher paying customers by offering consulting services.

Consulting services amount to private sessions for the purpose of educating. When you offer information about your primary products, you can also offer notice about the consulting you offer. You can offer consulting on the phone, online, via email, or even in person. Be sure about the hours you wish to make available when you offer private consultations. Your time is valuable, so use it wisely!

8.7   Coaching programs.

Similar to consulting, you may offer coaching programs to your customers as well. You may offer a coaching program to more than one person at a time. This increases the efficiency of your time and result in making more money. There's no hard or fast rule that coaching programs need be private, you are likely to sell this type of service as smaller classes of let's say five or six to 15 - 20 people maximum.

"If You Have An Email Account, Then You Have What it Takes to Prosper Beyond Your Wildest Dreams..."

For a limited time, the "secret weapon" behind the richest, most successful, and most envied marketers on the Internet is prepared to help take you to the next level... And beyond.

Copyright © 2007 http://www.copydoctor.com - All Rights Reserved

8.8   Mentoring programs.

Depending on the precise work you are doing, it is possible to offer mentoring programs as well. These are, again, very similar to consulting and coaching programs, but they are somewhat more specific. Mentoring programs offer you means of directing the progress of individuals to achieve certain ends within your niche market.

8.9   Speaking engagements (free or paid).

There's nothing like free publicity. Speaking engagements are one of the most effective ways of achieving free publicity. Plenty of people are interested in hearing from experts on any given subjects. If you're an expert on a particular hobby or a particular subject area, you can very well apply to community centers, museums, and other forums of public expression. If you offer to speak for free, you may well secure a lot of speaking engagements. You can, as part of the package, bring along plenty of marketing information, free handouts, and samples of your products to sell.

On the other hand, speaking for a fee can be just as beneficial and in some cases be extremely profitable - extremely!

8.10   Seminars.

What about reaching a hundred people at once? How about a thousand? A great backend marketing method, seminars can be offered in person and, thanks to sites like www.goinwebinar.com, you can also host seminars over the internet to online participants.

Copyright © 2007 http://www.bigseminar.com - All Rights Reserved

You can also offer seminars as part of your free publicity, posting information on your website and in other forums as well. You can refer to your seminars in your advertisements as an invitation to potential customers to review your products.

8.11   Similar niche products.

Of course, other backend marketing methods involve offering a range of niche products. If you can target a niche market with confidence and build up a series of eBooks, courses, videos, audio files, or software products that target your chosen market, you're set! ☺ The objective of producing niche products is to achieve repeat customers if possible. The successful development of such a backend marketing method, is the development of a beneficial and extremely lucrative business building tool!

Follow These Action Steps:

- ✪ Create additional profit-making alternatives:

    - ▶ **Upsell.**

    - ▶ **OTO.**

    - ▶ **Recommendations.**

    - ▶ **e-Course lessons.**

    - ▶ **'How-to-do-it' products.**

- **Consulting.**

- **Coaching.**

- **Mentoring.**

- **Speaking engagements.**

- **Seminars.**

- **Similar niche products.**

Chapter 9
Testing Phase - then Go LIVE!

9.1 Test, Test, Test.

Before you invest your money on advertising your programs or promoting your website, you must track and test your progress. You must track your initial visitors. You must track your initial marketing methods and ensure that they are working.

You must also test your website. That is, you must actually test the physical structure of your site. The site map of your site must be checked. You should ensure that your links are functioning. You must test your copy, and you must ensure that it's going to work. You must also test your delivery methods, your advertising methods, and your ordering options. You can bet if one or other of these elements isn't working, you'll lose customers.

9.2 Browser tests using Explorer, Firefox, Netscape.

You must test the appearance of your website on the primary browsers, such as Internet Explorer, Netscape, and Firefox. These three web browsers behave differently and they have a tendency to pick up different problems with a site. Some will not show pictures properly and there may be problems with your links within the site. The only way to ensure that these are working properly is to test them.

9.3 Purchase Product Testing/Order Testing.

Of course, you must also test your purchase and order processes. The best way to test these elements is to try the process yourself. If you have a web designer, they should certainly be able to help you correct any problems with your website.

9.4 Delivery Testing.

The end stage of the ordering process focuses on the delivery process. This, too, must be tested. The most practical and effective delivery methods are automated. Once your customer has selected items and paid the appropriate price, once their payment is processed, they should receive the product or products they have purchased. There are, of course, several methods of delivery that apply online.

The first method of delivery is immediate download. Your customer enters their payment information and, once the payment has gone through, within a few seconds on average, the customer is directed to a webpage from which they can download the product they purchased. You must test this delivery method to ensure that the right links associated with the purchase of the products are correct and that any redirects to specific download pages work properly.

The second method of delivery is email delivery. The process of delivery differs after the payment has gone through. Instead of being directed to a webpage at which the customer can download the products they've bought, they are sent to a page that thanks them for their purchase, confirms the purchase, and indicates that they will shortly receive an email with the product download information.

To test this delivery method, you must be sure that the customers receive the appropriate information on the web pages after their purchase, including the confirmation number. Next, you need to check that the appropriate email is sent.

9.5   Product Testing.

The final part of your test process must focus on the product you are selling. You must, of course, give particular attention to software that relates to your purchase. It's rare, but sometimes there can be problems with files. You must ensure that your customers don't suffer from these types of problems. Ensure that your downloads work.

You should also give particular attention to your software. You must ensure that there is no issue with the software and that it functions on both PC and Mac computers. You should certainly enlist friends to test your software if you can't do it yourself, on both a Mac and PC system.

If all is working well, you can move on to review your advertising methods and prepare to find and send traffic to your website to encourage potential buyers to become paying customers.

Follow These Action Steps:

- ☑ Test, test, test!

  - ▶ test with different browsers.

  - ▶ test your purchase and order procedures.

  - ▶ test your delivery method.

  - ▶ test your product.

PHASE 5:

Generate Targeted Traffic

Chapter 10
Traffic Control

10.1   Attracting Targeted Traffic.

A question you must repeatedly revisit: "what is the purpose of my website?" Your buyers and your potential buyers, will be engaged in a multi-step buying decision process. They may not yet be ready to purchase from you if they are early in the process unless you are able to attract targeted traffic. As the name might suggest to you already, targeted visitors are already part way through the purchasing stage. They're ready to approach the next step in the purchase stage.

One way to attract targeted traffic is to have a presence on a variety of information sites that attract visitors in your targeted audience. With few exceptions, information site visitors are gathering information and evaluating their purchasing options as it is.

Of course, if you run an information section on your site by offering free information on your chosen subject, a large portion of your web site traffic will be interested in researching the subject. They may be early in the purchasing decision process but you can attract information seekers by structuring each page in your web site to give information on a specific topic. Another advantage to this: the richer your content, the further you will expand the list of key words using which searchers might find your site.

In any case, targeting Web site traffic in the "right" decision making stage creates a win-win situation. Your visitors find the information they need and you profit.

In this chapter, we're going to focus on using an affiliate program to promote your website, as studies have shown this to be a particularly effective method for multilevel marketing. Later, I'll provide a summary of other key advertising methods you can use to draw attention to your site - and your affiliate program - once you have both up and running.

So, here goes . . .

10.2 Defining an affiliate program.

The first thing to note is that affiliate programs are really nothing new. Companies have been offering incentives to third parties as a means of promoting and selling their products. Getting a cut of sales through referrals is not a radical idea. However, since the introduction of the internet and the use of websites, it's become easy to implement.

Affiliate programs have started to impact everyday people, by that I mean those who don't own some kind of commercial business that have the resources to offer products and services to consumers and make deals with suppliers.

Affiliate programs are basically a means of hiring people to promote your business and work on a commission, which could be as high as 100%! For many websites, large and small, affiliate marketing is a superb idea. For your website, it might just be your life-line. It pays to take your time thinking about the kind of affiliate program you want to set up and who you want to target.

Let's think about this for a moment. Affiliate programs need to be well defined so that you can attract associates to work for you. As there are many programs out there nowadays, people are getting increasingly sophisticated about the types of deals they sign into.

Defining your affiliate program means identifying how you are going to promote your business - what products, services, or packages you going to promote - and how you are going to compensate your affiliates.

In summary, your affiliate program is defined in terms of what you offer, the program model you use, the commission structure, the reporting and tracking methods you use, and the level of affiliate support you offer.

10.3   Develop Your Affiliate Program.

The first step in developing your program, once you've examined the competition, is to decide which of your product offerings to make available for sale by your associates. The best products for affiliate channels require little explanation beyond what you can provide on a Web site. They should be easily packaged and shipped, and are made from high-quality materials. Examples include books, CDs, movies, video games, apparel, software, and gifts. Another point: the products in your affiliate program should be the best-selling items from your own store.

There are several successful affiliate program models being used by e-commerce sites today, including the standard, two-tier, fee-per-ad or fee-per-click models. By examining each form in action, you can weigh their pros and cons and choose what best fits your style.

There are dozens of search engines that you can use to find online communities, but you should start with the most popular ones: Google, Yahoo!, AltaVista, Excite, Lycos and Hotbot.

If your program is difficult to join, you may be losing potential affiliates. Create a user-friendly registration area on your site for potential affiliates that includes instructions, benefits, terms, disclaimers, and contact information.

Be discerning about who you allow to become an affiliate. Accept only sites in certain categories that offer products and services that complement your own.

The following guidelines should help you evaluate potential sites:

✓   Does the site target your market?

✓   What reasons do your customers have to visit this site?

✓   Does the site feature content that is valuable to your target audience?

✓ Does that content change frequently?

✓ What reason do visitors have to return to the site?

✓ Is the site free from offensive or adult-oriented content?

✓ What kind of traffic does the site report?

✓ Where is that traffic coming from?

✓ What other kinds of efforts is the site making to bring people to their site?

✓ What other affiliates or linking relationships does the site host?

✓ What kind of traffic do they send to the other merchants' sites?

✓ How much revenue does the site generate for the other merchants' sites?

✓ Are you the only merchant in the category?

✓ Or will you be competing with a giant name brand?

Ideally, your affiliates will be generating a substantial volume of traffic; however, don't rule out smaller niche sites based on traffic counts alone. Remember, quality is just as important as quantity.

It may not be worth your time and effort to sell books on a Web site where Amazon already has a prime position. However, if the opportunity is good enough, this consideration may be outweighed by the potential of real sales.

There are 4 different ways you could set up your affiliate program to compensate your affiliates:

✓ **Pay-per-impression program** - this is where you pay your affiliates each time a banner or link is displayed to someone visiting your site. Usually payments of $0.01 to $0.03 are paid out per visitor, calculated per 1,000 impressions.

✓ **Pay-per-click program** - Commissions paid out to the affiliate each time a person clicks through to your website via a banner, a link or text link. Typically, payments are more than the pay-per-impression program - in the region of $0.01 to $0.25.

✓ **Pay-per-sale lead** - Payments made to your affiliate for each "lead" sent to you. These "leads" would be sent to you via online forms after it has been filled out by a visitor, usually through a displayed link or banner on your affiliate's site. An incentive to fill out the form could be a request for a service, a free trial offer, request for free info - whatever you decide.

✓ **Pay-per-sale program** - the most popular of the affiliate programs by far. The only model that guarantees you'll make a profit! You pay your affiliate ONLY when a sale is made - which means no money from your pocket is necessary. The money you end up paying in commission to your affiliate would be partly from the sale you've made via the affiliate - so no out of pocket expenses involved! That's why this affiliate structure is so beneficial.

10.4 Choosing your commission structure. (1-tier/2-tier).

One of the particularly strong selling points about affiliate programs is that they are pretty sophisticated. This has a lot to do with how long they've actually been around, online or otherwise. When you start to think about compensating those affiliates you want to join your team, you have a number of options available to consider.

Commission structure for affiliate programs is basically determined according to a tier structure. You can set up a system whereby your affiliates can market your affiliate program as well as your products, so that third parties can join on someone else's recommendation.

You can create a pyramid structure for your commission payments. That is, affiliates who join you directly, without previously being referred to your program, become first tier affiliates. They can then sell your products or services and promote your site, but they can also promote your affiliate program. If a visitor to the site of your first tier affiliate then decides to join the program you can establish them as second tier associates and provide some form of compensation to the first tier associate who made the "sale" of your affiliate program in the first place. IF this sounds like sharing a lot of your profits, think about it for a second. You only share money with your affiliates when there's actually money coming in through them, and the system is pretty difficult to cheat.

Also, the more affiliates you have, the better chance that your traffic increases, which in turn increases the chance of more sales! ☺

While you could, technically, introduce third and forth tiers, you're more likely to do well with just one or two tiers. I suggest you do not do more than 2. If you have a lot of people joining your affiliate program through first or second tier affiliates, you can offer a graduation system. After acquiring x-number of affiliates for your site, second tier affiliates become first tier, etc.

The specific details of your program are yours to set. The best way to make the necessary decisions is to research a couple of programs offered on sites similar to yours. Look specifically at the terms and conditions of the deal and implement the elements you like.

10.5 How to promote your affiliate program.

We've already mentioned one of the best ways to promote your affiliate program. That is, of course, by offering part commissions for affiliates who recruit third parties to join. This can take time to work, however, and it obviously doesn't solve the fairly immediate problem of how to promote your affiliate program to your first lot of potential affiliates.

Promotion is always about targeting the right audience. To promote your affiliate program in the most effective way possible, you need to think long and hard about your ideal affiliate. Who are they? What demographic do they belong to? What type of website do they own? Where and how might they promote their websites? What key words might they associate with?

Once you can identify your ideal affiliate, you can start to think about the best way of attracting their attention. You could, if you see a website you particularly want to associate with, make an offer directly. Explain the terms of your affiliate program either during a telephone conversation or in an e-mail that you set up. Make sure, if you reach out directly to a particular site, that you secure the attention of the person or one of the people that makes the decisions.

The best way to attract and keep your affiliate is through the use of a variety of tools. Instead of expecting your affiliates to 'build' their own tools - you need to provide them yourself. There is no better person to do this since you will know your product best - right!?

It's also a lot easier for the affiliate to promote your product when the necessary promotional tools have already been provided for them. All they need to do is simply post them to their site. If this is all they have to do - then it's a no-brainer for them, it'll be easy for them.

Here are some methods and tools you can provide for your affiliates so that they can use them to persuade visitors to click through to your site:

- ✓ **Product images.**

- ✓ **Text links.**

- ✓ **Banner ads.**

- ✓ **Articles.**

- ✓ **eZine ads.**

- ✓ **Pop-ups.**

- ✓ **Product reviews.**

- ✓ **Interviews.**

- ✓ **Email promotions.**

You can also mention the program prominently on your website and somehow in relation to your products. You're bound to attract some affiliates by marketing the program to potential and existing customers of your niche market website, since they are likely to be very enthusiastic about the market area you're targeting anyway. If your customers or potential customers have a website, the chances are that it's relevant to yours.

10.6 Deciding on your reward system.

When a potential affiliate approaches you or when you approach an affiliate, the most important thing that they will question you on is, "what's in it for me?"

So, you have to be able to answer this question immediately so that they don't go somewhere else!

Your rewards system will obviously reflect your tier system, at least in part. The reward offered in standard affiliate programs is a percentage of any sales made by a party referred to your site by your affiliate. In most cases, the value is worked out as a percentage of whatever the final purchase price was for the sale.

The percentage can be anything from as little as 5% perhaps, to about, say 75%. I'm pulling these numbers out from what I've seen and experienced personally, but most programs offer between 40% and about 60% of the sale. It's important to remember that, the higher the percentage, the more likely you are to attract affiliates, although this truth is tempered somewhat by the need for your affiliates to actually make sales with your best products and services in the first place!

Apart from the obvious affiliate commission you're going to reward them with; there will be other aspects they will have questions about. If you can answer their questions adequately, they will want to join your program:

- ✓ Will it take long to set up the program on my site?

- ✓ When will I get paid my affiliate commission - and how often?

- ✓ Do I have to pay for something?

- ✓ Will the sign-up application process take long?

- ✓ Are there graphics and banners I can use to promote your product?

- ✓ How do I find out if I made a successful recommendation?

- ✓ Where do I go to see the results of the promotions for your product?

Everyone who signs up to your program will have a different reason for doing so. Some may put no effort whatsoever in promoting your product while others will do everything they can to promote your product. These affiliates will make up a small part of your army of affiliates but will bring you most of the profits.

It's been researched that 20% of your affiliates will generate 80% of your profits. These are the people you want to keep happy! ☺ Establishing a relationship with them would be very important. The following are a few ideas you should consider doing in order to keep from going elsewhere:

- ✓ Occasionally thanking them with a gift or card, perhaps at Christmas or other time.

- ✓ Providing a bonus for selling a certain amount of your products.

✓ Make sure you provide them 'first dibbs' on any of your new promotions or new products.

✓ Don't' just keep in touch via email but occasionally call them and ask how they are.

Do what it takes to establish a relationship with your super affiliates to ensure that your high profit makers stay with you!

10.7 Putting your affiliate program on autopilot.

Like any other system, it pays for your affiliate program to be automated as much as possible. That means, people should be able to sign up to the program automatically (without you having to necessarily oversee every application) and they should be able to secure their commission through sales without you having to peer over anyone's shoulder and check the figures and sales.

There are many different reasons why your affiliate program should run on autopilot. You need a adequate enough program to carry out the necessary tasks. Here are a few of them:

✓ Track your affiliates using html, cgi, or cookies.

✓ Affiliate sign-up process should be automated (work while you are sleeping).

✓ Need an automated contact system.

✓ The necessity for real-time statistics.

✓ Counting visitors and sales.

✓ The all-important affiliate payment process.

So how do you put your affiliate program on autopilot?

You have the choice of running an affiliate program by outsourcing it or by doing it in-house. Both can accomplish the necessary actions as explained above, however, one is more expensive than the other!

You should find affiliate software programs that will suit your needs. There are many, many of them on the net. Some good - many not good at all! If you choose the right host, you'll get the software included within your hosting package. If you decide to purchase an individual affiliate software package, everything you can possibly think of will be included in the package.

You should outsource your affiliate program if you have no interest in running your own or if you have a large operating budget. Now assuming you are a small business owner, I'm going to safely assume that your budget is not going to be a bottomless pit! However, if it is - here are some options you can choose from if you decide to outsource your affiliate program:

▪ Commission Junction - http://www.cj.com

- Be Free - http://www.befree.com

- LinkShare - http://www.linkshare.com

Start up costs will be somewhat expensive and if you choose later to switch to your own affiliate program in-house, it will be more difficult to do.

If you decide to run an in-house affiliate program, there are some advantages:

✓ You are 100% in control of the program (who joins, payment structure, and so on)

✓ You get to keep 100% of the profits (no paying LinkShare or Commission Junction fees).

✓ Enjoy the same if not more features that the in-house program provides.

Your ideal situation is to run an affiliate program that doesn't take too much time and effort. You certainly have other things that need attention in your business.

You'll need an all-in-one solution that'll handle everything with ease and will not need constant babysitting. So choose a hosting company that has an affiliate program included with it, such as **Thirdshere**: http://www.Thirdsphere.com, a very reputable hosting company - I mentioned this company earlier on.

Then there is **AssocTrac**, from Internet Marketing Center. I highly recommend it - it's one of the best affiliate programs you could get your hands on: http://www.marketingtips.com/assoc/.

10.8 How to search for potential affiliates.

Finding potential affiliates can be a four-fold effort! See, look here . . .

✓ Investigate potential affiliates.

✓ Investigate websites that are similar.

✓ Investigate your competition.

✓ Investigate Joint Venture (JV) partners.

At this point, I'm sure you are asking:

> "O.k., who are potentially good affiliates or JV partners and how do I find them?"

Great question!

Before I answer that for you, understand this - while you are looking for affiliate partners, keep in mind that some of these individuals are better off as Super Affiliates and further still as Joint Venture partners.

You can decide on these differences as you learn more about each individual and it pretty much comes down to how much they can 'bring to the table.'

Characteristics of Good Affiliates and/or JV Partners

Product Owners - assuming they have a good product that is selling well. This creates the possibility of a large enough list of people to sell YOUR product to.

In most cases, it may not be wise to try to partner with someone who has the same product as you. However, it will be potentially profitable for you if you find that your products compliment each other.

Product owners usually (in most cases enjoy customer loyalty. This can be extremely beneficial.

How?

Usually on average, you can get 1.3% of subscribers/customers to buy the product when presented to them. Now if an owner has a product that he has previously sold to customers, because of his customer loyalty, it wouldn't be unusual to see a sales ratio of 15% to 30% and even more! That could be very profitable for anyone partnering with this owner.

EZine Owner - these fine individuals usually have a large number of opt-in subscribers who read and listen to the advice given by the owner. This could also prove to be profitable for you depending on the subscriber loyalty of the eZine owner. If the eZine owner has the support, you are more than likely going to profit well from an endorsement of your product that he sends to his list.

High Traffic Websites - generally speaking, the higher the traffic, the more visitors there are, the higher probability you have of selling your product. Larger market = larger profits.

However, you cannot just target high traffic sites. The websites you should be targeting have to be markets that are similar in nature to what you are offering.

Experts and Forum Moderators - they have been around long enough that their knowledge and experience is sought after. Many individuals respect them and trust whatever they have to say. As a result, these individuals could really add to your profits.

Now that you know WHO to contact, WHERE do you find these good people!? :☺

There are a couple of good choices to choose from, one of which I've used extensively for many of my campaigns throughout the years.

Directory of EZines - http://www.directoryofezines.com: This is hands down the best resource you'll ever find that'll assist you in your endeavors to finding suitable eZine publishers as well as Joint Venture partners.

Everything you want to know about a specific eZine publisher is provided in a logical, clean and organized format that makes your research and choosing of your potential partner sooo easy . . . !

Here are a few important items you'll want to know about an eZine publisher before you decide to partner with this individual (this is a small sample of what DOE provides to make your decision an informed one) prior to your decision:

Publication	Publisher's Name	Category	HTML or Text Format
Web Site Format	Blog Format	RSS Format	Circulation
Publication Frequency	Free Ads	Solo Ad Cost	Top Ad Cost
Middle Ad Cost	Bottom Ad Cost	Classified Ad Cost	Ads per Issue
JVs accepted	Past Issues Available	Articles Accepted	DOE Discount

The image below gives you just a glimpse into the search feature at Directory of EZines:

Publication	
Publisher's First Name	
Publisher's Last Name	
Category	Writing / Publishing
HTML Format?	
Text Format?	
Web Site Format?	
Blog Format?	
RSS Format?	
Circulation	
Country	Any

Copyright © 2007 http://www.directoryofezines.com - All Rights Reserved

Here are the results of a search query that you would have made after looking for a publisher (Again, this is a sample of what DOE can do) and I've also erased a few details to keep the information private.

	Publication	First Name	Last Name	Category	Circulation	Free Ad	Articles	Discount	Last Updated
View	Newsletter			Writing / Publishing,Business General	80,000		Y	Y	08-30-2007
View				Advertising / Marketing,Writing / Publishing	6,000	Y			09-20-2006
View	Newsletter			Internet Marketing,Writing / Publishing	320,000		Y	Y	08-30-2007
View				Writing / Publishing,Writing / Publishing	2,200		Y		10-31-2006
View				Writing / Publishing,Writing / Publishing	2,400		Y		10-31-2006
View				Poetry,Writing / Publishing	900		Y		10-29-2006
View				Advertising / Marketing,Writing / Publishing	1,200				01-16-2007
View				Writing / Publishing,News	1,500	Y	Y		09-20-2006

Copyright © 2007 http://www.directoryofezines.com - All Rights Reserved

The image above is a view of a sample result from the 'Writing/Publishing Category.

The sample images below are of a specific eZine publication results page after 'View' is clicked.

Publication View

Publication Name	
Subject Content	A leading resource of site promotion tips for webmasters and small business owners, specializing in website submission, promotion, internet marketing, and optimization in the search engines
Categories	Internet Marketing / Writing / Publishing
Publication Format (s)	HTML / TEXT / WEBSITE
Circulation	320,000
First Published	October 1998

Copyright © 2007 http://www.directoryofezines.com - All Rights Reserved

Contact Information

Publishing Firm Name	
Contact First Name	
Contact Last Name	
Address	
City	
State/Province	
Zip	
Country	USA
Phone	
Extension	
Fax	
Contact Email	
EZine Home Page URL	

Ad Types & Cost of Ad Space

Ad Type	Ad Cost	Ad Rules
Solo Ad	$2,900	Max 50 lines,65 char/line
Sponsor Top	$900	Max 8 lines,65 char/line
Sponsor Middle	$600	Max 8 lines, 65 char/line
Other	Side Spots $900/month	2-3 Side Spots/month

Restrictions or additional ad space cost and rules:
Must be targeted to webmasters and small-business owners. Minimum order is $300. Media Kit avaiable at
http://www.

15% off of first purchase
10% off when purchasing 2 - 4 ads
15% off when purchasing 5 - 9 ads
20% off when purchasing 10 -14 ads
25% off when purchasing 15 or more ads

no adult, no profanity

Submit Ad to:
# of Ads Run per Issue:2 max

Copyright © 2007 http://www.directoryofezines.com - All Rights Reserved

Payment Options		
All Credit Cards / VISA / MasterCard / American Express / PayPal		
How Do Advertisers Pay You? For ad payment/submission questions		

Do you accept joint ventures?

Joint ventures accepted	No	
Contact		

Copyright © 2007 http://www.directoryofezines.com - All Rights Reserved

As I mentioned before - this is by far one of the best resources you'll ever need to find eZine Publishers and or Joint Venture partners.

Read more about DOE here: http://www.directoryofezines.com

The Directory Of Ezines

A Well Researched and Up to Date List of Internet Newsletters That Accept Classified Advertising!

Publisher's Publication List Form

Edit	Publication Name	Delete
Edit		Delete
Edit		Delete
Edit		Delete

Copyright © 2007 http://www.directoryofezines.com - All Rights Reserved

If you happen to be an eZine Publisher yourself and you'd like to be listed in a directory such as this - no problem! ☺ The owner, Charlie Page, obviously provides this added feature as well to accommodate individuals like you.

The eZine Publisher can easily add a newsletter to the data base like as you see below and enter all the required data as requested.

This is an extremely useful tool for both You, the eZine Publisher, Joint Venturers! ☺

If you want to beat your competition or 'swim with the Big Dogs,' Charlie Page's Directory of EZines will give you the upper hand! ☺ Don't promote your business the hard way . . . You'll be able to sell more and earn more by using eZine Publishers and Joint Venturers as a tool for your success, this is your path to getting targeted traffic and eager customers! ☺

Look - I'm a Lifetime member! And it's provided a considerable amount of profit for me in return! ☺

You should at least consider a one year subscription or even sign up as a life-time member!

The longer you wait to decide, the more money you lose! http://www.directoryofezines.com.

Here are a few other resources you can use to find eZine Publishers and potential Joint Venture partners:

EmailUniverse - http://www.emailuniverse.com

E-ZineZ - http://www.e-zinez.com

BestEzines - http://www.bestezines.com

10.9 Communicating with your affiliates.

Communicating with your affiliates is extremely important so it has to be done properly. Keeping this in mind, you must maintain regular contact with them. This includes telling them what's selling and what works. You need to tell them what links, banners and slogans do best and where. You should know because you know your business best.

Motivating your affiliates will be a major part of your success, so you should put it at the top of your priority list. This means you have to think of different ways to educate and motivate your 'little bees!' How and what you should do is what I'll describe next.

Signing up to your affiliate program should be easily accessible to your potential partners and more importantly easy to sign up as an affiliate. As soon as your affiliate becomes a member of your program, you should have an email that goes out to them right away (preferably using an autoresponder) that contains enough information for them to get started promoting your product.

The same host I mentioned earlier, **Thirdsphere**, can also provide you with a useful autoresponder. I would encourage and recommend that you use **Thirdsphere**, it's a very robust hosting company that's inexpensive. If you are not hosted there yet, you should: http://www.Thirdsphere.com. These extra features come with the hosting package at no extra charge! If you are hosted with a hosting company already, here is a good autoresponder service, it's called **AutoResponsePlus**, http://www.autoresponseplus.com, one of the best autoresponder services on the net!

At a minimum, the following should be included in this package or at least should be sent over a period of a couple of days:

- ✓ **A welcome letter.**

- ✓ **Tutorial and/or Tips articles.**

- ✓ **Frequently Asked Question.**

- ✓ **Create a regular affiliate newsletter.**

By properly using your email - all of this can be done. The best way to go about this is by sending out a general e-mail to reach out to all your affiliates, or you can contact individual affiliates using the contact information they provided as part of their sign-up. Either way, a proper autoresponder will be needed to accomplish this task when your membership of affiliates grows.

10.10 Summary of Non-Affiliate Advertising Techniques.

Press Release - The issuance of a press release is a valuable tool, regardless of whether it is reprinted in newspapers and other publications. The press release becomes part of the permanent "media book" for the company and may be featured on the company web site and in other promotional material.

While the press release may be sent to large national and regional publications, it should be targeted primarily to specialty publications such as trade journals. Attempt to be timely by announcing an event such as a product launch or store opening with a date shortly after the issuance of the release. In the body of the text, include the "who, what, when, where and why." - Leave 'em laughing. Buy low, sell high. Emphasize your main point throughout the piece. 10% of your customers provide 50% of your business. You never know where your next lead is coming from. Avoid clichés.

Email Advertising - This is most effective when sent to targeted customers. The best prospects are those you develop yourself, such as visitors to your web-site that leave their name and e-mail in response to your request for registration information. Beware of companies that offer to sell you email lists. You might well end up blacklisted for spamming. With few exceptions, you really should get permission from your potential customers before you start bombarding them with material.

If you only use email advertising when a potential customer has indicated an interest in your business - giving their name and email address on your site - you not only save yourself from potential repercussions of spamming, you can seriously enhance your credibility.

Article Advertising - The best advertising often doesn't appear to be advertising. Editorial coverage in a newspaper or magazine (a news or more typically feature article about your product, firm or principal) is often provided by the publisher to small advertisers as a key inducement. Play like the big boys and get feature coverage when you place an ad in your local paper.

Even if you look to write and publish a whole host of articles to advertise your business, there's no reason that this should take up too much of your time. On the contrary, one of the advantages to article advertising is that you can literally pull content from your existing material, rewrite it slightly as necessary, add a tag about who you are and where you sell your products (you must list your website address!), and you're good to go.

If you want to submit to article listing directories, try some of these:

- www.ideamarketers.com

- www.bestezines.com

- www.makingprofit.com

- www.ezadsuccess.com

- www.goarticles.com

- www.marketing-seek.com

- www.connectionteam.com

- www.homebiztools.com

- www.addto.com

- www.netterweb.com

- www.ezinearticles.com

You can also submit your articles to a variety of eZine directories:

- www.ezinesearch.com

- www.diysearch.com

- www.newz2me.com

- www.ezine-universe.com

- www.zineconnection.com

- www.ezinelocator.com

- www.ezinesplus.com

- www.bestezines.com

JV Advertising - Joint Ventures are probably considered one of the most powerful techniques in the business world. They can significantly increase your profits and extend your 'net' of partners even further by acquiring or attracting more customers.

Joint Ventures provide extra bang for your advertising dollar. Get two other advertisers to split the cost of a t-shirt or hat promotion, and place your own logo alongside. The cost can be carried by two advertisers, while you ride "piggy-back" for free.

While it sounds pretty elaborate, joint-venture advertising is increasingly popular and effective online and offline. Choose your associates carefully. They shouldn't be in direct competition with you but they should certainly cater to the same niche market.

Say you're offering an eBook and an eCourse on caring for a horse. You cover everything from purchasing to finding an appropriate stables, grooming and riding techniques. You have a pretty extensive product. You also have a range of possible associates for joint venture marketing, starting with, say, stores that sell horse related gear. You can also advertise with riding stables, horse breeders, and even the writers of other books and eBooks relating to horse riding. Perhaps you can find a writer who focuses on entering and winning horse shoes of various sizes. Such a writer wouldn't be in direct competition with you - your book and eCourse cover something totally different - but they would have a very similar audience to yours. You could easily establish a mutually beneficial partnership for the purpose of advertising.

Another form of JV'ing that most if not all internet marketers are familiar with is agreeing to sharing the cost half way with whoever you choose to partner with.

Also, you may have a product but not a list of potential customers/subscribers. You could partner with someone who has a list and agree to split the profits with the sales that are made as a result.

You basically use the same principals to find Joint Venture partners as you did with affiliates and Super Affiliates. However, there is one aspect that can make a huge difference in your recruiting of Joint Venture partners.

You really need to have some sort of working relationship or friendship with them first. This will increase your chances of gaining them as partners exponentially!

So what do I mean by this?

First, you need to 'single out' some eZine publishers or product owners who promote to a similar market as yours. If they write a commentary, an eZine, or a blog, sign up to it! Read their material. Also, check out their website and read any tips or articles that they've written.

After you've become familiar with their work, you'll want to contact the owner and compliment them on their work, articles, their techniques, whatever you decide. It has to be an honest assessment, it CANNOT be a 'template', it must be a unique letter addressed directly to them and only them! Otherwise, the owner will 'see' right through your purpose and you will not get a response.

Contacting eZine publishers should not be too hard to accomplish, as they usually provide contact information in their newsletters or provide a contact form on their websites.

At this point, you really should hold off any mention of JV'ing with them. You first want to establish contact and get into a comfort zone before you ask anything from them.

After a few letters are exchanged, then go about asking if they'd be willing to JV with you. However, it's important that initial introductions have been made and some correspondence has passed between the both of you.

It's very important that you keep this in mind. In my experience, I've found that following this procedure results in better partners! Your potential partners are not put 'on-guard' at first contact because instead, you are complimenting them - and everyone likes compliments! ☺

Here is an example of how this process works; it's part of an original email I sent to an individual who later became a great partner:

(Notice how I've complimented her, indicating that the content she provides is very beneficial. Now, I wasn't specific but I should have been. So, make sure you let the potential partner know what information you are talking about, call out the actual source or article and what it was about it that you enjoyed! ☺ Doing this will make the compliment more 'real' and increase your credibility. Then I requested a link exchange, mentioning it could help is both with traffic to our sites. Notice how no mention is made of any Joint Venture in this email. Getting a response from her is the first priority!)

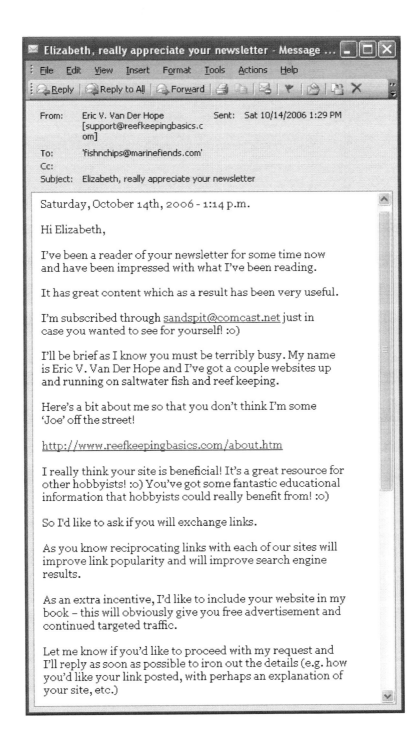

Elizabeth, really appreciate your newsletter - Message ...

File   Edit   View   Insert   Format   Tools   Actions   Help

Reply | Reply to All | Forward |

From: Eric V. Van Der Hope   Sent: Sat 10/14/2006 1:29 PM
          [support@reefkeepingbasics.c
          om]
To: 'fishnchips@marinefiends.com'
Cc:
Subject: Elizabeth, really appreciate your newsletter

Saturday, October 14th, 2006 - 1:14 p.m.

Hi Elizabeth,

I've been a reader of your newsletter for some time now
and have been impressed with what I've been reading.

It has great content which as a result has been very useful.

I'm subscribed through sandspit@comcast.net just in
case you wanted to see for yourself! :o)

I'll be brief as I know you must be terribly busy. My name
is Eric V. Van Der Hope and I've got a couple websites up
and running on saltwater fish and reef keeping.

Here's a bit about me so that you don't think I'm some
'Joe' off the street!

http://www.reefkeepingbasics.com/about.htm

I really think your site is beneficial! It's a great resource for
other hobbyists! :o) You've got some fantastic educational
information that hobbyists could really benefit from! :o)

So I'd like to ask if you will exchange links.

As you know reciprocating links with each of our sites will
improve link popularity and will improve search engine
results.

As an extra incentive, I'd like to include your website in my
book – this will obviously give you free advertisement and
continued targeted traffic.

Let me know if you'd like to proceed with my request and
I'll reply as soon as possible to iron out the details (e.g. how
you'd like your link posted, with perhaps an explanation of
your site, etc.)

Earlier, I explained how you could find potential affiliates and potential partners through a site called **Directory of EZines**. That's not the only tool you could use . . . another resource that'll help your search for partners is a tool called **Alexa**, which you may or may not have heard of before. You can download and install it on your computer easily and the best part - it's FREE! If you don't have it, then here is a link to it: http://www.alexa.com.

Alexa - http://www.alexa.com, is a search tool that provides detailed information about the site you are visiting, such as contact information, traffic rank and related links. This will prove to be an extremely powerful tool to finding potential partners, whether they are affiliate or Joint Venture possibilities.

Here are a few views of how it can be used:

Copyright © 2007 http://www.alexa.com - All Rights Reserved

The other option is by contacting people 'out of the blue,' which means you've never contacted them prior to your first contact. It's much harder to ask someone for something if you've never had contact or 'met' them before. However, this option is really the only alternative if you do not have 'warm' prospects. Usually, this would apply to 'newbies' (those new to the internet marketing community), who have little or no contacts.

Alexa Toolbar

Quick Tour

After you install the Alexa Toolbar, you will have a new toolbar built into your browser that looks like this:

The Alexa Toolbar is a free search and navigation companion that accompanies you as you surf, providing useful information about the sites you visit without interrupting your Web browsing.

Here is an example using Alexa on http://www.yahoo.com. You can find a quick summary of the site and contact info:

Yahoo.com - Yahoo!

yahoo.com

Personalized content and search options.
Chatrooms, free e-mail, clubs, and pager.

Yahoo.com has a traffic rank of: 1

Company Info for yahoo.com:

Yahoo!

Phone: 408 349 3300
webmaster [at] yahoo.com

Employees: **1K - 10K**
Ownership: **Private**
Revenue: **$6.43B**
Ticker: **NASDAQ: YHOO**

Copyright © 2007 http://www.alexa.com - All Rights Reserved

Including traffic history, rank and views:

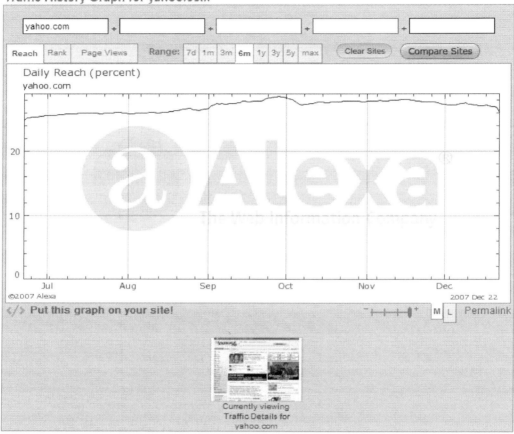

Reach for Yahoo.com: ⓘ
Percent of global Internet users who visit this site

Yesterday	1 wk. Avg.	3 mos. Avg.	3 mos. Change
26.1%	26.985001%	27.73%	⬆ 5%

Traffic Rank for Yahoo.com: ⓘ
Alexa traffic rank based on a combined measure of page views and users (reach)

Yesterday	1 wk. Avg.	3 mos. Avg.	3 mos. Change
1	1	1	No Change

Copyright © 2007 http://www.alexa.com - All Rights Reserved

Page Views per user for Yahoo.com: ⑦
The number of unique pages viewed per user per day for this site

Yesterday	1 wk. Avg.	3 mos. Avg.	3 mos. Change
11.5	12.8	13.3	⬇ 4%

Yahoo.com users come from these countries:
United States	19.4%
Taiwan	5.4%
Hong Kong	4.1%
Vietnam	3.8%
India	3.8%

More yahoo.com users...

Yahoo.com traffic rank in other countries:
Taiwan	1
Hong Kong	1
Vietnam	1
India	1
United States	2

More yahoo.com traffic rank...

Where people go on Yahoo.com: ⑦

* mail.yahoo.com - 47%
* search.yahoo.com - 13%
* 360.yahoo.com - 5%
* yahoo.com - 3%
* news.yahoo.com - 3%
* login.yahoo.com - 2%
* wrs.yahoo.com - 2%
* bid.yahoo.com - 2%
* answers.yahoo.com - 2%
* sports.yahoo.com - 1%

Copyright © 2007 http://www.alexa.com - All Rights Reserved

Includes other sites visited by the same individuals who've visited yahoo:

People who visit yahoo.com also visit:

Merchant Club Usa -- Home
aol.com
Site info for aol.com

Yahooligans
yahooligans.com
Site info for yahooligans.com

Google
google.com
Site info for google.com

Msn
msn.com
Site info for msn.com

Web Search - Webcrawler
webcrawler.com
Site info for webcrawler.com

Hotwired
lycos.com
Site info for lycos.com

Altavista
altavista.com
Site info for altavista.com

Your Ip Address Has Been Blocked!
hoovers.com
Site info for hoovers.com

Sohu.com
sohu.com
Site info for sohu.com

Baidu.com
baidu.com
Site info for baidu.com

Search.msn.com
search.msn.com
Site info for msn.com

Copyright © 2007 http://www.alexa.com - All Rights Reserved

Also includes sites that are linked to yahoo:

Google
Rank: 2

www.google.com:80/Top/Computers/Internet/On_the_We...
Site info for google.com 📄

Fotolog.com:80/TsR_BkR_TsR
Rank: 17

www.fotolog.com:80/TsR_BkR_TsR
Site info for fotolog.net 📄

無名小站
Rank: 39

www.wretch.cc:80/blog/csy4105939
Site info for wretch.cc 📄

Wikipedia
Rank: 8

en.wikipedia.org:80/wiki/AT&T_Yahoo!
Site info for wikipedia.org 📄

Post.baidu.com:80/f?kz=12133699
Rank: 16

post.baidu.com:80/f?kz=12133699
Site info for baidu.com 📄

Friendster
Rank: 14

www.friendster.com:80/10196746
Site info for friendster.com 📄

Search.yahoo.com:80
Rank: 1

search.yahoo.com:80
Site info for yahoo.com 📄

Copyright © 2007 http://www.alexa.com - All Rights Reserved

This resource can be an absolute gold mine for you! You get a quick snapshot of the site you are looking at, it could be a potential affiliate, a potential joint venture partner, or it could be your competition.

Within minutes you'll have a general picture of the site you are looking at!

Use this tool and you will be well on your way to establishing relationships with potential business partners and the growth of your business will surely grow!

PPC Advertising - Advertise on sites that participate in pay-per-click programs. Examples of these are Overture or Google AdWords. Seek PPC sites that offer a trial period. If you can engage in a trial period, you'll have the opportunity to see how much traffic it is producing. If you get a lot of referrals, you know you're on the right track. You can also check to see which of your selected keywords is attracting the most traffic and use that information to refine your keywords-based advertising efforts in the future.

There are basically 3 companies that you should look at for pay-per-click programs. They control most of where your traffic will go as a majority of the smaller search engines use them for finding their search results.

- ✓ Msn - Microsoft AdCenter

- ✓ Yahoo (formerly known as Goto and Overture) - Yahoo! Search Marketing

- ✓ Google - Google Adwords

https://adcenter.microsoft.com

Copyright © 2007 https://adcenter.microsoft.com - All Rights Reserved

http://www.marketingsolutions.yahoo.com

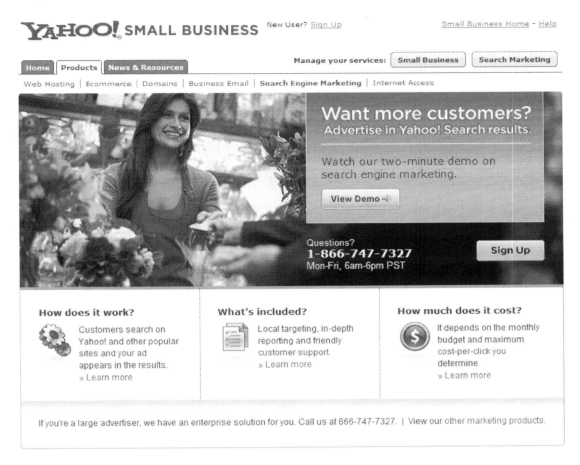

Copyright © 2007 http://searchmarketing.yahoo.com - All Rights Reserved

Remember, by using pay-per-click ads, you can actually be more effective as an advertiser by picking a whole host of cheap keywords. Spending $0.05 to $0.15 per click on a thousand or so key words, you have nothing to worry about. It might be more effective than spending several dollars each on just one or two clicks that receive a lot of hits and are used by big companies.

Here are some more PPC sites:

- www.7search.com

- www.search123.com

- www.goclick.com

- www.epilot.com

- www.kanoodle.com

Last but not least:

https://adwords.google.com/select/Login

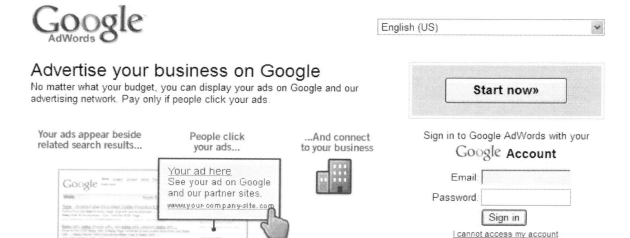

Copyright © 2007 https://adwords.google.com/select/Login - All Rights Reserved

These are a couple of screen shots of what it would look like once you've got your account running and you have set up your pay-per-click campaigns . . .

This is a Microsoft AdCenter campaign using a msn or affiliated search engine:

toys | **Search** | Advanced · Options

Web results 1-10 of 407,000,000

See also: Images, Video, News, Maps, MSN, More ▼

toys - Jellyfish.com   Sponsored sites
Shop & compare prices. Earn cash back when you shop on Jellyfish.com
American Express Shopping - www.bonuspointsmall.com
The Bonus Points Mall. An Exclusive Shopping Opportunity

Toys - Wal-Mart
Shop Low Prices on **Toys**, Gifts, Games from Fisher-Price, Lego, Bratz, Barbie Dolls, Disney,
Educational **Toys** for Girls & Boys
www.walmart.com/**toys** · Cached page

eBay – **Toys**, vintage **toys** and antique **toys** items on eBay.com. Find ...

Sponsored sites

Thousands of Great **Toys**
We don't sell all the **toys**, just the
highest quality and value.
www.fatbraintoys.com

Toys R S
Find Bargain Prices And Save Money
On **Toys** & Games!
bizrate.com

All the **Toys**
All the **Toys** & Fun Stuff for Kids
Smart Shoppers Start Here.
toys.allthebrands.com

toys
Find out which **Toys** are best with our
unbiased reviews.
www.consumerreports.org

Great Prices - KBtoys.com
Every kids' toy you can imagine! Send
great gifts for boys or girls
www.kbtoys.com

Copyright © 2007 http://search.msn.com - All Rights Reserved

This is a Yahoo! Search Marketing campaign using a yahoo or affiliated search engine:

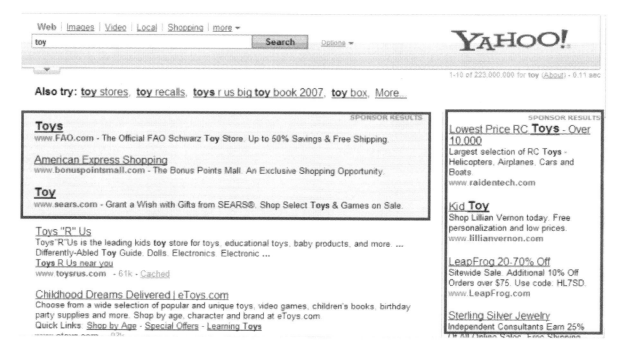

Copyright © 2007 http://search.yahoo.com – All Rights Reserved

This is a Google Adwords campaign using a Google or affiliated search engine:

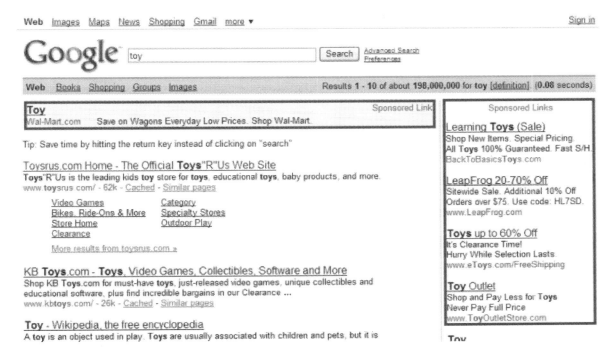

Copyright © 2007 http://www.google.com – All Rights Reserved

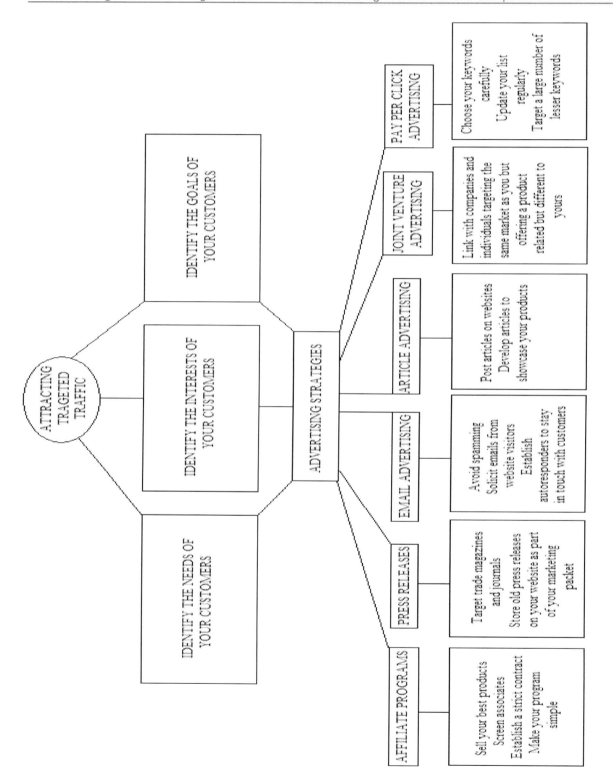

Follow These Action Steps:

- **Develop your own affiliate program.**

  - Decide how you will pay your affiliates.

  - Promote your affiliate program.

  - Search for potential affiliate candidates.

- **Develop a Press Release.**

- **Use email advertising.**

- **Advertise through use of articles.**

- **Use PPC advertising.**

- **Set up Joint Ventures.**

Chapter 11
Keeping Your Customers Happy - Exceed Their Expectations

11.1   Why? They represent YOUR business!

The principle feature of this big picture, if you haven't already given much thought to it, is your customer.

We've talked already about identifying your niche market. Your customers, of course, are an integral part of that. But the people that buy your products, that give you money in exchange for whatever it is you may offer, these people transcend your niche market in a way. They are the centerpiece of your business and guess what? You've got to keep them happy!

Your customers are parting with their money because you've told them your product is worth something. No one, no matter how rich, likes to part with money. Psychologically, it's not a feeling we enjoy. We like saving money, winning money, earning money. We don't like losing it, spending it, or forfeiting it one way or another. Use this little tip-bit of information to your advantage. Don't squander your customer's trust. Everyone has problems every now and again but that is not the norm. If you're selling products rather than services, you should be able to limit the impact that troubles have on your business, everything from family crisis all the way down to computer system failures.

You should have an automated system for advertising, following up on visits to your websites, orders, and requests for information. The better you can organize these processes to function without you, the more valuable your business will become and the more likely you are to avoid incurring the wrath of customers.

Bottom line, you must do everything in your power to ensure your customers are happy! ☺

11.2   What you MUST understand about YOUR customers.

The principle part of keeping your customer happy, particularly when you're operating in a niche market, involves understanding your customer's wants, needs, their problems, their goals, and their dreams. In short, you need to understand precisely who they are.

As part of your market research and product development, you will undoubtedly uncover a lot about your customers and get to know them well. You should, however, look to revisit these areas frequently.

The diagram below should help you to focus your research and stay in touch with your customers over time.

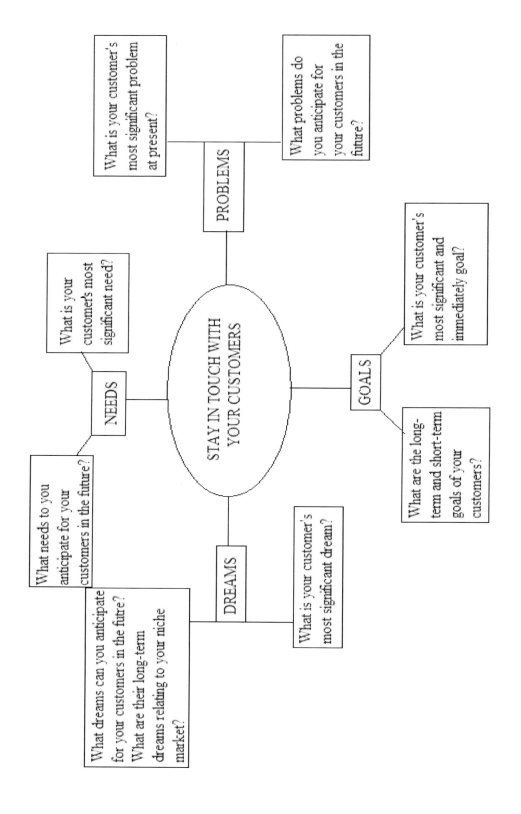

Follow These Action Steps:

✅ **Keep your customers happy.**

- ▶ Exceed their expectations.

- ▶ Your customers ARE YOUR business.

- ▶ LEARN what your customers WANT, then GIVE it to them!

PHASE 6:
Duplication of Process

Chapter 12
Multiple Streams of Income

Your success will improve dramatically if you complete the final step. Unfortunately most people tend to forget or completely ignore this essential step.

Once you have your first business model set up and you are making some money, all you need to do is repeat the process - completing the same steps you took with the previous model.

By duplicating a successful model, you can repeat the process and enter another market or try another niche. In other words, expand on your success by repeating a successful model.

By duplicating your successful model and putting your business on autopilot, you are setting yourself up to creating multiple streams of income!

That should be your ultimate goal. Having multiple streams of income will ensure that you are maximizing your profits.

The advantage of having multiple incomes is that if one of your income streams slows down, you'll still have others that'll continue to produce a profit. Also, by learning this process you can duplicate your success, assuming your first model worked! ☺

Each of the steps I've covered throughout this book requires that you actually follow through with them, no action = no results! You have to methodically follow each of the 6 steps to ensure your success.

Will the 6 steps that I've laid out and presented to you be enough for your success . . . ? Not necessarily.

Why?

Your success depends on your skill-set, in addition to the steps I've laid out in this book, as well as your desire to continually educate yourself with the proper resources and knowledge.

All successful business owners, no matter what kind of educational background or lack thereof, or whether they grew up less fortunate than others, or whether they grew up with a 'silver spoon' in their mouth, did everything in their power to learn the proper skills necessary to operate and manage their business.

Every business, whether offline or online, requires the proper tools to operate successfully. This means that it's absolutely essential to invest in the proper resources and be willing to educate yourself.

Hopefully, you will use this book as a foundation of your education by taking action on the process I've discussed - using the resources, the tools, and the suggestions or by simply 'filling in' the blanks where you feel is necessary - within your own business plan! ☺

The Wrap Up
Afterthoughts

The purpose of this section is to revisit the principle ideas that should be foremost in your mind. The information repeated here should also help you refocus and redefine your niche market business.

- **Develop your business plan**

To be successful in business you must be professional. You must be professional in your business approach, which means, before you do anything else, before you think of a name, before you develop a product, before you even take the first step to follow through on a niche market idea, you must establish a business plan.

You will not get anywhere if you do not know where you are going! ☹

A business plan, as mentioned earlier, ultimately consists of three distinct parts if you are thorough. The initial part is indeed the business plan. This outlines all of the key elements of the business you intend to develop. It also makes initial financial projections, indicates the intended structure, lists personnel to be recruited for the company, and other such sundry details.

The next section is the marketing plan. This will outline in detail the steps you intend to take to reach your target audience. Obviously, you're required here to define your target audience and describe your ideal customer. You must also draw up a preliminary budget for your advertising and indicate how your efforts will be monitored and refined over time.

The third section of your plan must outline the underlying strategy of your company. Your strategic plan should outline the values of your company and how you will incorporate those values into your business model.

- **Setting realistic milestones/goals**

Goal setting is an essential element to success. It applies as readily to success in a person's personal life as it does to business. There are, however, a few key points about goal setting that most people miss.

The most important note about goal setting is that you must be realistic in the milestones you create, whether they are for your business or for you personally. Challenge yourself by all means but don't set the bar so high that you can't possibly overtake it! Done correctly, goal setting should enhance your confidence in yourself and your ideas. It should also help you to see the positive as well as the negative elements of your business, improving both in turn.

- ### You must have the DESIRE to WANT the goals

Another essential ingredient to business success, of course, is the desire to achieve. There's absolutely no point in going into business for yourself unless this is something that you really want to do. Niche marketing is something you must be passionate about to do well at, like most other things.

You will have to do a lot of reading. You'll spend a lot of time reviewing this subject one way or another. If you don't really want to achieve it as a niche marketer (or whatever you choose), you're not going to enjoy the road to success.

Make sure your business is something that you really want before you go investing too much time into it!

- ### You must MENTALLY see your VISION & FOCUS on the possibilities

If you have a plan, you've set your goals, and you know you really want to have your own niche market business, you more than likely have the right mental vision and focus in mind. The more time you spend planning your niche market business, the clearer the process of your business will begin to look. The more clear and focused your vision, the more likely you are to take the appropriate action to achieve success in your niche market.

- ### You MUST be able to TAKE ACTION to produce your desired results

The final point, made throughout this book, one way or another, is that you must follow through on your plans to achieve a successful business. Taking action does not simply mean getting a website and writing an eBook on a chosen subject. It is a far broader notion than this and yet also far more specific. To be successful in business, you must calculate your approach. You must plan. When you act, your actions must also be calculated to achieve a desired effect. You must be conscious of the actions you take with relation to your business from day one. You must follow through on your plans but you must also be prepared to extend yourself, constantly testing and refining your business to maintain the most important component of business success . . . the good will of your customers.

I invite you now to visit the 'Further Resources' section of this book for more information about books related to starting up and running a small business, plus a whole host of websites and key terms you may find very useful as you move through the first crucial stages of business development.

Above all, keep your goals in mind and have fun!

About the Author

Eric V. Van Der Hope has quietly worked behind the scenes within the Internet Marketing community, developing little-known 'virtual real estate' niches. His passion and desire in helping marketers find their own 'niche' has been instrumental in their success. Many in the marketing 'arena' respect his 'tell-it-like-it-is' attitude as it brings a breath of fresh air to a competitive market.

Eric is honored and privileged to have contributed and partnered with many established and trusted internet marketers. He has participated/co-written in several book projects that have included well known online and offline marketers such as but not limited to Jeff Paul, Marc & Terry Goldman, Dr. Joe Vitale, Bob Silber, Michael Glaspie, Alan Bechtold, Bob Wilson, Joshua Shafran, Jim Fleck, Jason Mangrum, Kennon Fort, Jeff West, Bryan Kumar, Ewen Chia, Tellman Knudson, Gary Knuckles, Jason Anderson, Russell Brunson, Frank Mullen, Robert Puddy, Paul Barrs, Graham Hamer, Merle, Eva Brown Paterson, Codrut Turcanu, Thomas Olin, Irena Whitfield and a handful of other well known individuals.

Some of the work associated with these knowledgeable individuals was the result of working closely on projects with Shawn Casey, Patric Chan and Duncan Carver.

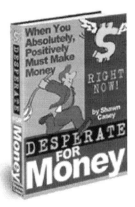

Eric V. Van Der Hope is a native of Southern California (born in Lancaster) and grew up in the foothills of Pearblossom in the Angeles National Forest. He basically grew up with the mountains in his backyard, within walking distance of a nearby county park named Devil's Punchbowl! (Wild name huh!?) Even though Mr. Van Der Hope grew up in a medical family - his grandfather was a surgical doctor, grandmother an R.N., mother an R.N., and father an administrator of a hospital, he was never interested in that line of work and ended up taking a different route! Before Mr. Van Der Hope was even 12, he traveled to New Zealand (by himself) and attended school there for a year. When he was a teenager, he attended an established English boarding school 65 miles southwest of London. The school is nestled in one of the most beautiful parts of the country on the South Downs in the town of Lavington, West Sussex.

Seaford College, West Sussex, England

While living and going to school in England, Mr. Van Der Hope had the opportunity to also visit and live in Europe, specifically - France and Germany. He found it to be a fabulous opportunity and while there he experienced life-changing events while living with a Turkish Ambassador to Germany.

Mr. Van Der Hope has worked in the construction field, health care field, both Civil and Structural Engineering fields, water utility field and participated in a religious sabbatical for 2 years. He is especially proud of serving his country as a member of the United States Military, contributing to the safe navigation of a United States Spruance Class Destroyer, USS Fife (DD-991). As a result, Mr. Van Der Hope traveled extensively throughout the world - from as far North in Sapporo - Japan, to the South including, Tokyo, Yokohama, Hiroshima, Nagasaki, Okinawa, Guam, the Philippians, and further still to Hobart - Tasmania. He was fortunate to visit his mother's country - Australia, and while there enjoyed Melbourne, Sydney, Esperance and Darwin. Mr. Van Der Hope also experienced the sites and sounds of Bali, Jakarta, Singapore (and many other Indonesian countries), as well as Thailand and Hong Kong.

United States Spruance Class Destroyer, USS Fife (DD-991)

Obviously, Mr. Van Der Hope has traveled extensively throughout the world and he's thankful for being American and more important, fortunate to experience what he has seen from his travels. He has gained a tremendous amount of appreciation and respect for all people who contribute in one way or another to our society of humankind. Mr. Van Der Hope feels that it's a shame that this world cannot get along with each other better - "all of us have something in common don't we . . . we're all human!?"

Mr. Van Der Hope is a strong supporter of people who follow their passion by doing what they love. There is nothing more fulfilling than seeing someone doing something they truly have a passion for and love. He is currently working on another website - but no ordinary one, a site that will bring people together so that they can share what their interests and passions are and how they in turn can help others as well.

Additional websites and products Eric has developed and managed:

Globalnet Publishing - http://www.globalnetpublishing.com
The Niche Sourcing Blueprint - http://www.nichesourcing.com
Reef Keeping Basics - http://www.reefkeepingbasics.com
Saltwater Fish Pets - http://www.saltwaterfishpets.com
Foundation of Success - http://www.foundationofsuccess.com

. . . and other niche specific money producing sites (Can't reveal all his sites to his competition!).

If you'd like additional information regarding these sites, refer to his portfolio at:

http://www.globalnetpublishing.com/portfolio.htm

You can learn more about the services he offers by visiting his Virtual Desk:

http://www.EricsDesk.com

Additional Resources

Publisher's Special Offer Page

As promised, you will be given access to products that if read, learned & used properly, it'll help you in the growth of your business.

This offer is **valid ONLY** if you are a customer of Eric V. Van Der Hope.

These products are currently **valued at $197** and it's highly probable that more products will be added, increasing the value of your gifts! ☺

Visit the following website and provide the required information to prevent any delay on your path to success:

http://www.masteringnichemarketing.com/vip/

EXTREMELY IMPORTANT . . . !

If you wish to receive these valuable resources, you **NEED** to visit the website indicated in the dashed box above. This will be the only way you'll be guaranteed access to the $197.00 worth of valuable information. So go there **NOW** before you forget! ☺ (It's HOW you use this material that will dictate the level of your success.)

118 Additional Sizzling Hot Niche Sourcing Methods You Can't Live Without!

If you still can't find a niche market from any of these revealing research sites, you probably shouldn't be in this business! I'm sure it sounds to you as though I'm being a real a** here, but with all these sites there should be no excuse at finding a business idea that could be put to use!

1. 43things.com
http://www.43things.com/
A site about people's goals. Reading the interests of other people may trigger ideas in your mind that you've not thought of before.

2. About A to Z list
http://www.azlist.about.com
This is the main directory of About.com, a great place to start! It's an excellent source to turn to when searching for content. No short supply here, over 600 expert "guides" to choose from written by experts with passion and expertise in their specific subject.

3. Alexa
http://www.alexa.com/browse
An excellent resource. You'll find a list of subjects further categorized into sub-categories. Each sub-category is broken down even further with a list of the 10 most popular/visited sites of each. One of the best sites you'll ever find that'll help you find your specialized niche.

4. Alexa Top 500
http://www.alexa.com/site/ds/top_500
The top/most popular sites on the web categorized by country, language, or subject.

5. Amazon Hot New Releases
http://www.amazon.com/gp/new-releases
The bestselling new & future releases on Amazon.com. Updated regularly. Actually lists product launches before they are released. Your opportunity to get a 'leg-up' on the most popular trends in the market place.

6. Amazon Magazines

http://www.amazon.com/exec/obidos/tg/browse/-/599858/ref=topnav_storetab_mag/105-2508564-0706831

If that link doesn't work, try this one: http://www.amazon.com/gp/site-directory/.

This will be the directory of all the stores, also known as "Shop All Departments". Every type of magazine or newspaper subscription you can think of. Categorized by new titles, best sellers, professional & trade, gift ideas, special offers, editors' picks, and more, updated and sent right to your inbox. In some cases it's updated hourly. A great resource to get a feel for the latest trends in the marketplace. You will find this to be an extremely powerful resource, search around a bit and you'll discover some great research tools just on this one site.

7. AOL Hot Searches

http://hotsearches.aol.com

You can quickly find out what's hot in celebrity news, breaking news, top electronics and gadgets, top vacation destinations, or whatever appears to get your attention - through AOL.

8. Archive.org

http://www.archive.org

A growing digital library on the internet. Access to a variety of subjects, even things such as cultural artifacts - all in digital format. Similar to a regular library, in that access is available to the general public and of course to scholars, historians, and researchers. Free to use.

9. Art Cyclopedia - The Guide to Great Art on the Internet

http://www.artcyclopedia.com

The site reveals the top artists, and provides information to articles, art news, art museums from around the world, and masterpieces. This site has become one of the most effective online guides to finding museum-quality fine art on the net. Provides a comprehensive index of a great number of artists represented at hundreds of museum sites, image archives, and other online resources. Since January 2006, the site has indexed over 2,300 art sites, offers nearly 100,000 links to an estimated 200,000 artworks by an estimated 10,000 well known artists. If your passion or expertise is here - this could be a great place to start your research!

10. Article Dashboard

http://www.articledashboard.com

This is an online article directory for publishers and authors and provides services for website owners, eZine publishers, and many others. An excellent place to brainstorm and finding ideas.

11. Articles Factory

http://www.articlesfactory.com

An excellent resource, simple to navigate and divided into categories to help zero in on your idea/niche.

12. Ask.com Top Searches

http://www.about.ask.com/en/docs/iq/iq.shtml

This site will reveal the results of the most popular search terms being used each week through the millions of searches being made through Ask.com.

13. Associates Directory

http://www.associateprograms.com/directory

You can do keyword research or you can find the products first, it's up to you. I've found it to be advantageous to see if there is a market for the product by researching into the product first. If there are several different products on a specific market you are looking at, there is a good chance it could be a profitable market. What AssociatePrograms.com can do for you is provide an extensive database to help you drill down into the content you are looking for quickly and easily.

14. Barnes & Noble Daily top Sellers

http://www.barnesandnoble.com/bestsellers/top10everything.asp

Get a glimpse into what people are interested in and looking for . . . this site provides an extensive list of the top 10 Bestsellers for more than 300 book subjects, and it's updated daily! Begin searching by category or simply jump into the multitude of subjects for each category.

15. Be a Guide Topics

http://beaguide.about.com/topics.htm

Choose from an extensive list of guide topics by highlighting the one that interests you and then use the detailed description of that topic to further your research.

16. Bella Online

http://www.bellaonline.com/misc/sitemap.asp

This is a site that caters to niches specifically for women. Provides a great resource with a women's point of view taking into account that their needs, wants and desires are different from men. This site provides helpful, high-quality information that is both honest and unbiased.

17. Best eZines

http://www.bestezines.com

An extensive database geared towards eZine (electronic magazine) publishers. It's got an enormous category selection to choose from and is updated regularly. Though it may seem that this is not relevant to your research, it is a great place to go to get fresh information that people have an interest in. At the time of this writing, this site's database consisted of over 2,162 eEzines which represented over 14,050,667+ permission-based email members!

18. Big Boards

http://rankings.big-boards.com/?p=all

This website is a directory that presents an enormous list of the most active forums (a.k.a. message boards) on the web. The site ranks forums by post count, by members count, and by post per member ratio. Data is gathered regularly, from the previous week, using the alexa.com ranking system or by traffic for the boards which have included one of the big-boards trackers. Only sites over 500,000 will actually be accepted (That's what it means by Big Boards)! This site can be a beneficial tool if you are searching for specific information or even if you are searching for an active community on a particular subject where many individuals are going to find answers!

19. BioMed Central

http://www.biomedcentral.com

If you have an interest in this field, there are certainly many individuals that are as well . . . This site contains 184 peer-reviewed open access journals in the biomedical field. Excellent tool for your research.

20. Blog Network List
http://www.blognetworklist.com

This site lists an extensive array of blogs on the net from around he world. They are tracked and ranked by performance. The site is probably contains the most comprehensive source of metrics and analysis for the global blog network.

21. Blog Search
http://www.blogsearch.google.com

As simple as it states . . . this is a research tool to find whatever blog you may be looking for. Google will find blogs published in the last hour, the last 12 hours, the last day, the past week, the past month, anytime! You will find up-to-date info and will be able to hunt trends in the market by using this tool that is constantly being updated.

22. BoingBoing
http://www.boingboing.net

This site actually started as a zine in 1988 by Mark Frauenfelder and Carla Sinclair, its issues were subtitled "The World's Greatest Neurozine"! Boing Boing has been an influence in the development of the cyberpunk subculture. Common themes that you will find here include technology, futurism, science fiction, gadgets, intellectual property, Disney and politics. A great tool to use to help open your mind to a variety of topics.

23. <u>Any Bookstore or Magazine Store (A Best ALL-Time Niche Sourcing Method!)</u>

24. CB Engine
http://www.cbengine.com

A source for ClickBank Marketplace products before the initial buzz and promotion, a tantalizing treasure chest of undiscovered, killer products you can actually get access to.

25. Clickbank Marketplace
http://www.clickbank.com/marketplace

This site is the largest retailer for digitally delivered products on the net. They offer eBooks to software. ClickBank leverages over 100,000 affiliates and as a result has become a global leader in the sale of digital goods completing over 20,000 orders from 200+ countries around the globe. An excellent place to brainstorm ideas for your niche!

26. CNet Buzz
http://www.reviews.cnet.com/4520-12578_7-6527356-1.html

Great site! Read up on what media brands involve and attract individuals through the things they love such as games, music, t.v., film, and technology. Editors review thousands of products by testing and using them and follow up with honest feedback as to the quality and value of each product.

27. Del.icio.us
http://www.del.icio.us/popular

One of the most popular bookmarking sites on the net. A great place to see what's being talked about the most. If it's popular, there is definitely potential for a profitable niche.

28. Depth Reporting

http://www.depthreporting.googlepages.com/websites.htm

You will find over 500 websites designated as "The most useful web sites for reporters". A powerful resource to benefit your brainstorming sessions.

29. Digg.com Popular Archive

http://www.digg.com/archive

Digg is a place for people to discover and share whatever they wish, from videos, to news, to podcasts, to images. Once individuals submit their entries it gets seen and reviewed by all those who use Digg. They get to decide on what they like best. The submission gets to the front of the line (the front page) if enough Diggs are received from people who like it and then results in the submission being seen by millions of visitors that visit the site! Powerful! This gives you a preview into what people like and have a passion or interest in.

30. Digg Spy

http://www.digg.com/spy

Cool stuff here man . . . ! Similar content as above but with one major difference . . . the content is updated in 'Real-Time'! Watch as hot and new content appears before your eyes almost every other second!

31. Digital History

http://www.digitalhistory.uh.edu

An extensive online digital history library sourced from court cases, historic newspapers, landmark documents and social history. Every type of historical data is contained within its pages provided through different ethnic groups and the even the educational media is interactive provided through e-lectures, film trailers, flash movies, and more. This is a fantastic site packed with an encyclopedia of ideas that can help you in your research.

32. Do It Yourself

http://www.doityourself.com

Time Magazine named this site as "One of the Top 50 Sites in the World"! You will find the most extensive list of topics having to do with home improvement on the net. You can get access to personalized advice from professionals in over 100 subjects. Find your passion and teach others what you do best - show and teach others how-to-do it.

33. DMOZ

http://www.dmoz.org

Here you will find the most comprehensive human-edited open source directory on the Web. At the time of this book being printed there were 4,830,584 sites listed by 75,151 editors making up over 590,000 categories! Whoa! Submissions are edited by real individuals who pride themselves on providing quality and comprehensiveness. Very, very useful resource on finding ideas that could be developed into something profitable.

34. Dummies Guides
http://www.dummies.com/WileyCDA/DummiesTitleAll/index.html
I'm sure you are familiar with this series of guides. However, if you think you've seen it all - you haven't! This is the most extensive directory of Dummy Guides on the net. These guides are a perfect fit for individuals frustrated with their problems. Technical jargon is turned into an easy to understand, down-to-earth, lighthearted style that makes it possible to learn just about anything while having fun in the process! Great resource to find ideas that you can turn into profits

35. eBay Hot Categories monthly report (pdf format)
http://www.pages.ebay.com/sellercentral/hotitems.pdf
This is a report, updated once a month, that lists what's Hot, Very Hot, and Super Hot on eBay! Get your hands on this and you'll be able to make profits without a sweat!

36. eBay Marketplace Research
http://www.pages.ebay.com/marketplace_research/index.html
This site assists buyers and sellers to gather critical information on the buying and selling trends in the eBay marketplace. You can view and analyze the top searches, average start prices of products, the average sold prices and much more. Access to historical data is provided over a 90day period. It helps you understand the demand of a product you will be planning to sell.

37. eBay Pulse
http://www.pulse.ebay.com
http://pages.ebay.com/help/buy/ebay-pulse.html
This site is basically a daily snapshot of the current trends, the hot picks, and the cool stuff being listed on eBay. It's a dynamic list that shows the most popular searches, the most popular stores, the most popular products, and the most watched items. This is a great resource to show you what's hot on eBay and what people are purchasing!

38. eBay Seller Central
http://www.pages.ebay.com/sellercentral
Your guide to eBay! Great place to find the latest tips, tools, information, and resources for selling on eBay! Categories include getting started, the best practices, advanced selling, category tips, what's hot, news & updates and resources.

39. eBay What's Hot
http://www.pages.ebay.com/sellercentral/whatshot.html
"Selling success often translates into being at the right place, at the right time, with the right product". This site will give you the upper hand by providing you with the latest and hottest items being promoted on eBay.

40. eBay Hot Hub
http://www.hub.ebay.com/buy
Advanced search directory to benefit your research on finding an item you wish to promote and or sell. Multiple categories to help you narrow in on your search.

41. eBay Pop - eBay Movers & Shakers

http://www.mpire.com/ebayPop.ivk

This cool little url will give you a peak into all that is 'moving and shaking' in the eBay marketplace. There is a 'niche pool' of unlimited items you could choose from to promote.

42. Ezine Articles

http://www.ezinearticles.com

EZine Articles is one of the largest article based sites on the net. There are more niches here that you can dream of! This is an extremely beneficial site that should trigger many good ideas in your head. What's even more powerful is that with each and every article there are about 30 similar niches to choose, split into 3 separate categories that include recent eZine articles, most viewed articles and most published in the category that you've chosen.

43. Face Book

http://www.facebook.com

Welcome to the greatest in social networking! This site can connect you with friends around the world. A great portal to discover the interests, hobbies and passions of others. This site can provide you an unlimited supply of niches by seeing what other people like, want and need. Connections can be made to individuals in their own specific networks. You can learn more about the people who work, live, or study around you. Powerful, very powerful resource and free to sign up!

44. Find Articles

http://findarticles.com

Another article database that contains millions of articles. You can browse by category or list of publication name. Pick from back issues of 900+ magazines, journals, trade publications and newspapers.

45. FreeIQ.com

http://www.freeiq.com

This is a fantastic site, better known as the "Marketplace for Ideas!" Something that is valuable to one person is valuable to another, what is valuable to a group of people is also valuable to another group of people. This site attracts the best of knowledge from a variety of sources. You and everyone else that visits this site share ideas among each other, you can learn from an unlimited number of experts. Fantastic resource to discover great ideas!

46. Furl

http://www.furl.net/furledPopular.jsp

This site is like your own personal information management system. And what's cool about it, is that it can be used as your own unlimited storage place that you can access at any time from anyplace on the net. You can bookmark any website of interest on Furl and refer to it later. This site lists the top most popular headlines over the past day, week, and month. This is one resource that'll tell you "where to look for what you need!" Learn and use what others have already started and make it better.

47. Gizmodo
http://www.gizmodo.com
Gizmodo is a blog known as the gadget guide. It's dedicated to writing all there is to know about every conceivable gadget known to earthlings! The latest gadgets and new toys all revealed here and in record time. Brings in over 50 million page views a month in traffic! Crap! What's up with that!? You can find everything you can think of here from cell phones, video games, computers, whatever . . . just about anything that has buttons you can push!

48. Go Articles
http://www.goarticles.com
Another site dedicated to listing articles within its search engine directory and done so daily. It's one of the largest free content databases on the net containing articles most of which focus on niche areas of interest to all marketers, webmasters, publishers, authors and entrepreneurs!

49. Google Catalogs
http://catalogs.google.com
Here is a tool that makes your search for ideas a bit easier. Provides you the opportunity to browse through 4517+ merchant online catalogs. You can simply browse through the catalog and see what interests you or you can type in a search term you are looking for and it'll show up in every place your term appears in the catalog.

50. Google Groups
http://groups.google.com
An excellent site to search or browse for information. If you are looking to learn something, anything - then this is a place you can start. Looking at learning how to build a tree house? Do you have a question on how to buy a car? You'll be able to find a group or discussion here that could help you out.

51. Google Groups Active
http://www.groups.google.com/groups/dir?&sel=0,83986080
Same site as above but different in that this specifically shows the most highly visited groups by activity. Grouped into separate categories such as topics, regions, languages and members. Do a bit of browsing and you'll quickly see what is being talked about and the trends that grow with popularity.

52. Google Keyword Tool
https://www.adwords.google.com/select/KeywordToolExternal
This is one of the most powerful tools you'll find that will narrow down your search for keywords, but also a wonderful resource to predict what markets have great potential. The tool also helps generate variations of your original keywords as well as synonyms. Using this will assist you in getting the most traffic you can with your specific keywords you are using for your specific niche.

53. Google News
http://www.news.google.com/news?ned=us&topic=po
Get up-to-date news from over 4500+ news sources! Amazing database of the most current stuff going on throughout the world. You can search or browse under the following categories: top stories, world, U.S., business, sci/tech, sports, entertainment, health and most popular.

54. Google Products
http://google.com/products
In order to find something to purchase, I recently conducted a search on this site and here are a few examples of the items being sold: baseball glove, windbrella, scsi card, cat collar, graphing calculator, dustbuster, fire extinguisher, remote control, glass vase, pashmina, scented candles, ibm, thinkpad t40, heart rate monitor, maytag refrigerator, night vision goggles, chopsticks, faucet, mustache trimmer, convertible crib, cpu fan, dog bed, chanel no 5, converse high tops, bill organizer, hangers. As you can see, there is certainly a variety of items that are being sold - and at a profit I might add. The internet is not all electronic media, it's in fact a medium that thousands, millions and even billions of dollars worth of tangible items are being sold.

55. Google Hot Trends
http://google.com/trends/hottrends
A great resource that Google developed to figure out the hottest trends. It uses approximations in attempting to follow specific search patterns being conducted on the Google network.

56. Google Scholar
http://scholar.google.com
This site is similar to the other Google search engines but differs in that it caters specifically to the more academic or scholarly topics that may be of interest.

57. Google Video
http://www.video.google.com/videoranking
This site displays the most blogged, the most shared, the most viewed, the biggest movers & the biggest shakers when it comes to videos on Google, a window into what people are interested in.

58. GoogSpy - powered by Velocityscape (also, refer to my review for Spyfu.com further on in this list)
http://www.googspy.com
This site will display a list of companies and keywords associated with the search term that you are using. It's an Adwords Competitor Research tool. Very cool! It processes approximately 5,688,130 search results - phew!

59. Hobbies List
http://www.hobbieslist.com
It's obvious what this site is all about! Lists hobbies by local, regional, and country searches. It also lists hobbies by popularity and lists the most current hot hobby trend. If this can't get ideas generating in your head, I'm not sure what will!

60. HomeBiz Tools
http://www.homebiztools.com
A great site and research tool to help individuals find the work they love and have a passion for and turning it into a profit. A great place to also gather information to use when up against your competition. There is a plentiful supply of tools and resources here for anyone to make a profit from what they love doing or have a passion for.

61. How To Do Things

http://www.howtodothings.com/browse-all-categories

A site dedicated to compiling as much information from people's experiences and expertise as possible into one place so that it can be used as a solution to others who don't have this exact information. This can be a very beneficial site to find important, reliable and trustworthy information on a variety of topics and subjects. You can easily extrapolate some ideas from this site and use it for your niche as it's providing solutions to what people are having problems with.

62. Idea Marketers

http://www.ideamarketers.com

As the site suggests . . . this is a place to find out and read about ideas! One of the most highly visited and quoted content sites on the net. Contains an extensive database of articles that cover more topics that you can imagine. A great resource and idea brainstorming tool. This will hopefully get your ideas flowing.

63. InfoMine

http://infomine.ucr.edu

Another scholarly internet resource search engine guide. This is a good one. A very comprehensive virtual library and reference tool. Provides search results for academic and scholarly Internet resources, web sites, electronic journals, bulletin boards, databases, listservs, articles, directories of researchers, online library card catalogs, and other types of electronic sources available throughout the internet.

64. Internet History Sourcebooks Project

http://www.fordham.edu/halsall

This site provides a non-advertising venue while it provides a collection of public domain and copy-permitted texts of historical significance. A very comprehensive site that contains very informative yet valuable information even if though it's historical in content.

65. Internet Movie Database

http://www.imdb.com

This site caters to the serious movie buff! A seriously competitive market, visited by over 50 million movie and TV lovers each and every month! The biggest and best movie and TV database on the net!

66. The Internet Public Library

http://www.ipl.org

Literally a library on the internet! Doesn't take much to wrap your head around this. This site is a public service organization and is a superb learning tool and provides an excellent teaching environment. Still can't substitute for the good ol' tangible library - but it'll do!

67. Intute

http://www.intute.ac.uk

This is another site dedicated to providing access to as many educational and research resources on the net. This resource reflects the type of site it is by the individuals and institutions that contribute to it, universities and other entities from the United Kingdom. You will find high quality information here - nothing less! This site sits on a growing database of 120,278 records!

68. Isnare Articles
http://isnare.com
This is an extensive article directory search engine as well as article distribution service provider. What the heck does that mean!? As well as being a directory of articles, this site submits articles to over 40,000 publishers! So articles that are hosted at this site are exposed to a tremendous amount of highly specific search traffic, direct traffic and organic traffic. The diversity in articles provides an excellent supply of ideas and niches for you to discover and potentially profit from!

69. iVillage
http://www.ivillage.com/archive/a2z
If you don't think women's issues make up a relevant niche that is the center of a growing market, I'm not sure what rock you've been hiding under! Yikes! This site is dedicated exclusively to connecting women at every stage of their lives that involves beauty, fitness, food, entertainment, health, parenting, pregnancy, relationships and more. The popularity of the site is proven by its 16 million + visitors that it receives and has become even more popular due to its interactive features that encourages networking and sharing of interests from women throughout the world. You will definitely discover some niches here and possibly some hidden gems as well!

70. Learning Annex
http://www.learningannex.com
Sign up for free and check out the online classes. A variety of Inexpensive classes are offered. Gives you great ideas on what you could teach if you put your mind to it. All of us have something we are good at! Browse the categories and see what some of the instructors are teaching, you'll be surprised. Even take a class you may be interested in - this will even give you a better idea what you could do to be successful.

71. Librarian's Internet Index
http://www.lii.org
Another fantastic online library! This is also a publicly-funded website and newsletters are sent out once a week. Since it's internet based, you don't have to live in any specific state, province or country to access it. This site has an extensive database that's actually organized by librarians! Many topics are covered such as current issues we deal with everyday, the holidays, interests of others and much more. Well over 40,000 subscribers read and use their site. At the time of this writing there were well over 20,000 entries organized into 14 main topics and subcategorized into 300+ related topics. Indeed, another great resource to get your thinking juices flowing!

72. Library of Congress
http://www.loc.gov/index.html
Probably one of the largest libraries in the world. Contains millions of books, recordings, maps, collections, photographs, and manuscripts. It's also the nation's (U.S.) oldest federal cultural institution and serves as the resource for Congress. By far, one of the best resources you will find - no matter where you are. The best advantage is that you don't have to go to the nations capital to use the library, you can do it online!

73. Live Search
http://www.live.com
Search engine features are becoming more and more interactive. If you are looking for video, news, images, maps, whatever - you can find it through this search engine.

74. Magazines
http://www.magazines.com
Printed magazines are expensive, yet millions are sold on every imaginable topic you can think of. So if you do your homework you can easily manage finding a profitable sub-niche without having to print tangible magazines instead producing something in digital form that can be copied over and over again with ease.

75. Marketing Seek
http://www.marketing-seek.com
A relatively small site compared to the many sites we've reviewed thus far. However, it's still a good place to go to search for ideas. The following is a sampling of categories in which a variety of topics are shared, some of which include: arts & humanities, business & finance, computers & internet, health and fitness, home and family, inspirational, recreation and sports, and many more.

76. Meetup Topics
http://www.meetup.com/topics
Here is a great tool to find out what people like and enjoy. A place where people meet and share the same passions in life. The extensive list of categories as well as the popular and growing topics should be a good resource to jumpstart your brain to think of potential niche ideas!

77. Men's Health
http://www.menshealth.com
Just as the women have many sites dedicated to their needs, so do men. Men obviously have their own market niche that caters to many facets of their life. Men's health for one! This site is obviously dedicated to men's health and covers every subject such as fitness, nutrition and sex to name just a few!

78. Metacafe
http://www.metacafe.com/most_popular
This site specializes in short-form original content - new, emerging talent and established Hollywood content. The site actually encourages interaction by engaging and empowering its audience. Most if not all content specializes in content that is made for the Internet. This site is dedicated to providing only material and content that is both entertaining and inspiring or that makes people laugh. Most if not all of the content that is uploaded is determined solely by its members, is user-generated, reviewed and selected by its users.

79. Movie Box Office Charts
http://www.movies.yahoo.com/mv/boxoffice
Lists the top 100 most popular movies in the country (U.S.). This is a great opportunity to see what people's interests are and what they are willing to pay for as far as entertainment goes. Indicates the gross profits made for the weekend, the cumulative gross profit, how many weeks the movie has been playing and in how many theaters the movie is being played.

80. Msn Groups
http://www.groups.msn.com
Similar site to Google groups. This is also an excellent site to search or browse for information. If you are looking to learn something, anything - then this is another place you can start. Looking at learning how to change an oil filter? Do you have a question on how to take care of an iguana? You'll be able to find a group or discussion here that could help you out!

81. My Goal
http://www.mygoals.com
This is a very cool site. This'll hopefully trigger your thoughts on a potential niche idea. This site provides pre-made plans on the goals of others. An extensive database of topics make up the site's foundation and it's organized by a variety of categories that include some of the following: family and relationships, health and fitness, career, education and training, recreation and leisure, home improvement and much, much more.

82. MySimon Categories
http://www.mysimon.com/4002-5_8-6273602.html?tag=ftr.glnav
A fabulous database! This site gives you the opportunity to compare the latest and hottest items on the net. You'll find the best deals on your favorite products as well as items that are hard to find, unique in every aspect. This resource is an exceptional tool to help you in your product hunt. Many categories to choose from and an endless supply of sub-categories to narrow in on the specific item of choice.

83. MySimon Top Searches
http://www.mysimon.com/9098-1_8-0.html
This is the same site but is a more targeted search that displays the top searches being attempted for the hottest items that are in demand. Whatever you think of you'll find here, from luggage to electric toothbrushes to stereos. You get to peer into the crystal ball and discover what other people are looking for! Find your hidden gem here!

84. Neilsen Net Ratings
http://www.nielsen-netratings.com/resources.jsp
If used wisely, you can discover some hidden markets here. This site has done the research for you by doing what it does, it analyzes and measures online audiences, consumer-generated media, consumer behavior, advertising, etc., and then packages it together in a format that can be understood by the user in order to make informed decisions. In otherwords, this site will give you the insight on what the market is doing and what it is looking for.

85. Netscape
http://www.netscape.aol.com
A one-stop source for everything you can think of. It's the latest news and everything in between from health and diet to real estate. Start hunting for your ideas here - it's a great tool. You should bookmark it or even use it as your homepage!

86. The News Directory
http://www.newsdirectory.com
Use this as your guide to your online media center. This is a free resource that provides information to as many media avenues you can think of including newspapers, magazines, television stations, colleges, visitor bureaus, governmental agencies and so forth. It'll help you find resources in any region you wish and provides the names and addresses of these media outlets so that you can further define your niche. You'll find that you can get access to thousands of written material throughout the world. This site links to over 3,600 newspapers, 4,800 magazines, hundreds of television stations and is linked to more than 14,500 sites. The sky is your limit here!

87. Nextmark
http://lists.nextmark.com
A good mailing list is hard to come by. This site makes it extremely easy to overcome this problem. But what does this have to do with you? Well, apart from the fact that you can use this service after you have a product to promote, it can also be used to discover what kind of lists are out there. If you know what kinds of lists there are, you can then 'spy' on your future competition. Learn of some good markets to get into after you see what the lists are targeting. There are more than 60,000 mailing list available! You can also use the mailing list search engine to find additional lists. All-in-all, you have a tremendous tool at your disposal! You can get access to virtually every mailing list in the market and as expressed earlier - this will give you insight into what is currently relevant in the market and what's the most popular in the market.

88. Niche-A-Day
http://www.NicheADay.com
Sign up and receive a new niche market every single day, 365 days a year - FOR FREE! Yep, you heard right! The email will contain a spreadsheet Excel file containing up to a thousand top keywords for the specific niche being sent. The email will also provide the monthly traffic the niche gets and the current Pay Per Click bid for that specific niche. This is an awesome deal! As you can see your brainstorming session has already been done for you! This is a no brainer - go ahead and sign up and get a niche a day!

89. Omgili
http://www.omgili.com
"Omgili is the best way in the known universe to find out what people are saying about anything and everything!" ☺ This is your source for finding opinions, debates, personal experiences, solutions, answers, discussions and just about everything in between. This site is a crawler based search engine that gathers millions of discussions from forums and can differentiate and separate different entities such as the topics, replies, discussion dates and titles!

90. Online Education Database
http://www.oedb.org/library/features/best-online-research-sites
This is another great online research sites out there on the net. This site's database consists of information from online accredited colleges and degree programs. It's an excellent research tool for the serious researcher. The site also hosts a variety of articles covering basic topics of attending online universities.

91. Popurls

http://www.furl.net/furledPopular.jsp

This site is like a personal information management system in one. What do you do when you find an interesting site . . . ? Make it a favorite? How do you find your favorite when you've got a 100 others to browse through? If you use a different machine this would pose a problem as well. By bookmarking whatever site of your choosing on Furl, you can easily annotate, find it later, refer to it, and share it with others. You are offered practically unlimited storage and it's accessible to you from anywhere on the web, for free. An excellent tool when you want to save niche rich websites.

92. Press Release Sites

http://www.IMNewsWatch.com
http://www.PRWeb.com
(refer to page 96 & 97 for more PR sites)

This is one of the leading PR sites on the Web apart from a couple others that I use regularly. You'll find just about every press release for distribution here. It's been used by approximately 40,000+ institutions and organizations. The benefit to using PR sites will result in greater visibility to the public and improve search engine rankings. This is another useful tool for finding information in demand.

93. Pricerunner

http://www.pricerunner.com

Another site that compares prices of products. Additionally you will find the best prices, coupon deals, expert and consumer reviews as well as buying advice. The site offers comparisons from a variety of products used every day as well as a score of others as well. Products that are compared include some of the following: digital cameras & camcorders, jewelry & watches, clothing & accessories, kids & family, computers & software, and so forth! The site also displays the top products, the top searches as well as the most popular categories.

94. <u>ANY Public Library! (A Best ALL-Time Niche Sourcing Method!)</u>

A surprising number of people do not use this resource - what a shame! Perhaps the best niche sourcing method anywhere. No where can you find more niches in one place under one roof!!

95. Reddit.com

http://www.reddit.com

This is a cool little site! It basically displays what's new and what's popular online. It collects data and then ranks this information according to how its users and members vote for it. This results in a site that displays information that people want to see or read and have an interest in due to its popularity.

96. A Research Guide for Students

http://www.aresearchguide.com

This is an exceptional resource site. Don't mind it saying 'student' research guide. It's a great place to browse subjects and get some fantastic ideas. Most of the 'tutorials' are well written. Most of the articles are geared towards the student, however, you may find a few ideas in there that you could exploit.

97. Search Engine Key Phrase Analysis

http://www.google.com
http://www.yahoo.com
http://www.msn.com

I'm expanding on the "keyword+forum" method as explained earlier on in this book. This particular method involves the use of the search engines. However, for all intents and purposes I'm only going to provide the 3 major search engines. The reason for this is that the majority of other search engines use the 3 major search engines to acquire their search results. You can of course use any search engine you wish using the same techniques that I'll describe to you. This technique is limited to how extensive your brainstorming can go - which could very well be unlimited!

To use this technique, simply add an action item, subject, idea, noun, or whatever you can think of to your keyword. To help get your thought process moving in the right direction, I've provided an example:

For a golf related niche, you could type the following phrase, or any other phrase you can think of, into the search engine (use quotes and a +):

"golf + articles"
"golf + experts"
"golf + lessons"
"golf + ideas"
"golf + interviews"
"golf + books"
"golf + magazines"
"golf + advertising"
"golf + questions"
"golf + websites"
"golf + problems"
"golf + answers"
"golf + solutions"
"golf + tips"
"golf + tactics"

98. SEObook Keyword Tool

http://tools.seobook.com/general/keyword

This is more of a search term tool than a niche sourcing tool, however, you can still take advantage of its abilities. When using a search term you've decided to use for your niche, you'll get an extensive list of keyword (or sub niche words) results, this could lead you down a path to finding something you think could be worth while pursuing!

99. SEOmoz

http://www.seomoz.org/popular-searches

A fantastic site to find content on the web that's being searched, viewed or enjoyed. Provides the top 10 searches from all the sources they use to obtain their results. This gives you an idea of what's hot the day of your search. Some of the sources that SEOmoz uses to aquire its content are: Technorati, Popular, Flickr Hot Tags, Del.icio.us Popular Tags, Yahoo! Buzz, Top Overall Searches, Google Hot Trends, eBay Pulse, AOL Hot Searches, Lycos Top 50, Amazon Movers and Shakers and much more. Provides an extensive cross section on what's getting the most attention on the net.

100. Spyfu.com

http://www.spyfu.com

This is a very cool resource to know about! :o) Want to know about your competition - this will do it for you! Spyfu gives you the opportunity of checking out what your competition is buying as far as their keywords are concerned. The competition optimizes their sites by purchasing specific keywords and you'll be able to find out what they are. Will list stats of your site such as organic search results, top organic competitors, top ad competitors, advertisements, subdomains, etc!! Good grief! :o) The site provides additional categories which could prove useful for your research as well such as top 100 organically ranked domains, the top 100 advertisers, and 100 most expensive keywords.

101. Squidoo

http://www.squidoo

http://www.squidoo.com/browse/top_lenses

This site is geared towards helping you make sense of your internet experience, whether it be if you are trying to search for something, buy something, hire someone, book something, or just about everything else! Most people tend to go online and search here, search there, trying to get an answer or two, or an explanation about something. Squidoo try's to make sense of things for you so that you can make an informed decision to take action - whatever that may be. Cool site to browse for a while and learn what it can do for you!

102. StumbleUpon Buzz

http://www.buzz.stumbleupon.com

This site helps you to discover websites that match your personal preferences, meaning - websites that are similar in nature to your likes and dislikes will be matched to you. When you use StumbleUpon, which is also known as stumbling or to stumble, you will only see pages which have been recommended by your friends or even yourself. The advantage is that you get to see sites you wouldn't normally see from using a search engine. As a result of your friend's recommendations, you'll see content that'll match your interests and personal preferences. There will be no need to search through pages and pages of search engine results, this site will help find content for you at ease. You'll discover sites not just recommended by you but also from surfers with similar interests to you. This what makes this site very powerful - you'll end up viewing content not just from friends you know but from hundreds or thousands of individuals around the world who have the same interests as you.

103. StumbleUpon Groups
http://group.stumbleupon.com
Obviously same as site above but categorized into groups - very powerful - you can surf directly to what your interests are. Very extensive. Take some time to browse here and I'm sure you'll find something you can put to use.

104. ThisNext
http://www.thisnext.com
http://www.thisnext.com/activity/map
You'll like this site . . . this is a 'real-time' Google-like map that shows you what is being purchased by whom and where! As soon as someone purchases a product (in the network community) you'll find out who is buying what and where they are located in the world! It's a visual 'real-time' look into what things are most popular and where it's popular. It's like a shop-casting network where you can discover, share or recommend the things you love. Play around with it a bit and you'll get the hang of it and discover how you can benefit from it.

105. Trendwatching
http://www.trendwatching.com
Just as the website name says - trendwatching! The site has a network of over 8,000 in more than 70 different countries that are watching and analyzing what the trends are. This can be one of the most powerful sites you ever visit - but you must use it to benefit from it content! If you are looking for ideas, products, or services, this site will give you the insight you'll need.

106. Top TV Shows
http://www.usatoday.com/life/television/news/nielsens-charts.htm
This is a great site that will give you a mental picture of what it is that people like watching on television. Find out what people are watching and you'll have a good idea what they like! The top shows are listed by popularity and other categories such as age groups 18-49 are listed. Gives you a great overall view of what the interests are for this age group.

107. TVEyes
http://consumer.tveyes.com
This site lets you search the Internet for TV and radio clips, it's a search engine for TV and radio and is searchable by keyword, phrase or topic - just like you'd use a normal search engine. A variety of languages are indexed and can be delivered real-time.

108. Yahoo Answers
http://www.answers.yahoo.com
Very powerful and beneficial site! Have questions - here are the answers! Very extensive database of answers! This site is a community of participants that ask questions and its participants answer them! A wide range of topics are available such as arts & humanities, beauty & style, business & finance, cars & transportation, computers & internet, dining out, environment, health, home & garden, pets, pregnancy & parenting, social science, and travel - and that's just to name a few! Finding a place such as this that individuals are sharing what they know is extremely beneficial. People are guided there and you'll be able to answer these questions for them. This is a great site to discover what people are asking - you get to provide the answer in the form of a product!? Someone could surely benefit from your knowledge, your opinion or your personal experience.

109. Yahoo Buzz

http://buzz.yahoo.com

A cool resource. This site will provide a buzz score, which is a percentage of Yahoo! Users searching for a particular topic on any given day! The results of which are put into a weekly top leaders format, ranked by subjects from hottest on down. Gives good insight into the popularity of the subject.

110. Yahoo Groups

http://www.groups.yahoo.com

This site is a wonderful resource similar to what Google offers. Here you can connect with people from around the world who share your passions, interests or whatever else that is similar to you. Sign up and you'll have access to millions of others who may have the same interests as you. Look for groups with high 'membership', usually this is a giveaway of a good idea or subject to concentrate on. Or you can look at small groups which have an extreme passion for the subject matter - this would be an easy niche to develop and profit from. Your market actually shouldn't be a large market where it can be extremely competitive, but a small market where there is little competition. Become the big fish in the little pond!

111. Yahoo Shopping

http://shopping.yahoo.com

This is an extremely cool site to help in your search for products that you may want to profit from. You can find, you can compare, you can read reviews & you can choose to buy whatever you want here! You can build your own store and then sell whatever you decide! Great categories to choose from and browse to look for sub-niches. This site can be very informative if you are trying to decide if selling tangible items will work for you.

112. Viral Video Chart

http://www.viralvideochart.com

Chart of the most popular viral videos on the internet. You'll find the hottest stuff here from YouTube, MySpace, Google, Metacafe, Daily Motion and Break.com.

113. ViewDo

http://www.viewdo.com

This is a free video library on how to do a wide variety of things. If the written word is not working for you nor are images getting the point across, turn to ViewDo to give you the proper clarity and understanding of how to get a job done the right way!

114. Whonu

http://www.whonu.com

Many of the search engines and the technologies associated with them have their own strengths and weaknesses. This site brings all these entities together by harnessing everything together in one place. As a result, an extremely powerful tool has been created that becomes the source of idea-making, discovery and research! Check it out - you'll be impressed.

115. WikiHow

http://www.wikihow.com/Categories

This is a site that anyone can write and anyone can edit. It's similar to Wikipedia. Any visitor who visits wikiHow can create a new page to write about how to do something . . . anything! It's basically an enormous how-to manual that contains every subject you can imagine and its growth is dependent on individuals from the public editing it as time goes on. Any visitor can make their own edits which then improves the overall quality of the submission. If you wish to generate new ideas, this is another resource that could benefit your efforts.

116. Wikipedia

http://www.en.wikipedia.org/wiki/Lists_of_topics

Similar to the site above but has been around longer, therefore the site is larger and the quantity of topics far surpasses anything else you will find on the net. An extremely useful tool - but like with everything I've described in this section - you need to use it for it to actually work for you - duh! If used correctly, you can narrow-in on sub-niches by taking advantage of the many links/references that it provides.

117. WordTracker.com

http://www.freekeywords.wordtracker.com

This is another search term tool rather than a niche sourcing tool, but can still accomplish the task that you'd like - which is to benefit your search in finding your niche idea and or product. By using this site you will be able to narrow in on sub-niches that could be potentially profitable for you.

118. YouTube

http://www.youtube.com/browse?s=mp

Not sure where you've been if you've never seen this awesome site! You think you've seen it all - nope! Not until you see some craziness here! You can view videos here on every single subject or topic you can think of - or not think of! Take some time to browse here and you will no doubt be able to generate some ideas!

BOOK RECOMMENDATIONS

- *Anatomy of a Start-Up: Why Some Businesses Succeed and Others Fail* by Randy Fields and Debbi Fields.

- *Business Law* by Robert Emerson.

- *Business Plans That Work For Your Small Business* by Alice Magos and Steve Crow.

- *Crossing the Chasm* by Geoffrey Moore.

- *E-Trepreneur* by Lamont Wood and Sherry Szydlik.

- *Everyone's Guide to Copyrights Trademarks, and Patents.*

- *Financing Your Small Business* by Robert Walter.

- *Founders at Work: Stories of Startups' Early Days* by Jessica Livingston.

- *Guide to Limited Liability Companies* by CCH Incorporated.

- *How to Buy, Sell and Profit on E-Bay: Kick-Start Your Home Based Business in Just 30 Days* by Adam Ginsberg.

- *How to Get Your Business On the Web* by Fred Steingold.

- *How to Really Start Your Business* by David Gumpert.

- *Incorporate Your Business* by Anthony Mancuso.

- *Legal Forms and Agreements* by Charles Chernofsky and Griffith deNoyelles.

- *Limited Liability Company: Small Business Start-Up Kit* by Daniel Sitarz.

- *Patenting Art and Entertainment* by Gregory Aharonia and Richard Stim.

- *Protecting Your Company's Intellectual Property: A Practical Guide to Trademarks, Copyrights, Patents, and Trade Secrets* by Deborah Bouchoux.

- *Small Business Taxes Made Easy* by Eva Rosenberg.

- *Start Your Own E-Business* by Entrepreneur Press.

- *Tax Smarts for Small Business* by James Parker.

- *The Small Business Kit for Dummies* by Richard Harroch.

- *The Entrepreneur's Internet Handbook* by Hugo Barreca and Julia O'Neil.

- *The Everything Online Business Book* by Rob Liflander.

- *The Guide to Retail Business Planning* by Warren Purdy.

- *The Innovator's Dilemma* by Clayton Christensen.

- *The Small Business Owner's Manual: Everything You Need to Know to Start Up and Run Your Business* by Joe Kennedy.

- *The Small Business Survival Guide* by Robert Fleury.

- *The Ultimate Small Business Guide* by Basic Books.

- *Web and Software Development* by Stephen Fishman.

- *Working for Yourself* by Stephen Fishman.

- *Write Your Own Business Contracts* by E. Thorp Barrett.

- *Your Limited Liability Company* by Anthony Mancuso.

WEBSITE RECOMMENDATIONS

I've provided some resources here that may not have been discussed earlier on in this book, however, just because I may not have mentioned them does not mean I haven't used them! These are additional sites that I've found to be very valuable have directly contributed to the growth of my business.

Hosting Companies

- Dreamhost - http://www.dreamhost.com
- Host Evaluator - http://www.hostevaluator.com
- Dot Easy - http://www.doteasy.com
- Third Sphere Hosting - http://www.thirdspherehosting.com
- Host 4 Profit - http://www.host4profit.com

Tutorials

- W3 Schools - http://www.w3schools.com

Word Processing

- TextPad - http://www.textpad.com
- UltraEdit - http://www.ultraedit.com
- NoteTab - http://www.notetab.com
- OpenOffice - http://www.openoffice.org

PDF Formating

- Adobe - http://www.createpdf.adobe.com
- PrimoPDF - http://www.primopdf.com
- HTMLDoc - http://www.easysw.com/htmldoc

Research Tools

- Alexa - http://www.alexa.com
- WordTracker - http://www.wordtracker.com
- Overture - http://inventory.overture.com/d/searchinventory/suggestion/
- NicheBot - http://www.nichebot.com

Outsourcing

- Script Lance - http://www.scriptlance.com
- Rent a Coder - http://www.rentacoder.com
- Web Design Lance - http://www.webdesignlance.com

Free Webtemplates

- Easy Website Page Builder - http://www.easy-web-page-creator.com
- Free Web Templates - http://www.freewebtemplates.com
- Free Site Templates - http://www.freesitetemplates.com
- Nvu – WYSIWYG (What You See Is What You Get) Software - http://www.nvu.com
- Free Layouts - http://www.freelayouts.com

Paid Webtemplates

- Template Monster - http://www.templatemonster.com
- Basic Web Templates - http://www.BasicWebTemplates.com
- Design Galaxy - http://www.designgalaxy.net

Copywriter

- Success Doctor - http://www.successdoctor.com

Best Tracking Service

- Web Trends Live - http://www.webtrendslive.com

MP3 Splitter

- EZ Soft Magic - http://www.ezsoftmagic.com

Audio Hardware

- Audacity - http://audacity.sourceforge.net
- Sound Pages - http://www.soundpages.com
- SwiffRecorder - http://www.powerbullet.com/swiffrec
- Internet Audio Guy - http://www.internetaudioguy.com
- Powerbullet - http://www.powerbullet.com

Email Capture/Autoresponder Services and Software

- Opt-in Automator - http://www.optinautomator.com
- Get Response - http://www.getresponse.com
- Pegasus - http://www.pmail.com
- Profit Responder - www.profitresponder.com/basics
- SendFree - http://www.sendfree.com
- Auto Response Plus - http://www.autoresponseplus.com
- Aweber - http://www.aweber.com

Graphic Artists

- Anthony Fesalbon - http://www.hypercover.com
- Killer Covers - http://www.killercovers.com
- Max Rylski - http://www.maxcovers.com
- Ebook Wow - http://www.ebookwow.com

Graphic Software

- Real Draw - http://www.realdraw.com
- Photoplus - http://www.freeserifsoftware.com
- Media Chance - http://www.mediachance.com
- Gimp - http://www.gimp.org
- The Graphic Organizer - http://www.graphic.org
- CuteDraw - http://www.cutedraw.com

Payment Processors

- PayDotCom - http://www.paydotcom.com
- Clickbank - http://www.clickbank.com/affiliateAccountSignup.htm
- PayPal - http://www.paypal.com
- 2Checkout - http://www.2Checkout.com

FTP Tutorial

- FTP Planet - http://www.ftpplanet.com/tutorial
- FileZilla - http://www.sourceforge.net/projects/filezilla/
- Download - http://www.download.com (Search for WSFTP LE)
- Cam Unzip - http://www.camunzip.com

NICHE MARKET IDEA KEYWORDS TO GET YOU STARTED

Recipes	Dog Training	Candles
Golf	Satellite TV	Gourmet Foods
Fishing	Beauty Tips	Gambling
Health and Fitness	Astrology	Mortgages
Travel	Cats	Credit Cards
Collectibles	Bartending	Music
Dating	Alternative Health	Jewelry
Security	Sex	Power
Immortality	Wealth	Happiness
Safety	Health	Recognition
Love	Parenting	Redecorating
Traveling	Foreign Languages	Dancing
Music	Children	Games
Fashion Ideas	Small Business Start-ups	Financial Management